THE INTERFACE BETWEEN SOCIAL WORK AND SOCIAL POLICY

Edited by Shulamit Ramon

VENTURE PRESS

Published by
VENTURE PRESS
16 Kent Street
Birmingham
B5 6RD

British Library Cataloguing-in-Publication Data
A catalogue record for this book is available from the British Library

ISBN 1 873878 86 9   (paperback)

Cover design by:
Western Arts
194 Goswell Road
London
EC1V 7DT

Printed in Great Britain

TO THE STAR YOU SEE FOR THE LAST TIME

Acknowledgements

I wish to thank the contributors to this book for their generosity and patience. Mrs Julie Brunton helped greatly in putting the disparate chapters into a unified format.

Thanks to Teodor, David, Michele, Nira, Shirley, Zvia, Zohar and Miriam for their unflinching support during this turbulent period.

Contents

Social Work in a Changing World

Introduction to the series

Since the end of the 1980s we have witnessed considerable political, economic, social and cultural change in east, west, and central Europe.

The scope and depth of change have been particularly dramatic in the former Communist countries, of which Russia is the biggest and the most influential.

These changes have confronted all of us who are interested in the well-being of the citizens of Europe with new, unprecedented challenges.

A number of new groups have become vulnerable in a way they were not before, while the old systems of welfare crumbled and their inability to provide economic, social and psychological safety nets became manifest. This has led to a readiness by policymakers, welfare workers and academics to look for new ways of meeting the emerging needs of such populations. An appetite for learning has been encouraged by eastern Europeans visits to western Europe and the United States, whereby they gained access to some of the experiences and literature available in the West.

At times such visits were all too short; the material looked at not particularly relevant; the cultural differences felt unbridgeable; and issues of power and hegemony too uncomfortable to confront.

Professional social work is one new way of responding to the challenges, obstacles and opportunities presented by these new situations.

There have always been people who helped others informally and formally, such as child care inspectors and social pedagogues who focused on children and recreational activities, but professional social work did not exist in the Soviet Union. In some form social work existed in Czechoslovakia, Romania and Slovenia however.

The uniqueness of social work lies in its attempt to offer a personalised service which holds together the psycho-social levels of our existence. Services are provided by professionally qualified workers who also act as intermediaries between the service user and the State. Usually social workers are not policy makers, though they may - and in my view should - attempt to influence policy decisions. Social workers are accountable to their employers, but their first and foremost loyalty is to defending vulnerable people in our society.

They do so in a variety of ways which are based on knowledge of how people develop, interact, change, learn, become motivated or despair; of how societies influence the lives of individuals; and of how to tread that fragile boundary between influence and coercion and enabling people to determine their choices and to put these into practice.

Social workers are successful at times and unsuccessful at others. Therefore the knowledge of the evaluative evidence on social work is crucial for improving its effectiveness, as well as for ensuring that newcomers to social work will learn from mistakes made in western social work. They will not need to repeat the mistakes but only to make their own, new ones.

An important component of social work is the belief that usually we do not know what is the best choice for another person; that individuals know better than anyone else what is good for them, once they know a lot more about alternative possibilities, the relative advantages and disadvantages of alternative courses of action, and once they have learnt how to make decisions.

This belief contrasts sharply with the view of authoritarian regimes which espouse they have the right to dictate to people what each of them should do individually, and with traditions of top-to-bottom advice giving and handing out of benefits. To acquire the ability to encourage people in a crisis situation to express themselves, to weigh possibilities and to make decisions, and to support them in implementing these decisions, requires not only a non- authoritarian stance but also a genuine belief that all of us have the right and the ability to lead a reasonably satisfactory life, however varied the range of 'satisfactory' must be.

Social work does not exist outside of specific political and cultural contexts. In the west it originated within the context of liberal capitalism. As liberal capitalism is now challenged by the New Right and pro-'free' market orientation western social work finds itself in a serious crisis in terms of adherence to its values, and its conceptual and practice frameworks which come from its previously dominant ideology.

This fact must be baffling for east Europeans impressed by the richness of the fabric of services and professional activities of western social work. In fact they may see the notion of such a 'crisis' as western indulgence.

Often westerners do not share with their eastern European friends their knowledge of this crisis for fear that this may prevent the latter from being interested in social work at all.

The position taken throughout the series SOCIAL WORK IN A CHANGING WORLD is the wish to share our ideas about social work as honestly as possible, warts and all, crisis and disillusionment, in the belief that this is the best way forward for the development of social work, wherever it is taking place.

Therefore, the form which social work should take in any one country has to come out of the context of the specific country; imitation of models of social work used elsewhere is unlikely to work well without such an adaptation.

Yet this series is based on the belief that nevertheless the *core* of social work is international because it is based on *common human experience*, and provides a guide to the content and format of social work in any one country (Midgely and Khinduka, 1992).

That *core* consists first and foremost in social work values (Shardlow, 1989), including:

- the right of individuals to be supported by their communities and societies when facing adversity and becoming vulnerable;

- the right to be treated with respect and be offered dignity;

- the right to self-determination, as long as it does not entail risk to oneself and/or others;

- the right to fail, as well as the right to fulfil one's potential, is an integral component of the right to self- determination.

- the responsibility of individuals for their own actions.

This is followed by the generalised knowledge of:

- how people develop and change;

- the role played by society in such a process;

- how people respond to adversity;

- what helps people in a crisis and what does not;

- what supports people in a way which enables them to take greater control over their own reality and to use their own potential.

The core social work skills which are based on the professional values and knowledge consist of:

- the ability to communicate with people experiencing adversity;
- the ability to form good personalised yet *professional* relationships with clients in which empathy and genuineness are expressed on the one hand, and yet are free from exploitation on the other;
- the ability to connect people to existing networks and create new networks if required;
- the ability to advocate and intermediate;
- knowledge and use of a wide range of formal and informal resources in the community;
- the ability to counsel individuals, families and groups;
- the ability to live with the losses and pain experienced by others without succumbing to the impact of such suffering oneself.
- the ability to reflect on, and evaluate one's own work, and to change it in the light of the lessons thus learnt.

Furthermore, it is productive to learn about how other societies conceptualise and operationalise their social work framework, as such learning generates ideas and helps to prevent the repetition of mistakes.

Reading about different approaches to social work is the least coercive way to influence people interested in learning about social work in post-Communist countries, for it allows them to reflect on what they have read, decide on their own what appeals to them and how to use it.

In social work we believe that *reflection* is indispensable in taking stock of situations and processes, of our own activities and those of others, and as a necessary, but insufficient, condition for the provision of a personalised service (Schon, 1983).

Such a reflection is necessary for negotiating the eternal dilemmas which social workers face constantly. For example, it would be naïve and misleading to suggest that social work is providing support only to people in adversity; it is also one of the more sophisticated tools of social control invented by liberal capitalism.

Social work exercises social control in a variety of ways, exemplified by the coercive form of taking children away from their parents, recommending that people be admitted to psychiatric hospitals, and influencing people's views of themselves and others at the psychological level.

Indeed, the conflict between exercising care and control and the inevitability that care does not come without some type of control is one of the dilemmas which all social workers face in every society.

This dilemma relates to yet another problematic issue; namely with whom does the primary loyalty of the social worker lie: is it with the State? with the specific employer? with the identified client? with the society in which the worker operates? In terms of core social work values, this loyalty has to be first to the client, and then to society, with the loyalty to the employer and the State trailing behind. Such a commitment may be seriously tested at times, and social workers require considerable peer and professional support to stick by the loyalty to the client and to society in general.

A good text on any aspect of social work would need to pay attention to these dilemmas.

The new series is thus dedicated to the coverage of social work values, knowledge and skills, in the context of different needs, wishes, client groups, and social contexts.

It is not accidental that the series forms a part of the activities of the TRANSFOR-MATION PROJECT OF THE HUMANITIES AND THE SOCIAL SCIENCES of the Soros Cultural Initiatives Foundation in Moscow. It was the initiative of Professor Teodor Shanin - the director of the project until November 1994 - that put social work on the map of the Transformation Project. This alliance with the Russian Ministry of Higher Education has led to the beginning of the dialogue between British, American and Russian social work educators. The initiative has been supported systematically from its inception by the current director of the project, Mr Victor Galizin.

In a number of ways, the move to develop professional social work in post-Communist countries embodies the challenges, opportunities and obstacles with which we are confronted throughout Europe. Particularly in post-Communist societies. Social work challenges traditional beliefs on the relationships between citizens and officialdom; the role of officialdom; the rights and responsibilities of individuals versus, the rights and duties of the State; the relationships between individuals and their communities; the abilities and potential of vulnerable people; the often fragile balance between the rational and the emotional compo-nents of our existence; care and control; and the nature of professionalism (Payne, 1991).

Thus it befits the Transformation Project, dedicated to introducing tools to facilitate transformation in the Humanities and the Social Sciences, to include the introduction of social work as a social science discipline as one of its core activities.

Professor Shulamit Ramon
series editor

References

Midgely, J. Khinduka, S. Hokenstad, M. (eds.) (1992) *International Profiles of Social Work*, American Social Workers Association, Washington, D.C.

Payne, M. (1991) *Modern Social Work Theory: A Critical Introduction*, Macmillan, London.

Schon, D. (1983) *The Reflective Practitioner: How professionals think in action*, Basic Books, New York.

Shardlow, S. (1989) (ed.) *The Value of Change in Social Work*, Routledge, London.

The authors

Alur, Mithu: Director of the Spastics Society, Bombay, India.

Brandon, David: Professor of Care in the Community, Anglia Polytechnic University, Cambridge, UK.

Chamberlyne, Prue: Principal Lecturer in European Social Policy, Department of Social Policy, University of East London, London, UK.

Kingston, Paul: Lecturer in Nursing, School of Nursing, University of Keele, Keele, UK.

Kourktchian, Marina: Senior Lecturer in Social Policy and Sociology, Department of Sociology, Yerevan University, Yerevan, Armenia.

Lévai, Katalin: Head of Department of Social Policy, Debrezen University, Debrezen, Hungary.

Munday, Brian: Director of the European Institute and of Social Work Studies, Department of Social Work and Social Policy, Kent University, Canterbury, UK.

Oghasian, Marina: Lecturer in Sociology and Social Work, Department of Sociology, Yerevan University, Yerevan, Armenia.

Payne, Malcolm: Head of the Faculty of Applied Community Studies, Professor of Applied Community Studies, Manchester Metropolitan University, UK.

Penhale, Bridget: Lecturer in Social Sciences, Social Work Division, University of Hull, UK.

Ramon, Shulamit: Professor of Interprofessional Health and Social Studies, Anglia Polytechnic University, Cambridge, UK.

Shanin, Teodor: Director, Moscow School of Social and Economic Sciences, Professor of Sociology, Manchester University, UK.

Solovyov, Alexander: Lecturer in Social Work, Moscow School of Social and Economic Sciences, Russia.

Zaslavskaya, Tatiana: Director of Intercentre for Interdisciplinary Research in Social Sciences, Moscow, Academician, and Professor of Sociology, Russia.

Introduction

Both social work and social policy are activities claimed by outsiders to be common-sensible and already carried out by others. In the case of social work the others are the "do-gooders", informal carers, volunteers, and members of the other caring professions. In the case of social policy, politicians, journalists, each ministry and professionals in the disciplines related to them – such as economics, medicine, agriculture, employment – believe that they know what are good policies and how to structure, implement and evaluate new policies in their particular field.

This assertion reflects:

- the youth of the two disciplines
- their applied nature
- the dependency on other disciplines for basic knowledge
- the dependency on the welfare framework in which they are grounded
- the uncertainty of their value and knowledge base.

This state of affairs is particularly observable in countries where social work and social policy are being established just now, such as Russia, or where the disciplines and the welfare frameworks are undergoing considerable change. All of the countries represented in this volume - Armenia, Britain, Germany, Hungary, India and Russia - fall into either the first or the second category as, with no exception, all of them have undergone fundamental changes in the last decade.

The recent attempts to introduce radical changes in east and west, south and north welfare systems inevitably spill over to the two disciplines most closely related to these systems, namely social work and social policy.

This text focuses on such developments in eastern and western Europe, though examples from other continents are utilised too.

The directions of the change in western Europe include:

1. Moving to a market economy view of welfare services.
2. the voluntary sector (NGO) as a service arm to replace direct public sector services.
3. Relying on relatives to provide care without supporting them adequately.
4. Opting for a managerial approach to govern the delivery system.
5. Moving away from large scale institutions in preference for small scale facilities in the community.

6.   More emphasis on individualised services.

7.   Encouraging the development of a stronger voice for service users and their relatives, though doing so with considerable ambivalence.

8.   Developing a pan-European welfare policy through the European Union, which is more orientated towards affirmative community action than the policies of most member states are.

The directions of the change in eastern Europe are both similar yet different from those prevalent in the West:

In addition to the move towards the market economy and the development of the voluntary sector, the East is also attempting to:

1.   Introduce new disciplines and new, or renewed, professions and disciplines in the field of welfare, yet without having trainers able to adequately prepare the newcomers to the disciplines and the professions.

2.   Using the new disciplines as a stopgap for people who lost their previous job due to the political, economic and social changes which eastern Europe has gone through in the 90s.

3.   Introduce the non-governmental sector, both the not-for-profit and the for-profit facets, as a way of not only cutting public expenditure but also of involving the community and devolving power.

4.   Relying on relatives to provide extensive care, without adequate support and without a network of services.

5.   Reducing public expenditure on existing welfare services without replacing them in a systematic way, thus letting services crumble.

6.   While having a general concept of where the modified welfare system should move, there is no worked out social policy or the data base from which to reach decisions.

7.   The new services, as were the old services, are much less focused on individualising services, community action and encouraging users to have a voice than western European services are.

8.   Introducing social work as an alternative to the existing heavily bureaucratised and impersonal social security system.

Both West and East use social work and social policy as means of social care and control.

This book describes and analyses the converging and diverging contexts in which the changes in the two welfare systems are taking place. In the post-modern world in which we live, in which Communism has become largely a thing of the recent past and capitalism prevails triumphantly, the major role of both social work and social policy is to attend to the inherent flaws within capitalism and the market economy, to soften their impact, to contain them from ruining the whole system, and to reduce the price which individuals, families, groups and communities pay for the success of capitalism.

It needs to be asked why is this the first text to focus on the interface between social work and social policy, an issue usually given a paragraph in textbooks of each of the two disciplines. Such a paragraph treats the interface as taken for granted, unproblematic, and hence uninteresting.

More often than not social work is portrayed as the handmaiden of social policy, the group which delivers policies as it is told, less conceptually and less research-orientated, less prestigious because it is assumed to be less academic. Typically, social policy research rarely focuses on what the "handmaiden" thinks about the policies conceived by others, let alone the clients of these services. When social workers are asked by policy researchers for their views, it seems that the "wrong" questions are asked in terms of the focus, as the questions are not concerned with the ease or the difficulty of delivering a service, the usefulness of the service to the clients and their relatives, or their usefulness in solving the problems as seen by the social worker.

Social work literature treats social policy either as an integral part of social work and the welfare system or as an alien discipline, located on another planet.

To me, the two disciplines share the values underlying the post-Second World War welfare state, which can be traced to the nineteenth-century liberal tradition and especially to the post-First World War beliefs such as:

- equality of opportunities for citizens
- social structural conditions contribute more to social and personal deprivation than personal qualities
- society is responsible for all of its members, including those who are more vulnerable than others, for whichever reason.

Being applied disciplines, the proof of the pudding does not lie so much in elegant analysis as it does in formulating and implementing policies which enhance the values outlined above. Hence, they are in essence pragmatic disciplines.

The main differences between the disciplines seem to me to lie in:

1. Emphasised values. In addition to the values outlined above, social work strongly focuses on supporting individuals in a dignified way. It pays a lot of attention to the nature of the relationships with the clients, at times accused of insufficiently focusing on outcomes because of the focus on the process of work.

    Social policy is concerned with groups in the population, rather than with individuals, and is interested almost exclusively in outcomes, to the neglect of the processes by which these outcomes have been achieved.

    Furthermore, while social work focuses on work with groups described as socially residual and is imagined as "tainted" by association with these socially undesirable groups, social policy attempts to shake off such an image and wishes to be seen as pertaining to the majority of the population.

2. Preferred scientific paradigms. Although both are applied and pragmatic disciplines, social policy is much more wedded to positivist methodological paradigm, whereas social work hovers between positivist and hermeneutic methodological paradigms, in part as it sees itself as between the social sciences and the arts, whereas social policy does not see itself at all as following the legacy of the arts.

3. While social work is a profession and a discipline, social policy is a discipline rather than a profession.

The interface between social work and social policy does exist. The contributors to this volume believe that it is mutual in its potential impact, rather than unilateral, as many social policy analysts would like to believe. This book offers many apt examples of the multifaceted, dual interface.

Thus the attention to child and elder abuse was drawn forcefully by social workers before it became an issue for policy makers; advocacy is still largely a principle without clear policies or practices at the levels of either social work or social policy; the redistribution of wealth in Russia has major consequences for both its social policy and its social work; bus drivers in Yerevan are making a mockery of governmental policies (and income) and succeed thereby in not becoming clients of social work; informal carers in eastern and western Germany respond to policies and practices of service delivery, yet attempt to mould these according to their preferences and felt needs.

The chapters by Teodor Shanin (social worker, sociologist, historian) and Malcolm Payne (social and community worker, social work theorist, educator in applied social studies) set out the scene in which the dramatic context and processes of our times unfold side by side with their impact on social work and social policy, as well as the responses of the two disciplines.

Shanin offers a vast historical canvas, while focusing on the place of social work in the complex trends of post-modern western and eastern Europe.

Payne provides an analysis of recent developments to a centrally shared component of both social policy and social work, namely Community.

Munday (social work and social policy researcher) provides a timely contribution pertaining to the role of supra-state organisation, an element typical of the post-modern world, which rarely is looked at in most texts on either social work or social policy.

Tatiana Zslavskaya (economist and sociologist) outlines the impact of the rapid changes, together with the seemingly immovable features of Russian society on the re-distribution of wealth and welfare today. This portrait provides essential data for planning social policy and social work in Russia and other east European countries.

Alexander Solovyov, who recently moved from lecturering in psychology to social work, offers comparative perspectives of the development of professional social work and training for it in Britain, the US and Russia, highlighting the similarities and differences among the three leading countries.

Marina Kourcthkian (physicist turned political science and social policy researcher) enables us to see some of the comic aspects of an otherwise sombre situation, of how ordinary people out-manoeuvre their government and its policy, as well as how the Armenian government copes in an impossible scenario, some of it of its own making.

Katalin Levai (sociologist and social policy researcher) highlights the development of the not-for-profit sector in her country, Hungary. This country has been the forerunner in a number of social policy and social work developments since 1956. Her chapter focuses on a phenomenon which is now rapidly spreading across east and west Europe, illustrating the views of two (out of five) major stakeholders to this enterprise, namely local government officials and leaders of not-for-profit organisations of these developments.

David Brandon completes the broad-brush picture by focusing on advocacy as an old, yet revitalised, development of our post-modern time. He highlights the inherent difficulties of moving away from lip-service principles to fully operational policies in practice, the price paid by those who indeed attempt to implement these principles, and some of the achievements.

The contributions by Prue Chamberlyne and Shulamit Ramon demonstrate two sides of the same coin: the far-reaching implications of a change in social ideology translated into policy and into formal and informal modes of delivery in the paradigmatic case of the shift from institutional to community-based care for people with long-term disabilities.

Chamberlyne (sociologist and social policy researcher) contextualises some of her more general observations in the comparative research she carried out in pre-unification east and west Germanies, thus offering a unique opportunity to look at the impact of ideology and policy when history and culture are shared.

Ramon (social worker and community mental health researcher) compares the treatment of the concept and practice of deinstitutionalisation in social work and social policy (as well as in related disciplines), in addition to its implementation in east and west Europe.

The chapters by Oghasian, Penhale and Kingston, and Alur highlight the roles played by social policy and social work in rediscovering and responding to time-old social and personal problems, such as child neglect and abuse, elder abuse, and the social integration of disabled people.

Oghasion (sociologist who became recently a social work lecturer) illustrates the intricacy of applying western-produced knowledge to a post-Communist country with an Asian and European past, of the social barriers to the rediscovery of an issue as emotive as the way some members of that society treat their children, and the lack of a socially agreed response to this socially undesirable form.

Penhale and Kingston look at only slightly less emotive issues, namely elder abuse, the difficulty of coming to terms with its existence for professionals and the general public, and of possible responses to this disturbing problem.

Elder abuse has been partly rediscovered because of the success of western Europe in enabling people to live much longer than they do in eastern Europe, yet without sorting out the social (and often also the personal) purpose of such contrived longevity. Neither social policy nor social work sees it as its task to dwell on the issue of purpose.

Alur (educator and voluntary sector leader) offers the only example in this book of a society located far away from Europe, but which has been strongly influenced by its colonial British past. Alur is an activist in the field of disability in India who has established herself as an innovative service in the field of cerebral palsy. She outlines the development of policy and practice within the statutory and voluntary sectors, inclusive of unique innovative projects. With candour she looks at successes and failures, opportunities and obstacles as against principles and ideologies in this field.

The authors of these texts are a distinguished group of practitioners, scholars, researchers, and activists who have consistently challenged in their work unquestioning approaches to both social work and social policy in their own countries and beyond. Their publication lists are too numerous to be printed here, and so are the research, education and social action initiatives which they have led in the past, and those they continue to lead.

Of necessity, texts such as these are bound to remain insufficiently comprehensive in their cover of countries and relevant aspects. However, I hope that readers will find the breadth and depth of the contributions sufficient not only to whet their appetites to learn more but also to be able to apply the analysis provided here to other manifestations of the interface between social work and social policy.

The contributions to this volume offer innovative and in-depth insights into an issue which is at the core of each national welfare system, as well as of the global welfare framework. Each chapter, and the specific examples which are highlighted in them, also demonstrates not only scholarly achievement but also the ingenuity of the actors within complex and often uncomfortable situations.

I hope that they will spark off the debate the issue deserves, but which has been muted up to now.

Shulamit Ramon

Part I: The Place of Social Work and Social Policy in the Post-modern World: Towards a New Conceptual Framework

Placing Social Work within Social Theory and Political Practice

Teodor Shanin

I wish to thank Ruth Tennant and Irene Lema for their help, without which this paper would never have reached completion.

Cultural Space of an Equivocal
Profession at the turn of a Century: Situating Question

We are currently witnessing massive, dramatic and fully unpredicted social changes of the 1980s/90s. These include the end of the USSR and the economic crash of its parts; the sliding into chronic economic crisis of its western vanquishers in the Cold War; the "privatisations" and the running down of "welfare states"; the downturn in Africa and the upturn in South East Asia; and the globalisation on a par with vicious xenophobic particularisms the world over. Facing this, there has been the feeling that our capacity to make sense of the world around us is strained at the seams to the utmost. What are the "classical" liberals to do with their liberalism, socialists with their socialism, conservatives with their conservatism, Christians with their Christianity etc., – all in ideological crisis? One can multiply such questions of conceptual retooling without which orientation in an increasingly complex and unexpected world cannot be even perceived. A new "axle stage" where new paradigms and questions are set, new interpretations adopted, new goals considered may be signalled by the feeling of a chasm where general theories of society and history stood for generations.

Some "gathering of stones" may be seen in the beginnings of efforts to build a new, more realistic comprehension of the social world which surrounds us. A new general organising concept which has emerged so far is "Post-modernity". We shall return to it. It seems that another relevant contribution and insight may come here from the relatively new and heavily under-theorised discipline-cum-profession of Social Work (for some academics, not a discipline at all, for some of the established professions, not a profession). To all accounts, it is a major critical repository of social experience concerning human welfare and contemporary statehood.

The place of Social Work within social theory and practice, societal perceptions and ideals, can tell us also about contemporary "advanced" societies and vice versa. Both social theory and Social Work could benefit from such an effort.

In this text, we shall look at Social Work and the cultural space it inhabits. The actual characteristics of Social Work and of similarities in ways its practitioners act have been defined as well as constrained by the conception of professionalism, by highly ambivalent relations with the contemporary State, by a philosophy-cum-ideology of human rights and, increasingly, by the political contest between the "New Right" and a "New New Left". Let us consider in turn these structuring parameters of contemporary Social Work.

Social Work: Profession, Ambivalence and State Power
Where popular visions of social workers are concerned, the first thing which would strike an investigating outsider from another planet, would be the nearly universal sneer and the ill-tempered joke. The social worker of "West Side Story" - an image of an ineffectual, silly and eminently plausible scarecrow, has represented it well. Such perceptions turn ugly every time yet another child is reported abused or killed, old people left cold and friendless, with social workers held responsible for yet another human tragedy. Ministers and officials, journalists and policemen, clients of Social Work and social workers themselves, talk endlessly of Social Work failures. Yet, interestingly, nobody suggests or even imagines a "western" world without social workers - a professional category which, let us remember, in its current form was unrecognisable but a century ago (Jordan, 1984). Indeed, this profession proceeds to grow rapidly in size. Clearly, there are characteristics of the Social Work of today which secure its continuity, its ambiguities, as well as the popular resentments of it.

Social work carries a variety of images and assumptions which are wrong, yet remarkably persistent. These begin with social work's origins. Although social work developed from philanthropic organisations, it differs from charity in its basic goals, its consequent methods and structure linked to a specific training, i.e. in most of what makes social work into what it is. Charity was motivated and defined by the spiritual needs and the feeling of duty of those who offered it, usually to do with their conceptions of immortal soul and human nature - the need to be good. The extent of "giving" has been the measure of its achievements. As against that, the ultimate success of a contemporary social worker is being measured by the ability to work oneself out of the initial context of the helper and the helped, i.e. to achieve what different generations within Social Work called "rehabilitation", "normalisation", "readaptation" and the like. The aim is to restore to the "client" the ability to act independently within the given social context (Brown & Smith, 1990; Ramon, 1991). Social work routines and training centred accordingly on the "clients" individual psychology, family networks and broader societal context in their interdependence, aiming to enhance the client's autonomy. It is the charity-givers and their creed who have been standing in the centre of human interaction, referred to as charity. It is the client who is to stand there by the maxims by which social work defines itself.

Another way to put it (and a fundamental formula by which the élite of the profession of social workers provide for their self-definition) is to describe social work as a profession (Abbot, 1988). In their contemporary sense, professions are delimited by an established set of problems and by set procedures for their identification and resolution (Torstendahl & Burrage, 1990; Illich, 1968). Each profession carries, therefore, a system of knowledge which incorporates theory and practice as well as some indices of success in "problems resolution". It carries also a system of discrete professional ethics, defining the correct behaviour within the professional circle, in relations with clients as well as when facing total outsiders. These are enhanced by training schools, professional associations and official recognition within the law. Manifestly linking goal-resolution and professional ethics stands the category of professions, defined in contemporary English as "caring professions". These lay claim to science-like objectivity and detachment in observing, analysing and "engineering" human reality, to do so to serve a client. A major aspect of it is "a certain equilibrium between the universal and the particular" (Hughes, 1993). These behaviours, knowledge, self-imposed restrictions, assumptions and patterned plausibilities are passed from generation to generation through systematic university training, focusing on the development of particular skills, as well as through the transfer of tradition by some type of master:apprentice relationships between different generations of practitioners.

A "typical" professional personality is formed as much by systematic selection and self-selection into each profession as by continuous pressure to conform to the profession's *mores*, ideas of group interest, beliefs, prejudices and even forms of dress and specific jargon. Ways in which professional reputations as well as career ladders are formed offer a major carrot-and-stick system to secure the profession's structure and coherence. As a general rule of thumb which explains their persistence, the professions offer an effective way to use limited resources to solve the problems set within their self-definition. They also offer a powerful meaning-of-life focus, interpretations of choice and a measuring rod for occupational success. They offer as well a major way to put in the hands of the professions membership control of resources and privileges, which made Bourdieu (1988) talk of professional knowledge as property of a type. Finally, professions form powerful blinkers to those fully socialised into them when issues outside their scope of preferred experience are encountered.

The main historical change in the characteristics of professions was their gradual colonisation by the modern State. Members of "free professions" have increasingly become salary-receiving state employees. Yet, the described qualities of "professionalism" stayed largely intact.

The beginning of social work as a profession can be found more than a century ago when it evolved within some charitable organisations which looked for new, systematic ways to work with those thus supported. As against categorisations of "the poor" into "deserving", i.e. worthy of charity, and "undeserving", destined for damnation, come efforts "to take the side of the poor" and focus on them, with some of the new social workers settling in Christian communities in the city slums as missionaries to the underclass. But it was the "New Deal" of the US and the Welfare States of Europe which brought social work into being as a fully established profession and an academic discipline. It also brought to light some of its basic ambiguities. Assumptions of universal rights of humans as such to a minimum level of decent living, underwritten by the State and enshrined in law were adopted by the profession. The social worker's task was to offer an individualised safety net, designed to pick up human failures and rejects of "Welfare State" - all those cases when, even if good in its intentions and satisfactory in its provisions, the welfare-directed law, simply applied by simple bureaucrats, did not work. Contrary to the universalistic assumptions or pretensions of the Welfare State and its equivalents (even though much within the humanistic values underpinned it), a profession and a service were created. These were set up to have the application of welfare provisions and laws personalised, adjusted and indeed often circumscribed by a peculiar category of Welfare State practitioners.

Social workers have been those who carried extensive knowledge of the "machine" of welfare provisions and legislation, as well as specific "human knowledge" relevant to its "clients", applied psychology, often with a strong psycho-analytical component and some sociology and economics thrown in. The initial professional core of training which came to delimit Social Work from the other "caring professions", became known as "casework" (Hollis & Wood, 1981). This particular combination of theory and application, integrating insights, is drawn from different academic disciplines with massive generalised experience of help offered to families and individuals within the specific context of Social Work's main goals, practice and its definitions of successes and failures. Dynamics of individual responses and interactions with the social environment at the points of crisis were central to that general knowledge. The diffuse nature of newly established professional fields meant that apprentice training became an extensive part of the way social workers were being trained. However, it was also linked to rigorous academic tuition which was enhanced by the selection and self-selection of particular personality types for it. The nature of their work *vis-à-vis* large bureaucratic structures made social workers develop also skills of negotiation, advocacy, team-work and mediation, often within multidisciplinary teams, as well as of leadership, formal and informal.

Social workers as individuals, as an "imaginary community" as well as a structured establishment, were powerfully moved by the model and behavioural standards which the conception of "professionalism" defined for them. Despite a diversity of fields of specialisation, i.e. different categories of clients, different styles of work and different schools of thought, the characteristics of social work have been on the whole sufficient to make it into a recognisable profession, rather than a heterogeneous list of activities and institutions. In increasingly atomised societies of rapid change, with growing "minority" populations and individual marginalisations, the need for such a recognisable address to be used to unload "social problems" has been increasingly felt. At the same time, while becoming constituted as a profession with its own problems-set and stereotypes of solutions and training, Social Work has borne a number of characteristics which accounted for its enhanced ambiguity and problematic status. It operates in a field where certain knowledge of the intervention:outcome sequences is ever in doubt, while failures are easily exposed to the public eye. It is a new profession which makes it less sure of its footing and foothold within academic and administrative environments. Its claims to objectivity and scientificity *vis-à-vis* human predicament are ever suspect and often resented. So too is the claim to privileged professional knowledge where everybody's private experience does exist and may be preferred. On the other hand, it is an academically linked profession, but its status is continuously challenged by claims of its common-sensible rather than theoretical nature or else it being an intuitive art rather than a science.

The fact that Social Work actively infringes on established fields of human privacy and claims to substitute its "professionalism" for some of the human links of interdependence and emotions, such as family help and friends' advice, adds a particular dimension of irritation at its claims to privileged knowledge or status. Hence the sneer in the response to it. It also offers itself as an ideal "whipping boy" - when the family, the society and the State fail to fulfil their assumed roles and do so incomprehensibly, one can easiest blame the social workers.

But the core ambivalence of the profession lies in its interdependence with the current State within and without its bureaucratic welfare departments and functions. The symbiotic relations of social workers and the current Welfare State were strewn with ambiguity and it was that ambiguity which became a central characteristic of the profession as such. These technicians of the Welfare State - their main employer and generator of functions - were also often enough its most vociferous critics. The ambivalence was built into the very conceptual nature of Social Work. It carries a basic challenge to universalism which has been the very soul of the Welfare State; equal rights to minimal well-being were to be interpreted in it diversely, specifically and individually. The self-image of detachment befitting experts clashes with the powerful emotional content of the work shared by the social workers. Being placed between the State bureaucracy and "clients", i.e. between major impersonal power in the land and the most powerless of its citizens, led to the Janus-faced nature of the profession. They represented authorities as against the "welfare cases" but also their "clients" as against the authorities.

In the context of harsh criticism of the repressive nature of the contemporary State and/or capitalism, especially since the 1960s, an over-socialised supra-critical image of the profession of Social Work has grown up on the intellectual Left in "the west" by which social workers appear as simple executives of oppressive regimes which wish to control the fringes of their population - a category on a par with the police and the prison officers, enhancing the institutional cage of the modern society. One of such major current insights powerful enough to enlighten but also to blinker was expressed by the nowadays particularly influential works by Foucault, which made more specific the *One Dimensional Man* message of Marcuse in the 1960s (1968) while broadening that of the earlier - still image of institutions as prisons in *Asylums* by Goffman (1961). Foucault"s concept of "governmentalisation" (1977) as increasingly dominating history of the last two centuries is doubtlessly profound. An "ensemble" of institutions and procedures operating as a regulating mechanism of humans and human actions has been expressing a system of power. In such an analytical context, social work is but one more exercise in "governability". The reality has been more complex, however. Social workers were not only obedient servants of the State. Trade unions of social workers found themselves defending not only "salaries and conditions" of members but acting as union-substitutes for their ununionised clients and their interests. The profession of Social Work has indeed been functioning as a "soft" yet repressive control of marginal populations but also as their defender and at times as the organiser of their resistance (as well as, time and time again, their only voice) (Brandon *et al.*, 1995). Moreover, in a world in which the opaque glass wall of the mass media restricts the understanding of social problems over and above a piece of "news" or a scandal, the profession of Social Work carried and often disseminated extensive actual knowledge of marginality, repression, inequality and despair - a major potential of radicalising knowledge.

As with most of the "caring professions" in the last generation, the majority of social workers were employed by "the authorities" - governmental, semi-govern-mental and municipal. What made for the substantive difference between professionals and clerks so employed was the shared professional status and knowledge, which offered the base for critical appreciation, autonomous judgement and choice - an alternative to simple execution of "orders from above" or else to a utilitarian personal strategy of minimisation of effort, while maximis-ing benefits to oneself or to "the office". At the root of that shared professional knowledge of social work, legitimising and defining approaches and actions alter-native to simple bureaucratic obedience and utilitarian egoism, lay two fundamental concepts and/or ideological constructs. One was that of the "profes-sionalism" of social workers, the other that of the basic human rights this profession is called to serve.

Stages in Formulating Human Rights:
Citizenship, Welfare Individuation

On a par with "professionalism", a framework of human rights formed for Social Work its most relevant conceptual foundation. Broader still, it formed the main cognitive axis and legitimation of political reformism during the most reformistic era of human history. While well disguised within the prevailing common sense as natural and eternal, the philosophy of human rights is in fact remarkably new - an invention which, once established in western Europe and the US about two centuries ago, received a life of its own (Laqueur & Rubin, 1989). Despite con-siderable efforts to give it an empirical "scientific" base, e.g. the work of the Utilitarians, it remains indeed a philosophy in the sense of logically linked abstract principles, categories and values - an "inter-subjectivity" rooted in an unfolding consensus rather than reflection of natural instinct innate to "human nature", to an objective need or to simple self-interest. It was often used as a way to disguise interest of specific groups and as a propaganda device of political forces. But it was seldom just that.

At its core, the philosophy of human rights represents a set of assumptions con-cerning self-evident and universal rights of every human as such to privileges available in the past only to some families and social estates of western Europe (as against the totality of obedience within unlimited rule associated with concepts of "oriental despotism"). Put otherwise, the philosophy of rights was a process by which a coherent set of images concerning actual and ideal societies and of humans within them was generated, established and followed by a movement of peaceful or of revolutionary reformism, aiming to transform society, adjusting it to a model which was to address the substance of human predicament. The very realisation of such plans produced on the whole, growing criticism of the initial project and a massive challenge to it, in which a new perception of human rights and a new reformist programme were formed and a new cycle of reform eventually began. Up to now, one can identify two such cycles and the beginning of a third one, categorising these by the assumed focus of each: citizenship and political equality, welfare and social equalisation, individuation and choice.

Traces of basic assumptions of what was to become established as a philosophy of human rights can be found quite early in human history. Those who came to elaborate it in the eighteenth and nineteenth centuries have often referred to and compared their ideas with Ancient Greece and Rome. Indeed, the Greek city-state has established the concept of citizenship for some, linked to "direct democracy" while Rome's Stoicism developed assumptions of the basic equality of humans. Still, the idea of universal citizenship rights was substantively a seventeenth- and eighteenth-century product and invention, brought into focus by the American and French Revolutions and the ascendance of a British parliamentary tradition (as best expressed by Locke). It laid claim to a new and true understanding of human nature and the natural human place in the universe, carrying a powerful reformistic message of a better and more rational world due to be established. Such a world was one of nations of citizens rather than of kingdoms of subjects. In the philosophical language of Kant's ethics, this meant approaching all humans as ends rather than as means. The natural rights of people meant equality before the law and eventually a "one citizen one vote" principle, by which legitimations of governments were to be defined as of now.

While the reformist factions argued and fought over the specific nature of the new State, the qualifications for citizenship and the ways to enter the new world, they mostly shared the basic assumption of what the new liberty was to be. They also agreed on the way social inadequacies and wrongs outside of legal and political matters would be put to rights. The good sense of majority, once legally empowered, was to secure the most rational leadership, caring for the needs of the whole of the population. The social ills would be ironed out and fraternity would necessarily follow the equality of political rights defined within a constitution (which for a time made "constitutionalism" synonymous with the reform of the old regime, with the exception of Britain).

The crisis of the programme and of the system which came to express this philosophy of rights focused on legal equality which was part and parcel of its realisation. The new worlds of the American and French republics came rapidly to display how much the growing equality of political and legal rights does not result "naturally" in actual equality of citizenry. The collapse of the customary dependencies meant also the loss of traditional safety nets and the pauperisation of major parts of the population. New times resulted in growing social polarisation between the rich and the poor. The onset of the Industrial Revolution meant the creation of a working class and extensive slums of mass poverty and despondency. The new underclass was growing, increasingly finding expression in the works of the more sensitive and more honest representatives of the literati of the upper classes. If the red-hot revolutionary of the turn of the eighteenth century, Thomas Payne, still professed what would be to us a constitutionalist creed of all-solving franchise, the major theorist of nineteenth-century liberalism, J. S. Mills, moved by the end of his life to its explicitly socialist criticisms.

The substance of the next cycle in the philosophy of rights and of its reformistic derivations was well expressed in the name adopted by a major group of its supporters - the Social Democratic Workers Party of Germany (Eley, 1984). These were adherents to democracy in its initial sense of constitutionalist reforms. But they added to it a "social" dimension of the reforms aimed at. In the context of an industrialising society, they came to see themselves as the party of the working class, i.e. industrial wage workers - to them, the future majority of the world's population (even though such delimitations were never simple - Social Democracy was as popular with craftsmen, intellectuals and, at times, peasants and radical bourgeoisie). The socialist Second International they dominated set out in full the new extended vision of basic human rights and necessary social reforms. Under Marx's powerful impact, they called it "Revolution", but Kautsky's *One Day After the Social Revolution* established the actual nature of the anticipations involved (1902). It was to be the result of a remorseless but spontaneous, slow and fundamentally peaceful evolution of forces of production, of the size of the working class and its socialist education, resulting in the "qualitative leap" in which the State, essentially as it was, would become an instrument of the working class and its party - their tool for the anticipated social reforms.

The substance of human rights as not only a civic but a "social" proposition lay in the assumption of a minimum income and security of well-being for all as due within any enlightened and civilised society. Within the rapidly urbanising and industrialising countries this meant invalidity, illness and old age pensions, and unemployment benefits, as well as access to free health care, education and minimal lodging (Wilensky, 1975, Flora, 1981).

The Social Democrats were not on their own in their consideration of a "social dimension" to whatever political strategy was on the cards. It was being adopted by socialism's political enemies, often in an effort to steal their political thunder. It was also more than that. Many assumptions concerning goals and means of the new reformist design should be treated as *Zeitgeist*, a general "view of the age" bridging the usual ideological divisions, relevant as much to scholarships and ideological programmes as in popular common sense and to different political factions and tendencies. For the radicals of the socialist movement, it was to link with a decisive shift of social power towards the powerless producers - in Marx's words, the "disalienation" of the proletariat. On the political Right, to Bismarck, such *varzurgung*, i.e. patriarchal care expressed in State-induced reforms was to enhance the German Empire. The more radical brands of twentieth-century liberalism, be it Lloyd George's or Roosevelt's, developed their own forms, sub-interpretations and agendas of it. Even Winston Churchill was to remark on the need to take "a big slice of Bismarckianism" into the policies of the government in which he served. A major difference to socialists, even as mild as the British Fabian Prime Minister, Attlee, it was part of a process due to abolish or transform capitalism as known and to radically redistribute public wealth (hence extensive "nationalisation" of means of production which was to represent it). To their Liberal and right-wing opponents, capitalism was good or good enough but in need of some rectification and reining in for its own sake by some rational welfare policies. Right, Left and Centre, the definitions of human needs and human rights became remarkably similar and so was the major tool due to specify and secure them. The instrument for the execution of the "social" agenda and its universalisation was the State and State bureaucracy in its broad sense (i.e. inclusive of local authorities and "quangos").

The Bolshevik Revolution of 1917 and the creation of the USSR split the socialist movement into its communist and social-democratic adherents which meant also a sharp division in their interpretation of the human rights agenda. The Social Democrats approached the "social" rights as a further development of citizen rights achieved at the earlier stage of reforms, while their communist enemies viewed these civic rights and legislation as bourgeois sham, to be eradicated and replaced rather than built on. The "dictatorship of the proletariat" became rapidly a synonym of a police state aiming at the eradication of any dissent. The Soviet party-state was its actual expression. Yet, once again, some basic ideological similarities cut across party-political frontiers in matters concerning the rights to social welfare, public education, etc. State-socialism and state-welfarism were remarkably close in the social rights declared and actually activated: from inexpensive lodgings, universal invalidity and old age pensions to free education and public medicine. This second cycle in development of the philosophy of human rights came to its full maturity by the end of the Second World War. The British christened it the Welfare State. It was by then already established in outline in parts of Scandinavia and a few more places and was to spread rapidly through western Europe. It was to eradicate all social ills described by Beveridge (the planner of the British Welfare State) as those of ignorance, squalor, disease, enforced idleness and want. Within two years, Roosevelts "Economic Bill of Rights" in the US spoke of it as "freedom from want" linked to "freedom from fear". Two points should be made here. One, the cross-party fundamental consensus as the Welfare State was being established, was well expressed in the fact that its basic laws in the United Kingdom were written by a Liberal for a Conservative-majority government to be implemented eventually by the Labour Party (and to become its ideological "jewel in the crown", yet never challenged also by the Conservative governments between the 1950s and 1970s). Second, to read the USSR constitutional provisions together with the Beveridge programme of the Welfare State, Keynes's economic analysis concerning policies of full employment in the UK and the laws of Roosevelt's New Deal is to find them remarkably similar in basics. Nor was it propaganda sham - both Soviet and western educational and health services, pension provisions were by the mid-twentieth century real and universal, based on free access, state-budgeted and granted as mandatory citizen rights.

Once again, it was the success, i.e. their actual execution, which exposed and brought to the fore the limitations as well as the criticism of reforms expressed in the conception of the Welfare State. Two generations or so of state welfarism and state socialism proved them unsatisfactory on a number of counts *vis-à-vis* their own programmes and agendas as well as difficult to sustain economically, at least in their bureaucratic forms. To compare in human terms nineteenth-century capitalist advance through contemporary pictures drawn by Engels, Booth and Dickens, Gorkii and Uspenskii or the 1930s' soup-kitchens for the unemployed millions (while governments sat on their hands) with the "welfarist" 1950s is to see a dramatic measure of improvement for the majority of the populations. But the long-term 1950s-1970s boom of the post-war cycle in the West and the pirate-like use of resources the world over, were followed by economic slow-down, social instability and sharp and debilitating ecological decline. While the nineteenth century's optimism assuming endlessly growing resources was disappearing, the call on them within regimes committed to universal welfare was increasing through ageing populations and chronic unemployment as much as the bureaucratic overhang in welfare provisions. And despite all efforts and resources spent, social ills and needs seemed bottomless.

In the increasingly dualised post-Second World War world the crisis of the USSR ran an interesting parallel to that of "the West". A crisis of resources *vis-à-vis* welfare provisions, the objective poverty, subjective distress, growing intersubjective tensions, inability of an overgrown state to address those issues over and above simply brushing them under the carpet of censorship or self-delusions were there on both sides, even though to different degrees (Aganbegyan, 1986; Zaslavskaya, 1987). The official goal to catch up with and to outrun the West in terms of the well-being of populations - declared by Stalin and relaunched by Krushchev - made the failures to deliver on its commitments by the Soviet system the more explicit.

It is important to recognise here that the growing crisis of "West" and of "East" alike (the "South" of so-called "developing societies" would need a particular exposition) was expressed not only in the way it related to economic dynamics of populations and resources. It was the very conception of the eradication of human predicament by state-run universal welfarism which was being exposed through its execution as clearly inadequate, especially so for "marginals" and "minorities" in a rapidly globalising and diversifying world. Yet, it has been a world where in every population "minorities" were increasingly becoming a majority. What used to be seen as the main road to the final resolution of human predicament has grown oblique. General doubts concerning universalist solutions were growing while their chosen instrument - the State - came increasingly to be seen as the major force negating human liberty, equality and fraternity, that is, the very tools with which reformist and revolutionary exponents of the philosophy of human rights set out to create a better world.

The new collective perception, new cycle in the vision of human rights came as a growing challenge to the universalism and "statism" of the older system. These came increasingly to be seen as restricting human choice, incapable of addressing specific, i.e. individual, human problems, oblivious of "minorities" - a new dictatorship of experts, bureaucrats and generalisations over actual human needs, a regime which often suffocated and harmed "by kindness". Fundamental assumptions of predictability, underlining bureaucratic planning, of totality of rationalism in interpretation of human relations, of panacea-like powers of laws and regulations addressing every aspect of human livelihood, the very visions of solutions via bureaucratic intervention came increasingly to be doubted. So was the fundamental optimism of the idea of Progress by which forward ever meant up and up, better and better, more and more universal and more and more rational (Shanin, 1996). The parallel advance of a long-term economic crisis of the capitalist industrial societies, of the decline and collapse of the Soviet regime, of awareness of global ecological limitations as much as the failure of scholarly prediction of all these put in doubt the self-evident nature of all previous assumptions. Eventually, an international offensive by the New Right came to challenge the Welfare State itself, the assumption of universality of rights to social services free of charge and called for their running down, for sharp restriction of welfare budgets and "privatisation" of services. Once again, the general vision was cutting across the formal party divisions as it did at the upsurge of welfare-statism. The influential parties of the Left, now in ideological retreat, have been adopting fairly similar views to those of their political foes.

Social Work *vis-à-vis* Postmodernism, the New Right and a New New Left
The discussion above attempted to place Social Work as a discipline and a profession in the context of long-term development of prevailing understanding of the world around us - the two and a half centuries or so of "modern times". Let us bring our essay to its end by relating Social Work of the 90s to the turn of the twentieth century's major perceptions and ideologies: postmodernism, the New Right and, for lack of a better description, the New New Left. One cannot do justice here to so broad a field over and above a short introduction to the way these interlink, that is, both overlap and clash with contemporary social work.

During the last decade, Postmodernism emerged as a major new interpretation of society - a claim to a new stage in cultural history and a major alternative vision of inter-subjective relations (especially of language), critical of established academic scholarship (Bauman, 1992; Parton, 1994). It dismissed as "essentialism" monolithic models of society, "grand narratives" of its perception and to a considerable degree, the very intelligibility of human history. The subject matter was being seen as fragmented, fluid, "decentred". The view rejects totalising knowledge and any *a priori* claims of causality (especially of an economic nature), while accentuating minorities, margins, uncertainty and choice. A way to place it is to see Postmodernism as a major intellectual response to the transformation of industrial society as we knew it, with globalisation and "internetting" linked to the turning of the welfare-and-social-equality stage of the consensus philosophy of human rights. It can be put with other critics of "modernity" and modernisation theories, such as those by Ivan Illich (1978), Polanyi's earlier critique of the eternal nature of markets (Polanyi, 1957) and with ideologies of the "new movements" such as Greenpeace or for the defence of native rights.

Social work as a profession, i.e. both as practice and as a conceptual construct, represented all along an unrecognised yet major expression of what could be named after Zygmunt Bauman "intimations of Postmodernity". While seldom aware of the extent of its own contradictory nature (as a heavily undertheorised discipline would be) social work carried within "modernity" and its universal welfarisation programmes or dreams, the message of the necessity of individuation. This linked to perceptions of deeply set unpredictability, randomness, marginalisation, anomy and alienation within the whole sphere of human livelihood as accentuated particularly within the social workers' clientele. These and other aspects of what can be seen as postmodernity type of thought came early into the professional attention and training of the social workers. The distrust of "grand narratives" and universalistic behaviour models, information treated as a basic resource of human action, an applied ethics and emotional colouring accepted as central to the analytical viewing of social reality rather than a footnote to its "objective" nature - were part and parcel of what the élite of social workers and their educators took for granted. Much before the fashion struck academia, words such as "deconstruction of a narrative" (human - of the "clients" wordings as well as the official one of laws and regulations) would have sounded abstract but not substantively odd to the core of professional social workers. One can put it otherwise by claiming and tracing back concerns of Postmodernity and Social Work alike to the sociologies of social fragments and fragmentation by G. Simmel and M. Weber as well as the whole of the neo-Kantian and anti-Positivistic tradition at the beginning of the twentieth century (Weber & Wolff, 1964).

The professional and academic self-images of social work often went together with accentuation of its apolitical nature, its objectivity befitting generalised humanism and scientificity. To look more closely at political confrontations of the Philosophy of Rights' third stage is to see why it is not quite so. Social Work was neither but a tool or a slogan of a political party, nor has it been politically neutral.

The call for and vision of individuation as a challenge to the major ideology of goals and means within the social-democratic half a century ("liberal" in the language of US politics) became at least initially the banner and the official strategy of a New Right. There is irony of history there, for the first massive criticism and challenge to bureaucratic state-socialism and state-welfarism alike and to the potential of repressive dynamics of human interaction as an "alienating" force came mostly from the Left. The New Left as dramatically expressed in the heady days of 1968 in Paris and Prague, at the Anglo-Saxon campuses, the anti-Vietnam-war marches and "communities of living" (Suarle & McConville, 1968). It was expressed as well by extensive literature both new - be it Marcuse,

Laing, Macluhan or C. W. Mills and "rediscovered" - be it the "young Marx", Chayanov or Benjamin. In a major challenge to the State as a universal tool and final legitimation as well as the chief provider and "definer" of needs, they raised the banner of defensive individuation within society due to be differently shaped and integrated. Students of Paris or the United States and supporters of the "Prague Spring" of "socialism with a human face" carried a very similar message. The rights of the minorities and the marginals, indeed the right to be a minority and a marginal without being repressed or categorised out of existence was the major component of this "New Left" creed. New perceptions of ecological restrictions of the globe and the role those played in its structures of inequality entered it also - a new red:green alliance and set of ideas (Coldwell, 1977).

The response of those in power to the 1968 New Left wave was clear, effective and successful in bringing the unexpected challenge under control - the Soviet tanks moving into Prague were matched by the threat of French tank divisions moving from Germany towards Paris, the police brutality in Belgrade and the National Guard bullets at the Kent campus of the US. In the West, as befits its political traditions, enough of compromise was also offered to calm some minds while the war in Vietnam was rapidly brought to an end to remove a major destabilising influence. Not less relevant to the outcome was the response of the official radical opposition to the west European regimes. The French Communists, their impact made central by the Parisian students' revolt, did their utmost to bring it into accepted channels, while refusing to respond to its radical message. In the "East", Soviet Communism responded with routine brutality of arrests, ostracism and mental hospitals. It was the eventual defeat of the New Left "sixty-eighters" as much as the way the official Left brushed their message aside which gave the field to the right wing radicals. It also spelt rapid decline and dissipation of the "Old Left" - within the new context and *zeitgeist* it came now to look shabby and hypocritical. The radical potential of growing anti-statism, the growing doubts as to the usefulness and sustainability of generalised welfare provisions where human predicament is concerned, gave the "moral highground" of policies of social reconstruction in the interest of greater liberty for the most active to a New Right. There, it was wedded to the belief in "free markets" and policies of radical monetarism as mechanisms of liberation as much as engines of "economic growth".

Initially, the New Right borrowed its clothes from the classical liberal tradition - the past radical challengers to the seventeenth and eighteenth centuries' *ancien régime*, their message reinvigorated by the rapid advance of the New Leviathan - the modern and "total" state. This vision came in particular through the voices of the academic survivors of Nazism such as Hayek (1944) and Popper (1962). Their critique, which was eventually to cut the ground from under the self-evident nature of the design of universal state-executed accomplishment of human rights through "social welfare", began as a few voices crying in the wilderness to turn by a remarkable *tour de force* into the prevailing ideological language of Thatcherism and Reaganism - a "revolution from above" by the powers that be. This is still actuating actual policies of governments and the IMF and their intellectual advisers.

The political project of re-empowerment of property holders *vis-à-vis* the modern state was put forward as the one secure way for the enhancement of individual rights of choice. The disintegration of the Soviet regime was offered as added proof of the fundamental unrealism of socialist and welfarist designs. Massive privatisation programmes served well new capitalists of speculative riches but also found a ready response or at least indifference in the mass of a welfarised population, increasingly hateful and doubtful of the State and its bureaucrats, as well as of "social" institutions and of nationalised industries state-bureaucratised to the core. Claims of decentralisation and "getting the State off one's back" were clearly what the sympathetic electors wanted to hear. Yet, the actual ethos and practice of new reformers was increasingly departing from its official old-liberal ideology. It was characterised by State bureaucratic interventions, endless changes "by order" from above, naked managerialism, which would have horrified Adam Smith. Moreover, the marketisation-induced free-for-all and economic polarisation made new waves of criminalism and a beggars-in-the-streets syndrome surface, against which the ready response of repression of all who do not fit, was brought to bear - programmatically adopted by the New Right and popular with many who feared social disorder without understanding its roots. The incompatability of the actual "keep the lowly down" strategies with liberal posture was disregarded. The actual growth of the repressive powers of the State under the New Right regimes to which the force of multinationals should be added has been surfacing from under the rhetoric of decentralisation (Hutton, 1995).

In many ways, the New Right has been, therefore, the opposite to the Old Right - conservative in its preferences for stability, for tradition, for non-state communal authorities and paternalism. It also differs from the moralistic assumption of classical liberalism. An exclusive image of humanity as the eternal, universal and optimal market lies at the roots of the New Right vision of humans. Manipulative management of humans, aethical and engine-like, becomes its *modus operandi*. At the root of it all stands a behavioural model assuming depersonalised market and self-directed benefit-maximisation of individuals as the only springs of human action. All else becomes accordingly Utopian or conservative - the very notion "conservative" increasingly used negatively as exclusive market-radicalism becomes the proof of the New and true Right. Objections by the "caring professions" to naked managerialism are categorised accordingly. Poverty is being assumed once again to be a natural result of self-indulgence, incompetence and lack of character - carriers of such qualities to be tightly controlled nationally and internationally (with provisions for the "deserving poor only" taking place of universal citizen rights to welfare services). Meaningful reforms are equated now with "bitter medicine" which is "good" for "them"- the "them" representing lower brackets of populations, both nationally and internationally.

Once the dust of the crush of the USSR regime settled and the "end of history" triumphalism ran its course, the old fundamental Right:Left divisions of political visions re-emerged, adjusting to a new context. The new type of Left, or at least its outline, was gradually taking shape. It is far removed from the "statism" of the "Old Left" and the mystique of an anticipated proletarian rule (with actual bureaucratic controls and privileges to go with it). It is not quite the New Left of the 1950s and 1960s either, calling "a plague on both houses" of the two superpowers and envisaging its task mainly as the purification of nineteenth-century ideologies of human liberation. While clearly linked to the New Left of 1956 and 1968 in its critique, the New New Left of the turn of the twentieth century is being defined and shaped by the character of the New Right and its domination during the 1985-95 decade.

At the core of contemporary anti-Right argument stands the assumption of treating depersonalised market relations and self-directed profit maximisation and managerial controls as the only real springs of human action. Altruism interlinked with collective solidarity is seen as significant and to be preferred, where human action is considered. The New New Left assumes individuation as part of non-state collectivism or communalism as the effective guarantors of individual liberty. It is the assumed community which is under debate. While to some on the New New Left it has been seen as the direct relationship of solidarity of neighbours or members of co-operatives, it was the gender or the race in a self-defence posture which seemed to play that role for most of its contemporary adherents. This was expressed in continuous pressure for "positive discrimination" of populations considered under-privileged as the main political strategy these views generated up to now. While taking its cues from liberal, populist and socialist traditions of the past, this approach added its demand for actual empowerment "from below" of humans *vis-à-vis* the welfare state and the free market alike - a radical democratisation. It also added the demand for open information as part of that empowerment and democratisation (or redemocratisation) (Rowbotham & Wainwright, 1979; Williams, 1989).

Much of the Left's argument, present and past, has been set up as moral dilemmas directly relevant to political decision-making: maximisation of profits versus the quality and aesthetics of life of the majority, humans as objects of effective management versus humans as subjects of history, ecology versus the profit-maximisation, etc. Matters of human dignity stood high on such agendas. One more way to look at the contemporary Right:Left divide is to consider what each side believes to be unrealistic. To the New Right, the Left agenda is Utopianism dressed up as "soft" social sciences or social ethics. To the New New Left, the agenda of the New Right is an ideological dressing-up of the egoism of the privileged and of meanness presented as good management practice and/or laws of economics.

Social Work: Matters of Conceptual Survival
Social workers have been entering this world of new conditions, images and political confrontations quite unprepared. Their professional self-images militated as much against speculative debate as against direct involvement in party politics. Yet, increasingly, they found themselves confronting such matters. This mostly meant, in fact, confronting the New Right policies of the State, while delimiting its own stand *vis-à-vis* Postmodernity and the New New Left visions. One can, of course, trace similarities as well as diversity between all those entities sharing social and cultural space.

The resources at the social workers' disposal are being defined not only by general economic trends but by political and ideological decisions as to " how to slice the cake" of public wealth. The last decade was particularly bad in that sense. Economic pressures came into the field of Social Work together with endless demands to have its expenses justified in terms of "real results" while the signposts of what are these "real results" were vague and shifted endlessly. Cuts in welfare budgets and imposition from above of constant changes in the rules of the game to their disadvantage made social workers feel, with particular strength, the many aspects of ambivalence of their profession-cum-discipline.

At least in terms of rhetorical declarations, the New Right shared Social Work's implicit criticism by deed of suprauniversalistic assumptions of welfarism - the assumed need to treat "clients" as endlessly diverse. The emphasis on personal fulfilment and family responsibility in the New Right programmes would also overlap with much of what the "casework" training and social work routines would take for granted. However, the New Right's consistent antagonism towards public expenditure on state welfare, its belief in the ability of faceless market forces, once freely applied, to resolve all social problems, ran directly contrary to what social workers knew and documented from daily professional encounters.

The same applied to managerialism increasingly adopted by the New Right state as the single guide to managing human affairs. To quote a recent study, "targetled management has no ethic beyond achieving its set goals and no identity beyond the organisation and whoever controls that organisation. It controls and it is controlled". Its rules of the game thereby, have "no parallel in ethical professional practice, whatever the profession" (Barr, 1992). The same can be said about social workers' professional training to support the empowerment of the lowly and vulnerable, to minimise interference and to treat "clients" as subjects.

While social workers have often been politically quite naïve, the New Right ideologues and politicians were quick to recognise social work as a potentially hostile force ("conservative" in the new language of radical marketers who measure "progress" by the indices of dewelfarisation and of "privatisation" of services). Within a model of economics in which the state economy and services are equated with the "spending burden" (and only the privately owned enterprises are defined as "productive"), social work is by definition the spender *par excellence* due for "cuts" in the interests of "the economy" and the nation. A profession which additionally carries ethical doubts and continuous evidence of pauperisation by major parts of the population, was to be restricted and tamed. Part of the ideological justification for that has been the images of the profession as a conspiracy against laity. The taming was to be carried out by a new breed of extra-professional welfare managers and through bureaucratic control via protocols and "guidelines" rather than the professional standards, to which extensive "marketisation" of public services has been added (Simic, 1995; BMJ, 1994; Hudson, 1994). This has been making it all a matter of existence to the social workers as such for what may be at stake is creeping de-establishment of social work as a profession and an academic discipline with its functions taken over by the clerks and executives of state and corporative bureaucracies.

As to the Postmodernity idiom and thought, many of its major components were accepted well in advance by the mainstream of Social Work (Taylor-Gooby, 1993). There has been spontaneous acceptance of the significance of "short narratives" and of the subjective and diverse meanings attached to objective reality when humans are concerned. But at the same time, the profession was built on an assumption and centrality of a fundamental "grand narrative" of human rights: the right of humans as such to minimal levels of well-being, underwritten by society as a whole. While carrying within itself the experience of relativity and of diversity of ways in which help to humans can be offered and interpreted, the core of social workers assumed and elaborated a "grand narrative" of practical altruism as a basic part of communal human living. This has been a consistent immovable at the core of the professional persona of the social worker in direct contradiction with the "shifting sands" feeling of social reality which the post-modernity paradigm has been promoting.

As to the New New Left, still in the process of establishing itself as a programme and an agenda (rather than just a contra-shadow of the New Right), many of its arguments against the New Right policies overlapped with the fundamental codes of Social Work: the defence of those in need with particular attention given to minorities and their rights to full expression. The argument for the extension of "communal Social Work" besides the "casework" as part of Social Work training, comes close to much one can hear also from the New New Left. However, the New New Left come-what-may militancy on behalf of specific groups of the underprivileged and the argument for ever-advancing democratisation clash with the academic and professional tendencies and credentials of Social Work. Professionalism carries assumptions of objectivity and admits an in-built unequal relationship. The keeping of distance and eventual disappearance from the scene by the "professional" is fundamental for his brief of "rehabilitation"-cum-"normalisation" of the "client". Also, it is the individual and family which are Social Work's central focus rather than a generalised social category such as gender, race or "the underprivileged" *in toto* (Williams, 1989).

Within the constant administrative and financial upheaval of the contemporary state and its dependencies, the future of social work, its ability to survive as a distinct profession and discipline is being defined by its ability to sustain its particularity as a concept, a function, and institutional framework, a section of the "budget" and a self-reproducing cadre. Under the pressures simply to obey "those above", facing indifference and often hostility outside its ranks, social work very much depends on its content, on the loyalties it generates and on the ability to train newcomers, and to defend "its corner" from constant administrative interferences and from its own internal feelings of futility. Social work has carried into the era of New Right governments and prevailing ideologies a brief of integrated social policy with an individual edge where the vulnerable members of society are concerned. At the core of its self-definition, proceeds to stand an interpretation of human rights and of professionalism linked into a still broader and more diffuse image of applied altruism within societies in which altruism carries a major positive value. Its functional expression is rehabilitation-cum-normalisation as a concentrated effort to enhance the human autonomy of those vulnerable. Its concept of professionalism as virtue is shared with other "caring professions" but with a somewhat more generic and society-bound vision of human needs and an interprofessional tendency to match.

Social work specifically and the "caring professions" in general, carry particular potential of dissent and of challenge to the powers that be and social realities as those are. To spell it out, one may as well reach back to the Hippocratic oath, introduced many centuries ago by the first "caring profession" to recognise itself as such. The wording in its current edition, if we remove the very few of its specifically medical components, sounds as follows:

I solemnly pledge myself to consecrate my life to the service of humanity

I will give my teachers the respect and gratitude which is their due

I will practise my profession with conscience and dignity

. . . my patient will be my first consideration

I will respect the secrets which are confided in me. . .

I will maintain by all the means in my power the honour and the noble tradition of the profession

My colleagues will be my brothers

I will not permit considerations of religion, nationality, race, party politics or social standing to intervene between my duty and my patients

Even under threat, I will not use my knowledge contrary to the laws of humanity.

I make these promises solemnly, freely and upon my honour.

Notice - not profit but service. Notice - not the dutiful execution of a work contract or orders by "the authorities" but the consecration of one's life. Notice - nothing to stand between one's duty and one's patient, irrespective.... Notice - this promise being made upon one's honour. Such declarations are seldom fully matched by reality but this does not mean that they represent empty promises either. As well stated in a major UN document, "Ethical codes ever precede ethical conduct......If it had not been for the enunciation of principles that were difficult to fulfil, the progress which has been made...... would not exist" (Laqueur & Rubin, 1989). One should consider contemporary Social Work and its "survivability", which is in balance, in those terms.

References

Abbot, A. (1988) T*he System of Professions*. Chicago, University of Chicago Press.

Aganbegyan, A. (1986) *The Challenge: Economics of Perestroika*. London, Tauris.

Barr, N. (1992) Economic Theory and the Welfare State, *Journal of Economic Literature;* Vol XXX, pp 741-803.

Bauman, Z. (1992) *Intimations of Post Modernity*. London, Routledge.

Bourdieu, P. (1988) *Homo Academicus*. Cambridge, Cambridge University Press

Bourdieu, P. (1991) *Language and Symbolic Power*. Cambridge, Cambridge University Press.

Brandon, D., Brandon, A., Brandon A. (1995) *Advocacy: Power to People*. Birmingham, Venture Press.

British Medical Journal, The Rise of Stalinism in NHS (editorial), 16 Dec 1994.

Brown, H., Smith, H. (ed) (1990) *Normalisation: A Reader for the 1990s*. London, Routledge.

Coldwell, M. (1977) *The Wealth of Some Nations*. London, Zed.

Eley, G. (1984) "Combining Two Histories: SPD and the German Working Class before 1914", *Radical History Review.*

Flora, P. (1981) *The Development of Welfare States in Europe and America*. Brunswick, Transaction Books.

Foucault, M. (1977) *Discipline and Punishment*. London, Tavistock.

Goffman, E. (1961) *Asylums*. New York, Anchor.

Hayek, F. A. (1944) *The Road to Serfdom* London, Routledge.

Hollis, F. Woods, M. E. (1981) *Casework, a psycho-social therapy.*New York, Randon House.

Hudson, B. (1994) Management and Finance in N. Malin, *Implementing Community Care*. OU Press, Milton Keynes.

Hughes, C. F. (1993) *The Sociological Eye*. New Brunswick, Transaction Books, p 378.

Hutton, W. (1995) *The State We're In*. London, Jonathan Cape.

Illich, I. (ed) (1968) *Disabling Professions*. London, Marion Boyars.

Illich, I. (1978) *Towards a History of Needs*. Berkeley, Berkeley University Press.

Jordan, B. (1984) *Invitation to Social Work*. Oxford, Polity Press.

Kautsky, K. (1902) One Day After The Social Revolution.Moscow, *Iskra* no 18.

Laqueur, W., (1989) Rubin, B. *Human Rights Reader*. New York, Scribner.

Marcuse, H. (1968) *One Dimensional Man*. London, Heinemann.

Parton, N. (1994) "Problematics of Government, (Post) Modernity and Social Work", *British Journal of Social Work*. 24, 9-32.

Polanyi, K. (1957) *The Great Transformation: The Political and Economic Origins of Our Time*.Beacon Press, Boston.

Popper, (1962) *The Open Society and its Enemies*. Routledge.

Ramon, S. (ed) (1991) *Beyond Community Care: Normalisation and Integration Work*. London, Mind Macmillan.

Rowbotham, S., Wainwright, H. (1979) *Beyond the Fragments*. London, The Womens Press, Merlin Press.

Shanin, T. "The Idea of Progress" in M. Rahname and V. Bawtree, (1996) *The Post-Development Reader. London*, Zed.

Simic, P. What"s in a Word: From Social "Worker" to Care "Manager", *Practice* Vol 7, No 3 (1995) pp 10-11.

Suarle, P., McConville, M. (1968) *French Revolution* Harmondsworth, Penguin.

Taylor-Gooby, P. (1993) Post Modernism and Social Policy: a Great Leap Backward? *Journal of Social Policy*.Vol 21, no 3, pp 385-404.

Torstendahl, R., Burrage, M. (1990) *The Formation of Professions*.Beverly Hills, Sage.

Weber, M., Wolff, K. H. (1964) *The Sociology of George Simmel* New York, The Free Press.

Wilensky, H. (1975) *The Welfare State and Equality: Structure and Ideological Roots of Public Expenditure*.Berkeley, Berkeley University Press.

Williams, F. (1989) *Social Policy: A Critical Introduction*. Cambridge, Polity Press.

Zaslavskaya, T. (1987) *The Second Socialist Revolution*. London, Tauris.

"Community" as a Basis for Social Policy and Social Action

Malcolm Payne

The importance of "community"

The idea of "community" has been an important one in politics, social welfare and social policy. It is still important, as we can see from the recent espousal of "communitarianism" as an answer to the ills of modern societies (Etzioni, 1995). Willmott (1989) in a study of 1980s community initiatives in Britain identified community care, community policing, community architecture, community work, community organisations, community development, community arts, community media, community social work, community education, community business all as current attempts to implement an idea of community within some other aspect of social policy. He also identified many reports of other organisations and projects which referred to "community" as the basis of their work.

Butcher (1983) identifies three types of explanation for this recurring enthusiasm for the concept of community in policy:

"Community" is used pragmatically in building policy which responds to current trends and attitudes to society. Its use draws on common ideas and values and enables policy-makers and workers within services to identify and present alternatives to current policy and practice in a way which reflects these accepted values.

The need to use "community" derives from legitimation, performance and fiscal crises of the State. People are less prepared to accept the right of state planning and services to intervene in their lives - this is seen as less legitimate than in the past. Centralised state services are seen as ineffective and bureaucratised, and there are problems in funding them to a level adequate to provide the desired level of service - their performance and financing are increasingly problematic. Moving to a community ideal suggests other solutions which are seen as more acceptable, more efficient and less demanding of state finance; or at least this is potentially so.

Devolving services and policy-making to a community level reflects a change in the nature of society towards a "post-modern" or "post-industrial" one. We can no longer see nation states as all-embracing, centralised units, meeting all their citizens" needs. Employment and industrial development are not in large companies or state organisations offering jobs for life. They are beginning to fragment, become more plural. Life is more individualised, privatised - that is, our ways of living and commitments are hidden from others and are pursued alone or in small groups rather than as part of wide-scale political and social organisations.

All these changes are affecting societies throughout the world. We can see similar developments in policy-making, similar legitimation, performance and fiscal crises and similar moves towards breakdown of bureaucracies and centralised industrial management in the capitalist systems of western Europe and north America, in the former communist states of Europe and Asia, in the newly developing economies of the Pacific rim and in developing countries of Africa, Asia and Latin America. It is not clear whether it is an unstoppable movement of social change which is enforcing changes in management and policy, or whether it is a political change deriving from preference for self-identification with less-all-embracing social structures. It may be a complex mixture of the two trends. People see around them the consequences of global change deriving from the information revolution and technological change and respond to the opportunity for a different way of life by demanding and creating social change. Managers and policy-makers respond both to these social pressures and to the economic and industrial changes which derive from technological change. All societies struggle to make sense of and bring together the aspirations of their people and the consequences of social phenomena. "Community" enables them to do so.

Ideas of community
The ideal of community is drawn from a variety of sources. Willmott (1986, p83) argues that it is derived from having things in common. In the classic statement by Tönnies (1955) "community" (*gemeinschaft*) is characterised by many mutual links, shared values, dependence and an accepted, almost natural status hierarchy. The alternative "association" (*gesellschaft*) has relationships characterised by formal rules and conventions. Community implies interpersonal solidarity based upon features of the social environment; association is less natural and has to be constructed.

Among the sources of community in the environment, we may identify the following:

Place communities" based on shared location (Willmott, 1986). People in them have *frequent interaction* over a *range of aspects of life* in common because life takes place in the same locality. But community is more than shared locality - these communities are seen to possess characteristics of shared experience and value which goes beyond mere proximity. There is an image of particular *social lifestyles*. People have beliefs about and valuations of particular lifestyles which they have experienced and lost or of which they are aware and value.

The traditional community is the residential religious and Utopian one. The Christian monastery and convent in which people live communally, giving up individual possessions and participating in a joint commitment to a social ideal is replicated in religious communities throughout the world. Many social movements over the centuries have sought to create ideal communities in which the self becomes committed to the communal, sometimes with political sometimes with social objectives (see, for example, Kanter, 1972; Mercer, 1984). All strands of life, the family, employment, leisure, religion and politics are brought together and shared. This is a continuing thread of idealists the world over. Israeli *kibbutzim*, sixties hippy communes (Abrams and McCullouch, 1976) and their continuation as part of the Green movement, seeking self-sufficiency in the face of the evils of industrialisation (Pepper, 1991), and communist collective farms reflect this ideal of shared residence and identity. We can see this implemented in the ideal of asylum for mentally ill people in the nineteenth century and in modern-day techniques such as the therapeutic community (Jones, 1968; Jansen, 1982; Manning, 1989; Kennard, 1983). In planned therapeutic environments (Righton, 1979) such as therapeutic communities, people are cured of social and personal ills by learning the skills of sharing and interpersonal responsiveness through experience of them in controlled settings.

Another valued lifestyle is the claimed rural idyll of the pre-industrial phase of society. The ideal is of a natural rural community in which everyone knows everyone else, everyone has a place and a contribution and can live within the boundaries of a local economy and localised social network. Having a "place", of course, implies more than a residence and a social role, but a position in a defined hierarchy and social order in such societies. Frankenberg's (1957) study of an isolated rural community in the 1950s is a classic example, and connects with much anthropological work throughout the world.

Finally, in this category of thinking about community, there is reference to an urban community lifestyle associated with working class areas in previous generations. Important American studies of Middleton in the 1920s and '30s idealised the communities of small-town America. In the 1950s and '60s, there were a number of famous studies (Frankenberg, 1969) of urban British life. There has been much criticism of this kind of work, since the findings are of a particular time, place and point of view. It is difficult to say anything definitive about the nature of these communities. What we can identify is the sense of a mutually supportive social life organised in relation to local industrial shared employment for men and shared adversity in maintaining household and family life for women.

Communities of interest (Willmott, 1986) arise because people have interests in common. These may be leisure, work or other social contacts.

Important communities of interest may derive from important social characteristics or relations, such as having the same ethnic origin. People may see themselves as part of the African-Caribbean, Chinese or Indian community, even if they are not in close proximity. People see a boundary which defines a group and strong interpersonal social relations which create a social network within that group. Equally, we talk about "the business community" recognising that the kind of people involved in business have shared interests and attitudes, even though they do not live in a particular locality. They may form a community through social relations within a variety of interlocking groups even though all businessmen are not in touch with all others. People recognise and acknowledge shared *boundaries and connections* within social life.

Community as *gemeinschaft* is seen as natural, but an alternative view claims that all understandings of how society is are constructed. Community is a symbol, an idea created by people of some forms of social life. In discussing place communities, I have suggested that particular lifestyles have been idealised as "community" lifestyles of various kinds. They are "reality" to people who are involved in these lifestyles, or who are observers of these or other lifestyles, or who are commentators and identify or construct these types of lifestyle. This reality is a shared perception and understanding of how things are. It is a construction, made up from ideals and perceptions of life. The construction is social in the sense that it is shared, agreed and understood between people. Agreement and shared conception lead to a shared reality about the nature and value of community. As we disentangle the strands of thought, we may come to see another reality of a more complex kind, but the more simple social construction has the advantage of being able to engage commitment and understanding from people. It may, therefore become a powerful motivator for action. Also it is a positive, rather than negative, motivator because of the absence of negative connotations to the concept and of opposite conceptions to set against the idea of community (Williams, 1983, pp 75-6).

Because community is a social construction, a shared conception, it gives people one way of understanding and defining aspects of a complex life in comprehensible ways, as ideas of "family" or "nation" sometimes do. Comprehension permits action. Important aspects of the idea of community are that it allows people to see boundaries around certain social relations and connections between people within those boundaries as more significant than connections across the boundaries. This allows people to understand where they fit into place communities.

These ideas are not solely western ones, and western thought often limits our conceptions of community. Ripathi (1988), for example, argues that western views of the group treat it as separate from the individual. There are interactions between them. An Indian view sees the individual as integral to the group. The group is, in essence, a wider boundary of the individual. The individual is a boundary within the group. If we are truly part of a group, its essence becomes part of us and our participation endows the group with our characteristics. Our conception of the group includes our conception of ourselves, and our "self" contains our understanding of the group. This view of our personal interaction with the groups which we are part of helps us understand that our symbolic construction of the communities that we can identify includes ourselves, and our construction of our "self" includes the communities that we understand ourselves as being part of.

"Community of attachment" (Willmott, 1986), where people identify with particular *social interests*.

Community is about self-identity. Community exists where people perceive or experience themselves as being in association with each other in special ways. People in a community, whether of place or of interest, share attachments. They are social attachments in two different senses. We have seen that they imply interpersonal interconnections in a network. The social attachments also imply shared social interests. We noted above that one origin of the idea of place communities was the character of working class communities. Such communities with close supportive relationships often came from shared adversity, shared interests in the face of conflict or pressure. Here we may see community as being oppositional. Attachment came about because it is necessary in the face of opposing social interests. Thus, as we saw in relation to communities of interest, feeling a sense of community in the face of racism or social oppression can be an important aspect of life which cements attachment to a community. Williams (1993) shows, similarly, that women can feel "confined" in a community by their domestic responsibilities. The business community has particular social and political interests which the interlocking organisations that form the community pursue. We can thus see "community" as a political entity. It is political in the sense that the network of relationships exists partly to pursue the interests of those involved by exercising influence and power on their behalf and often contrary to the interests of those who might oppose it.

Nartsupha (1991) explores the "community culture" school of thought in Thailand. Within this view, we can see the western idealisation of rural community as the basis for an idealisation of social relations which might be effective for social action. However, this school of thought counterposes such rural communities against state intervention as part of a "capitalist" culture. In this view, middle and upper class élites in society construct social relations around an industrialised, globalised culture which develops an economic and employment system that is different from the interpersonal, face-to-face interactions of a rural culture. The rural culture is seen as a much more fundamental form of social relations than the capitalist culture. Community thus implies an anti-state and non-capitalist mode of social relations. An important aspect of this view of community is its perception of community as part of a political discourse about what kinds of social relations may be valued in society.

Transferring this back to western society, we can see much more clearly how the ideal of community is a social and political critique of current state and capitalist constructions of social relations. If we take up social policies and forms of social action which rely on the concept of community, we are taking up a critical stance and a critical form of social action. Community sometimes acts against the State and against depersonalising and alienating forms of social relations, although through creating shared stereotypes of social relations such as homosexuality it may strengthen oppressive social ideas about people too. This is Etzioni's (1995) view. He proposes communitarianism as an alternative way of achieving social relations which will attain effective, committed participation in social progress and which will be an alternative to bureaucratised and alienating centralised social relations. Understanding this, we can also evaluate the sort of state annexation of community in the list of "community . . ." services derived from Willmott's (1989) study with which I started this essay. If community is a critique of the State, to annex it is to attempt to incorporate potential criticism into the State's social order, and deprive any alternative social order of the opportunity of gaining attachment to community.

Community initiatives in social policy
From these conceptual considerations, we can now turn to the role of community initiatives in social policy. I have argued that incorporating community into social policy initiatives seeks to annex a potential and potent force of opposition or source of alternative values into state social policy. It also attempts to recruit to the interests of the State the power and commitment of attachment and interest which comes from people's constructions of community in their lives and

lifestyles. Instead of seeing community as "natural", as Tönnies might, if it is constructed, we can create new constructions that produce the ideals which we seek to achieve in our societies. We can see how this might be possible by exploring different forms of community initiative.

Willmott (1989, p25) identifies four types of localised community initiative, distinguished by the extent to which they are internally created or externally recruited. He sees *neighbourhood life* as daily activities which take place without formal organisation. Community policy initiatives seek to enhance, re-create and recruit neighbourhood life to the social purpose of promoting social cohesion and presenting social dislocation. *Community action* is also internally created, but is more formally organised. It might comprise a playgroup or a residents' association. Community policy initiatives seek to enhance such action to create social cohesion, to provide a conduit for social concerns. Such a conduit might reduce the need for state action to respond to the concerns and prevent social conflict arising from them. *Community development* involves enthusiasts and professionals in supporting indigenous efforts in local social life. This suggests that external support is needed to enable more-complex activities to take place. Arts activities or community centres require more financial or physical resources and a wider range of skills than may be immediately available within a place or interest community. The community policy initiative is undertaken on the assumption that the greater economic and social value of more-complex activities will realise greater returns in cohesion and commitment than might be achieved by indigenous community life or action. Alternatively, development directs or redirects indigenous action in the fulfilment of social purposes which are of value to policymakers, but which might be a lower priority to indigenous people. Finally, *community policies* implement external policies in ways which seek to recruit participation from indigenous people in externally created objectives. A number of examples include neighbourhood watch, in which local groups are organised to protect each other's property and assist the police in preventing crime from taking place by promoting watchfulness. We might also include "community care", the idea of promoting informal networks as the major basis for personal care of people with long-term caring needs.

Willmott was only concerned with local initiatives, but it is possible to identify two further types of external community initiative. These are *community services* in which a public service is organised or reconstructed to emphasise local responsiveness. Community policing is an example. The service continues to be an official one. It is not intended that this should be carried out by indigenous people, but that their support should be engendered by presenting the service with an emphasis on commitment to local responsiveness in organisation and philosophy. *Community programmes* are public or broad-scale services and policies which are not constructed to provide for place or interest communities, but emphasise the elements of their purposes which seek social cohesion and commitment. So, many businesses have "community affairs" departments, many of which are information or public relations organisations. They are designed to facilitate a social environment which enables the business more easily to pursue its profit-making aims by presenting its objectives in ways which emphasise the social purposes and advantages of successful business enterprise.

There is a history throughout the world of community initiatives of all these kinds. A few examples are as follows:

The settlement movement of the late-nineteenth century sought to create rural mutual relationships within very deprived urban settings, and so cut across class divides and inequalities (Meacham, 1987). Houses were set up in deprived urban neighbourhoods in which middle-class people, particularly university students, would live for a while, during which time they would provide help to the poor people around them. They would live as a Utopian community, in communal surroundings, and in close contact with the class which would otherwise be so distant from them. Many universities established such facilities in Britain and the USA and many strands of social work emerged from them.

In the 1930s in Britain and the USA there was an economic recession leading to considerable hardship. This led to both political action by workers' organisations and social responses by local organisations, setting up employment projects and practical help for local unemployed people. These movements reflected collective and community action based on localities and a sense of community derived from shared adversity. Such experiences led to pressure for the creation of organised welfare provision in the 1950s and '60s. Similar experiences in the 1980s and '90s have led to a similar flowering of social responses and projects, but a fragmentation of organised welfare because of the failure of political action by and on behalf of those affected. Organised welfare has fragmented because of the promotion of the idea that welfare and social security services were overloaded by the pressure of these events and had become ineffective because of bureaucratisation. There has been a consequential political movement in favour of reducing and restricting welfare provision until it is affordable, responsive to individualised demands and separated from the State. Part of this political response identified the failure of the community response apparent in the 1930s.

This was blamed on the effect of the welfare provision developed in the 1950s and '60s which was perceived as "inhibiting" community responses. There were attempts to substitute organised voluntary and informal responses for this supposed failing.

In summary, recently we have seen a reaction against community-oriented developments associated with political action by oppressed peoples because the welfare state achievements of such action in the past are being rejected as unaffordable. This has led to attempts to substitute constructed forms of community life promoted simply because they are affordable. However, these are viewed as false by oppressed people because they do not conform to the experiences of shared social lifestyles and shared understanding of the world which, as we have seen above, is inherent in people's experience of the meaning of "community".

An important aspect of much community thinking has been voluntary provision for caring, assumed to be based on altruism and a preference for community living. In the nineteenth century, much social provision arose from charitable work by rich or middle-class people caring for those with evidently great need. Many organised services were developed, using volunteer labour – that is, people undertaking work without receiving payment for the value of it. Volunteers both managed and provided much social service and campaigned for their own replacement by effective public services. The creation of fairly comprehensive organised public services in the 1950s led to a change in focus whereby the "voluntary sector" of organisations concentrated on the "vanguard role" establishing the validity of services responding to new needs, which might then be taken over by public provision. They also dealt with people on the margins of society, such as drug addicts, the homeless or prostitutes whose care was not accepted as a valid expense to taxpayers.

In the 1960s and '70s, attempts were made to reproduce altruistic volunteer neighbourhood care through organised local services (Abrams *et al.* 1989). There was a movement to help social networks to strengthen "natural" helping networks and enable them to be more effective in providing care for larger numbers of people or undertake more-difficult caring tasks. Many such developments foundered or had limited results because of evidence that actual or assumed reciprocity is more important than altruism in informing and motivating voluntary action. People expect something in exchange, and undertake voluntary work out of personal satisfaction, past experience of someone else providing for them or the expectation that they can and will call on similar help in the future. Social changes have also meant that local networks are less important to many people and cannot provide for care needs. There is also a good deal of evidence that the need for social links does not mean that they are necessarily created. Many people prefer privacy and confidentiality. All of these issues are reviewed by Bulmer (1987).

The perception, then, that voluntarism is a characteristic of a sense of community seems false. Similarly, there is little validity in the idea that it might be created by the improvement of community or that community might be developed from strengthening voluntarism. From another point of view, voluntarism may be contrasted with community. We have noted above that much of the experience of voluntarism comes from a class-based form of provision. It has stemmed from "haves" providing for "have nots". Political and workers' action has focused more on achieving and maintaining general social provision. Extensive need for voluntary provision might therefore be taken as a sign of division and inequality in societies rather than of cohesion and mutual assistance.

Evidence of substantial division and deprivation has also led to community initiatives from government. In the 1960s, concern about the breakdown in social relations and in particularly high levels of crime and environmental degradation in urban areas, in both inner cities and peripheral housing estates developed in the 1950s, led to movements in both Britain and the USA to focus on those communities. An aspect of these was community work, which is considered briefly below. Conflict about the aims of these projects arose. Their focus on the needs of particular areas was criticised because their problems arose from wider social inequalities and failings of government social programmes. Drawing attention to these inadequacies led to conflict with governments funding the programmes in the UK (Loney, 1983). More-recent attempts at such activities have focused more clearly on economic development, and the idea of creating more successful social relations has taken a back place.

Present concerns about community focus on the needs of particular groups. In urban areas, these are often minority ethnic groups which in many western societies are particularly disadvantaged and oppressed compared with the host community (Ely and Denney, 1987). However, internationally, there is also a strong focus on the needs of women and disabled people (Coleridge, 1993; Harcourt 1994). Public concern is also focused on high crime rates, on the evident criminality asociated with drug addicts, and on frequent teenage offenders. The problems of each of these groups are taken as at least partly a failing of community and the response is often to promote community support. Again, these groups are identifiable and therefore their condition may be worsened by stigmatisation and social relations which take for granted that such groups may be oppressed, because of cultural expectations or social convention. Such cultural and social pressures are often bolstered by the way in which social structures favour people who are already economically and socially advantaged.

This account of a variety of community issues and initiatives which have arisen in the recent history of social provision draws attention to the ways in which community is often seen as a response to social division and inequality, and social problems are seen as a failing in community. However, we have also seen how community initiatives assume the maintenance of social inequality and division. This issue is also evident if we turn to examine various forms of intervention in community.

Community as an element of social intervention

Because of its social importance as an ideal and mode of organisation, community has also formed an element in many different constructions of social intervention. In the previous sections, we explored projects, agencies and initiatives which include community as a social construction of their objectives. Community is also used in constructing methods of social intervention. I explore in this section ways in which community has been used as the basis of various forms of social intervention: in social casework, in different models of community work, in community social work and in community care through care or case management. We have already briefly examined therapeutic communities above.

Social casework is one of the basic forms of social work, and is usually considered to comprise work with individuals and families where the aim is to prevent, cure or reduce the consequences of various social ills. Its individual and treatment focus tends to emphasise the expert professional helping a disadvantaged or problematic person or persons. This tends to exclude it from consideration as a community intervention. The community context is best expressed in the classic form of "the person-in-situation" as the objective of psychosocial casework theory (Hollis, 1970). Here the individual work responds to the situation of the person being helped. That situation affects how the person sees their problem, how the problem affects them and the resources available both within themselves and in their surrounding social relationships to deal with the problem. The social worker tries to affect not only the person (as a psychiatrist, counsellor or psychologist would) but the situation also and seeks changes in the situation in concert with the changes in the individual. Social systems theory extends this concept. It prescribes formal assessment and involvement of different networks of social relations around the individual client (Pincus and Minahan, 1973). These may be changed and effected separately: it is assumed that as these are changed they affect the client indirectly. Systems theory, then, proposes that work in social relations not involving the client may affect not only the "situation" but also the client, whereas psychosocial theory requires work with both the client and situation and focuses on the client and their interactions with the situation.

The community focus among the objectives and values of social casework comes from the contexts in which this service is typically implemented. It is used on the boundaries of institutions such as hospitals and prisons to prevent admission or to facilitate discharge and to deal with the social consequences of institutionalisation. Thus, social work is typically used to foster movement into and out of institutions and to consider the external rather than maintenance of the institutions themselves. Doctors, nurses and prison officers, on the other hand, focus on the running of the institution and the provision of its treatment or social control purposes.

However, social casework seeks to maintain individuals within communities rather than enhancing community and communities. This is more clearly the focus of another fundamental element of social work: community work. Neither is community work restricted to alliance with social work agencies. It is used in association with other public services, particularly education, planning and housing services to support their activities also.

More broadly, it has, at times, been used as a means of social and economic development. This has taken place in developed countries such as Britain and the USA in attempts to respond to severe urban, and occasionally rural, deprivation. The 1960s War on Poverty in the USA (Brager and Purcell, 1967) and community development programmes in the UK (Loney, 1983) focused on very-run-down city centres, where multiple deprivation among people and seriously deteriorated environments seems to require special action. Recently, it has been used in more focused ways, for example to engage substantial numbers of the population in a region to prevent crime in areas where it has been a severe problem. Such work has been defined as community development because of a very clear focus on locality, since place communities are easily understood as a focus for community initiatives.

In developing countries, community development has a long history. In colonial times, it was a way of responding to social dislocation arising from rapid social change and destruction by colonial powers of traditional social relations (Midgley, 1995). Community development maintained such traditional social relations as continued to exist and sought to translate them into new social objectives by promoting participation in economic and industrial development. More recently, the focus has been on economic development and social consequences have been neglected: however, this failing has been perceived as damaging efforts at economic development and attempts are being made to redress the balance (Midgley, 1995). Social development techniques used in developing countries are equally applicable in many developed countries because, fundamentally, they seek to deal with major social and economic inequalities.

Present-day community work contains these and further models of practice. All these, in various ways, seek to develop the sense of community among defined groups by increasing the number and frequency of links and contacts between organisations, groups and individuals within a defined community, and usually increasing skills and capacities to deal with problems which arise for organisations, groups and individuals within that community. Popple (1995) identifies eight:

- community organisation aimed at improving co-ordination between agencies

- community development aimed at helping groups to gain skills and confidence to participate in community life and at decisions affecting them

- social and community planning aimed at analysing social conditions, setting goals and evaluating services in areas being redeveloped

- community education aimed at bringing education and community into closer relationships

- community action being a class-based conflict-style approach to resolving local problems

- feminist community work aimed at improving women's welfare and developing collective responses to women's inequality

- black and anti-racist community work aimed at responding to the needs of black groups and challenging racism

- community care aimed at developing self-help, social networks and voluntary services in support of caring provision.

Community as a middle-range policy objective

So far, I have been arguing that the idea of community has been an attractive one in many societies. It is a symbol of particularly valued relations. Those relations are characterised by a high degree of interconnection between individuals: they meet and relate in a variety of social contexts rather than just one. Community policies, then, set out to construct additional linkages among people with some reason for contact in order to form a "community" where one did not exist, or develop it where it may be identified. Thus, special things are done in a residential care home to create a "community" which is therapeutic, rather than merely housing and sustaining the members. Additional connections are made within social links to add caring and protective functions through community care provision. In various forms of community work, locality or interest is used as a starting point, and additional relationships are created to increase the number and range of links within that locality or interest group.

Much social policy and political thinking is concerned with the nation state and its needs. Thus, economic, defence and foreign policy objectives are an important aspect of political and public life. We also think of services designed to meet personal needs, for shelter, sustenance in adversity, education and health. Though these are for individuals, they are intended to meet various social objectives. It is in the economic interests of a nation to ensure that its people are able to work, by being healthy, well trained and housed. A successful nation will also need public order, so there is a public policy interest in democratic participation, policing and civil regulation. Similarly, it is possible to see that personal services which support the social order of the family will help sustain and support young people and elderly or disabled people.

Not all needs for social regulation can be achieved, however, with political intervention in the economic or justice system or by meeting individuals' needs directly or through sustaining kinship networks. "Community" forms a social construction at an intermediate level between societal objectives and interventions and family and personal supports. It offers a comprehensible and potentially supportive social system to which individuals might look in the absence of personal and kinship supports as an alternative, or to which they might look as an additional element in their world.

Pinker (1990) argues that community is embraced as an objective at least in part because it represents the opportunity to interweave formal with informal services. There is a good deal of evidence that people prefer to receive social caring services in their own homes, from people who are close in relationship to them rather than from paid officials in organised programmes of service. State services benefit from this preference, since the need to pay for public services is avoided or reduced. Social relations are developed to support this preference within society. For example, it is seen as stigmatising to be unable to provide for oneself and one's family. The degree of disapproval varies among societies, but is rarely absent altogether. Relations of this kind revolve around interpersonal relations and power relations in societies, so that the preference benefits and maintains élites whose power defines such social discourses. When family, the preferred source of personal caring, is not available, other personal links may be pressed into action. The "community" is a social construction of those informal links, helping people understand and give meaning to what otherwise might be diffuse and incomprehensible. It may be given greater form through the creation of localities or more-complex interrelationships among more distant links. Thus, if there is little reason for links to be created among neighbours, it becomes worthwhile to construct them through the various forms of community work discussed above.

Endword: community as lived social order
However, the construction of community comes both from itself, from individuals and their personal needs and from the social structures with power to influence shared understandings of society and its make-up. We have seen throughout this chapter that community is constructed so as to make sense of potentially chaotic and incomprehensible social relations: it makes order out of confusion. It is presented by those who would embrace it as an answer to social problems as an alternative to the present social order, more attractive, more capable of engaging commitment. Sometimes it is explicitly a criticism of the nation state, or bureaucratised public welfare. In some conceptions, our community is a part of ourselves, just as our family, however conceived, is. The recruitment of community to public and organised services, to public social policy, is at once an acknowledgement of its power to gain commitment and involvement, of the failure of public and state services to engender such commitment and of a wish to achieve that elusive goal.

Yet the fact that community is in essence in opposition to the idea of organisation and official governance and yet is also associated with a social order of its own suggests an interpretation of its role in social life. Community is one of the ways in which people make sense of their own lives and create a social order out of the interconnected complexities of their way of living. Its recruitment to official purposes, to support of bureaucratic organisation, can only ever be seen as inadequate in comparison with the lived experience of community. Community in social policy expresses an ideal and a value objective for organised and official services, even if they are not successful in meeting the ideal: to achieve something approximating to people's lived experience of the social order "community", to offer interpersonal social support akin to that lived experience when it is not present. Consumers of services can know when they experience something of the sort, observers and professionals can identify some of its attributes and have a feeling of the whole. But it is people's lived experience of that social order which is the only way of knowing whether the ideal and value of community have been attained. And rules, regulations, systems and quality assurance mechanisms, so beloved of public service managers, will never be able to understand whether that lived experience has been attained unless they ask and accept the experience of the people who use the services provided.

References

Abrams, P., Abrams, S., Humphrey, R., Snaith, R. (1989) *Neighbourhood Care and Social Policy* London, HMSO.

Abrams, P., McCullouch, A. (1976) *Communes, sociology and society.* Cambridge, Cambridge University Press.

Brager, G., Purcell. (1967) *Community Action Against Poverty: Readings from the Mobilization for Youth Experience.* New Haven, College and University Press.

Bulmer, M. (1987) *The Social Basis of Community Care.* London, Allen and Unwin.

Butcher, H. (1983) "Why community policy? Some explanations for recent trends" in Butcher, H., Glen, A., Henderson, P. and Smith, J. *Community and Public Policy.* London, Pluto.

Coleridge, P. (1993) *Disability, Liberation and Development,* Oxford, Oxfam.

Collins, A. H., Pancoast, D. L (1993) *Natural Helping Networks: a strategy for prevention.* Washington DC, National Association of Social Workers.

Dennis, N., Henriques, F., Slaughter, C (1969) *Coal is Our Life: an analysis of a Yorkshire mining community.* London, Tavistock.

Ely, P., Denney (1987) *Social Work in a Multi-Racial Society.* Aldershot, Hants, Gower

Etzioni, A. (1995) *The Spirit of Community: rights, responsibilities and the Communitarian Agenda.* London, Fontana.

Frankenberg, R. F (1957) *Village on the Border: a social study of religion, politics and football in a North Wales community.* London, Cohen and West..

Frankenberg, R. F. (1969) *Communities in Britain: social life in town and country* Harmondsworth, Penguin.

Harcourt, W. (ed) (1994) *Feminist Perspectives on Sustainable Development.* London, Zed Books.

Hollis, F. (1970) "The psychosocial approach to the practice of casework" in Roberts, Robert W. and Nee, R. H. (eds) *Theories of Social Casework* Chicago, University of Chicago Press.

Jansen, E. (ed) (1982) *The Therapeutic Community Outside the Hospital.* London, Croom Helm.

Jones, M. (1968) *Social Psychiatry in Practice: the idea of the therapeutic community* Harmondsworth, Penguin.

Kanter, R. M (1972) *Commitment and Community: communes and utopias in sociological perspective.* Cambridge Mass, Harvard University Press.

Kennard, D. (1983) *An Introduction to Therapeutic Communities.* London, Routledge and Kegan Paul.

Loney, M. (1983) *Community Against Government.* London, Heinemann.

Lynd, R., Lynd, H (1929) *Middletown.* New York, Harcourt Brace.

Lynd, R., Lynd, H. (1937) *Middletown in Transition.* New York, Harcourt Brace.

Manning, N. (1989) *The Therapeutic Community Movement: charisma and routinization.* London, Routledge.

Meacham, S. (1987) *Toynbee Hall and Social Reform, 1880-1914: the search for community.* New Haven, Yale University Press.

Mercer, J. (1984) *Communes: a social history and guide.* Dorchester, Dorset, Prism.

Midgley, J. (1995) *Social Development: the developmental perspective in social welfare.* London, Sage.

Nartsupha, C. (1991) "The community culture school of thought" in Chitakasem, M. and Turton, A. (eds) *Thai Constructions of Knowledge.* London, School of Oriental and African Studies, University of London.

Pepper, D. (1991) *Communes and the Green Vision: counterculture, lifestyle and the New Age* London, Green Print

Pincus, A., Minahan A. (1973) *Social Work Practice: model and methods* Itasca, Ill., Peacock.

Pinker, R. (1990) "The quest for community: from the settlement movement to the Griffiths report" in Pinker, R. *Social Work in an Enterprise Society.* London, Routledge.

Popple, K. (1995) *Analysing Community Work: its theory and practice* Buckingham, Open University Press.

Righton, P. (1979) "Planned environment therapy: a reappraisal" in Righton, P. (ed) *Studies in Environment Therapy* Volume 3. Toddington, Glos, Planned Environment Therapy Trust.

Ripathi, R. C. (1988) "Aligning development to values in India" in Sinha, Durganand, and Kao, Henry S. R. (eds) *Social Values and Development: Asian perspectives.* New Delhi, Sage.

Tönnies, F. (1955) *Community and Association* London, Routledge and Kegan Paul.

Williams, F. (1993) "Women and community" in Bornat, J., Pereira, C., Pilgrim, D. & Williams, F. *Community Care: a reader* London, Macmillan, pp33-42.

Williams, R. (1983) *Keywords: a vocabulary of culture and society* London, Fontana.

Willmott, P. (1986) *Social Networks, Informal Care and Public Policy.* London, Policy Studies Institute (PSI Research Report 655),.

Willmott, P. (1989) *Community Initiatives: patterns and prospects.* London, Policy Studies Institute (PSI Research Report 698).

Young, M., Willmott, P (1957) *Family and Kinship in East London.* London, Routledge and Kegan Paul.

The Role of the Supra-State Organisations in Shaping, Contributing to and Controlling the Development of Social Policy and Social Work: The Case of the European Union

Brian Munday

Introduction

The European Union (EU) is only one of several highly influential supra-state organisations exercising very considerable influence on the economic and social policies of European countries in recent years. These countries include the now-fifteen member states of the EU, and increasingly the former communist countries in eastern and central Europe. The main supra-state organisations providing economic and social assistance are the World Bank, the International Monetary Fund (IMF) and the EU. The involvement of the United Nations, the Council of Europe and the International Labour Organization (ILO) is also important but their contributions to the development of European countries' social policies lack the powerful ingredient of substantial financial aid.

We need to understand more precisely the complex effects on European countries' social policies of the involvement of these powerful international bodies and to assess them from a critical standpoint. The everyday observation that "there is no such thing as a free lunch" surely applies to the conditions attached to massive loans from organisations such as the IMF and the World Bank. In his editorial to a special edition of the Journal of European Social Policy on eastern and central Europe, Deacon (1993) refers to developments in eastern and central Europe:

> A key aspect is the influence played by supra-national agencies in the devel-
> opment of post-communist social policy, notably by those that have
> financial purse strings. Poland's heavy indebtedness to the west has given a
> powerful leverage to conditions attached to IMF and World Bank loans,
> which have been used to set strict limits to successive Polish governments'
> public expenditure (p160)

Similar observations can be made about the effects of conditions imposed on other countries such as Hungary, Bulgaria, Romania and Albania. We should not be surprised by what Deacon describes as this "social policy conditionality" attached to financial assistance but it does need to be understood and questioned as necessary. There have already been signs in Poland, for example, that the price to be paid - in terms of strict control of economic and social policy - may be unacceptable as judged by voters' preferences in national elections.

The EU is in the "big league" of supra-state organisations effecting economic and social policies throughout the expanded Europe. It does so most obviously in the case of its member states but also increasingly with those countries wishing to join the EU and others whose economic and social conditions make membership a more distant possibility. Arguably, the EU is the most interesting supra-state organisation to study in respect of its role in shaping the development of social policy and social work, and this for two reasons. First, the EU has an extensive system of social aid programmes combining financial and non-financial resources. These are discussed later in this chapter. Secondly, the question of the EU's role in member states' social affairs is highly controversial and the subject of much debate: 1996 sees the second EU ministerial conference when major disagreements can be expected over the future involvement of the EU in social affairs in the context of the debate over closer European integration and a single currency.

The rest of this chapter will provide an overview of the EU's involvement in European social policy - including social work - together with some assessment of its impact and future directions.

The European Union and Social Affairs
The then "European Community" was created by the Treaty of Rome in 1957 as primarily an economic and business body, with strictly limited responsibilities for social policy, social welfare and social work. When the term "social affairs" is used by the EU it refers mainly to employment and work subjects rather than to components of social policy such as social protection, social services and social work. For example, the EU's Social Chapter is concerned primarily with the rights of workers. Textbooks on "social Europe" reveal this same bias towards employment, with limited reference to social welfare and social services.

The economic rationale for the creation and expansion of the EU is the need to create an increasingly integrated economic region able to compete successfully with the industrial giants of the USA, Japan and south-east Asia. This requires a major rationalisation of key industries such as steel, a painful process resulting in large scale unemployment in parts of Europe. In other words, there are serious *social* consequences flowing from economic policy, consequences which the previous President of the European Commission - Jacques Delors - concentrated upon in the increasing priority he gave to social policies and social programmes in the late 1980s. Delors had a vision for a "social Europe" with balanced economic and social progress within a frontier-free region. Delors's view was reflected in the influential Cecchini report (1988) which emphasised the social as well as the

*The Role of the Supra-State Organisations in Shaping, Contributing to
and Controlling the Development of Social Policy and Social Work:
The Case of the European Union*

economic dimension of the EU. The vision of a social or citizens' Europe which
will benefit *all* remains - if somewhat modified - but the implementation is slow
and controversial.

EU Social Policy and Social Care
This book is concerned primarily with the relationship between social policy and
social work. This writer considers social work within the context of "social care"
or "social services" as the organisation and practice of social work cannot be considered outside this context. As has been indicated above, social policy and the
social programmes of the EU are more to do with the world of employment and
unemployment than social care or social work, but nevertheless its involvement in
and impact upon these fields are significant.

The recent EU White Paper (1994) on "European Social Policy: a Way Forward
for the Union" takes forward the debate about the EU's acceptable role in social
policy, including social care. In a section on "Social Policy and Social Protection -
an Active Society for all" there is the recognition that the welfare state needs to be
maintained; greater support given to people denied the full rights of citizenship;
and that people such as the "active elderly" have a useful role to play in society.
Social care and social work are never specifically referred to, although problems
and needs of recipients of these services are addressed. For example, there is the
promise of more action to tackle the widespread problem of poverty and area
deprivation; and a commitment to continue work to enable disabled people to
enter or re-enter the labour market. Some prominence is given to the increasingly
important role of non-governmental organisations in social policy, the European
Commission recognising that most if not all European countries are placing
greater emphasis on the contribution of non-state organisations as part of their
development of mixed economies of welfare.

The European Commission's cautious approach to the development of its social
policy role is epitomised in its emphasis in the White Paper on acting as a facilitator and co-ordinator for the dissemination of new ideas and examples of good
practice in priority areas. This is made very clear in the Commission's follow-up
to the White Paper, namely its "Medium-Term Social Action Programme 1995-
97"(1995). Here the relative marginality of social care and social work is shown
in the proposal to launch a major initiative on the future of social protection (i.e.
cash benefits) the purpose of which is "to maximise exchanges of information,
experience and best practice in this area, with a view to enabling Member States to
develop and adjust their national systems on the basis of optimum understanding

of what is happening in other Member States". There is no recognition that cash and care services are frequently indivisible - for example in relation to elderly people - and so need joint study.

Guiding Principles for the EU's Involvement in Social Policy

The European Commission's recent problems of gaining approval in the European Parliament for specific funded social programmes illustrate its cautious and limited approach to involvement in social policy. Parliamentary approval for further programmes concerning both poverty and elderly people has been withheld because of objections by Germany and the United Kingdom. Their objections are mainly on the grounds of the principle of *subsidiarity* – a guiding principle in determining the allowable role of the EU not only in social policy but in many major aspects of the relationship between the EU and the fifteen member states. Subsidiarity sets limits to the powers of the EU in its relationship with Member States. As Swithinbank (1996) comments (p73):

The Maastricht Treaty added a new article to the Treaty of Rome, limiting the Union's powers to act only in circumstances where the objectives of the proposed action cannot be adequately achieved by the member states. Policies should always be made at the lowest possible level of government. Adherence to this principle of subsidiarity has made the EU reluctant to override national sovereignty by introducing any radical action in the field of social services. It will only become involved in areas in which member states cannot or will not act, or where pan-European action is absolutely necessary.

It was the German Länder, for example, who argued that anti-poverty programmes were their responsibility and best achieved by them, rather than by the EU. It is this principle of subsidiarity that requires the EU – and the Commission in particular – to beware of attempts to determine social policy in member states and largely explains why its direct involvement in social care and social work remains rather modest.

Two other principles governing the EU's role in social policy in Europe are *additionality* and *transparency*. The former principle states that the EU can only support activities which are additional to the normal operations of a member state's government; and EU funds may only be used for these stated and limited purposes. In the fields of social care and social work this means that EU funds are not available to pay for core services when a member state has problems in financing those services itself. The principle of "transparency" simply means that the EU is formally committed to a more open form of government in all its activities,

The Role of the Supra-State Organisations in Shaping, Contributing to
and Controlling the Development of Social Policy and Social Work:
The Case of the European Union

resulting - for example - in the White Paper on social policy which followed wide-spread consultation throughout the EU. As Swithinbank (op. cit.) observes (p74):

> Because of these principles the European Union has strictly limited compe-tencies in social care and is even more limited in its operation of those competencies. This is either because it must operate through national govern-ments and can only act where they do not, or it must make its procedures so open that it is hard to circumvent subsidiarity and additionality. The common impression of the European Union - and especially the Commission - as a huge bureaucracy overriding national sovereignty and imposing European-wide legislation against the member states is an exaggerated and prejudiced view.

In addition to these principles governing the EU's role in social policy, there are two important guiding concepts that feature in discussions of the EU and social policy. These concepts are *harmonisation* and *convergence*. Because of adherence to the principle of subsidiarity there is strong opposition from some member states at least to the EU attempting to use legislation and other devices to achieve unifor-mity in key areas of member states' responsibilities. This is particularly so in relation to social affairs, where any proposals for harmonisation across the EU are firmly resisted by Britain in particular. Convergence is the more accepted guiding concept in social affairs, with the Commission working within its gradualist role of facilitating the exchange of information on innovation and good practice. The expectation is that common agreed principles will emerge from this process to underpin the development of, say, social protection systems across the EU but each country retains the right to set levels of cash benefits appropriate to its economic and social circumstances. In many other fields – such as levels of allowable pollution in seawater – harmonisation through EU directives may be acceptable.

Convergence is applied in social policy in the EU in four ways. First, through the encouragement of each member state to adopt similar social policy objectives. These include the removal of poverty and the integration of disabled and disad-vantaged people into mainstream society. Secondly, convergence is achieved through the sharing of experience and good practice referred to above. Thirdly, member states are encouraged and enabled by EU support to co-operate in working on priority issues such as poverty, the needs of the family and the increas-ing proportion of elderly people. Finally, through a system to redistribute EU resources to the most economically deprived areas of the EU. This last measure can have significant benefits for the development of social care and social work in the poorer countries of the EU, such as Greece, Ireland and Portugal.

The European Commission makes considerable use of its system of networks and observatories to further its role in social policy. These are groups of experts from all member states selected to work on major policy subjects such as social exclusion, child care, elderly people and the family. The groups publish valuable information and data on their subjects across the EU and generally play an invaluable role in the process of influencing social policy and practice through gathering and making available knowledge of innovation and good practice. It is only unfortunate that their regular publications are not more widely available.

The discussion in this chapter now moves substantially to details of the many specific EU initiatives and programmes in the social policy field as they affect social care and social work. This includes the newer programmes designed to assist developments in eastern and central Europe. A broad but unstated definition of "social care" and "social work" underpins this discussion. The writer's view - based on much previous work in this field (e.g. Munday 1989 and 1996) - is that attempts at precise definitions of these terms are unsatisfactory, given differences across Europe in what services and responsibilities are included in social care; and which staff are included in the term "social worker". One very significant difference in social care arrangements is that in many European countries cash and care services are integrated in one administration, whereas in a country such as the United Kingdom local authority social services or social work departments are quite separate from the cash benefit social protection service.

Specific EU Social Programmes
As indicated earlier, a major priority for EU social policy now is to combat social exclusion through programmes designed to achieve the integration or reintegration of economically and socially marginalised groups. In practice this means EU-funded programmes aimed at young people, long term unemployed people, migrants and ethnic minorities, women, drug and alcohol dependants and people with disabilities.

Various means are used to assist people in these priority groups. These include vocational training to develop skills or retraining for people whose previous skills are no longer needed in the labour market; the creation of new jobs through small enterprises, including "social enterprises"; support for newly trained people to enter or re-enter the labour market; and providing the means for independent living for people whose disability could otherwise result in their exclusion in institutional living. A specific constraint limiting the involvement of the EU is that it cannot support projects designed to be only of value to people in one area of a single member state unless there are clear arrangements for the dissemination of the results of the project for the benefit of similar people in other EU countries. It is committed to the operation of the multiplier effect, for example through project partnerships between social care organisations in two or more member states to ensure a wider impact for EU-funded programmes.

Vocational training
This work has been financed mainly through the European Social Fund (ESF), one of the EU's three structural funds. This is one of the few EU programmes not requiring direct links with another country. The Social Fund is used by social care organisations for vocational training schemes for people with physical or learning disability, and also people with mental health problems. Some projects are large with substantial funding and of considerable benefit to the trainees. However, more recent emphasis on the acquisition of qualifications as a result of the training can make it difficult to include the most dependent and disabled people - whose needs may often be the greatest.

People with disabilities
For many years the needs of disabled people have been a high priority in the EU's social policy, with particular emphasis on promoting the integration of people with disabilities into the labour market. As Wilson (1996) observes (p185):

> HELIOS is the oldest of European Community programmes addressing the concerns of the disabled. It was a new step towards integration and independent living for disabled people in the European Community . . . HELIOS I and now HELIOS II seek to promote integration broadly by the dissemination of good practice between the member states. HELIOS II involves 676 disability organisations across the twelve member states participating in this programme which runs until December 1996.

HANDYNET is part of the HELIOS programme and is a computerised information system for disabled people and workers in this field. HORIZON was established in 1990 as part of the European Social Fund and is now finished. Its purpose was "to transfer expertise between member states through transnational projects which seek to improve access to the labour market for people with disabilities and those who are disadvantaged" (Wilson op cit. p 186). There have been two other EU programmes concerning disabled people, one concentrating the use of new technology for disabled and elderly people, the other on promoting artistic and creative projects involving people with disabilities.

People with disabilities have been critical of the EU's work in this field. For example, concerns have been expressed about the relatively small amounts of money allocated to the programmes, and the absence of disabled people from the officials responsible for the HELIOS programme. HELIOS II has been referred to as an uninspiring version of HELIOS I, while HANDYNET has been a disappointment to potential or actual users because of deficiencies in the content and organisation of the information for disabled people. There have been tangible gains, particularly with the emphasis on training and integration into the labour market, but there is a strong view that a more radical EU stance is required, including moves to establish a policy of human rights for disabled people.

Women
The European Commission's aim is to promote equal opportunities between men and women through several programmes. One – New Initiatives for Women (NOW) - is designed to improve women's qualifications and to enter or re-enter the labour market. This programme has been used in the field of social care to train community care or residential care staff to compete for jobs in the new style care services. IRIS is a network of women's training organisations sponsoring model projects to celebrate women at the top of their profession.

The EU's Women's Local Employment Initiatives (WLEI) supports women setting up their own enterprises, preferably employing women typically excluded from the labour market. It is argued with justification that women lack equal opportunities in social care work in that they are over-represented in basic day-to-day care work, but grossly under-represented in the middle and upper levels of management in social care agencies. Therefore, EU programmes in this field have special relevance to European social care.

Young people
Here again there is high priority given to programmes to assist young people into the labour market, given the high levels of unemployment amongst this group in several member states, e.g. Spain where the figure is alarmingly high. YOUTH-START, a major new initiative starting in 1995, supports training and placement programmes to assist young people's personal, vocational, entrepreneurial and linguistic skills. YOUTHSTART is seen as particularly suited to employment in social care services, including the employment of young people who have been in public care. There is the EU emphasis on transnational link-ups to enable young entrepreneurs to share ideas through trading agencies and networks. One expected outcome of this programme is the training of young mobile care workers able to

*The Role of the Supra-State Organisations in Shaping, Contributing to
and Controlling the Development of Social Policy and Social Work:
The Case of the European Union*

move across national boundaries to provide care for dependent people. It will be
interesting to see to what extent this ambition is achieved.

The longer established YOUTH FOR EUROPE programme concentrates on
developing a sense of European citizenship among young people through youth
exchanges, including with non-EU countries. It also encourages voluntary work
and the exchange of good practice in the youth services.

Elderly people
Elderly people have achieved a higher priority in EU social policy in recent years.
Perhaps this reflects increasing concern in member states over the implications of
demographic trends, together with effective pressure from organisations for and
of older people. EU policy has the twin aims of helping to change stigmatising
attitudes towards elderly people that sees them as a burden without an active role
in society; and to work with member states in examining cost effective ways of
providing long term health and social care for the increasing number of dependent
elderly people.

The EU has a "special year" approach to concentrating interest and projects on a
policy priority subject: 1993 was the European Year of Older People and
Solidarity between the Generations, encouraging a positive attitude towards
ageing and the relationship between older and younger people. This led to the
European Commission proposing a five year programme of follow-up work, with
an emphasis on people still at work but approaching retirement; retired people
able to lead active and independent lives; and elderly increasingly dependent
people. Unfortunately the implementation of this programme has been delayed or
even lost because of objections on the familiar grounds of subsidiarity.

Poverty
The prevention and alleviation of poverty have long been a major concern for
social policy and social work. Earlier reference was made to how this social
problem is addressed by the EU within the broader framework of social exclusion.
The EU has allocated substantial funds over many years to support experiments in
understanding and dealing with poverty, the results of which are not particularly
clear. This work has been conducted through three poverty programmes, proposals
for the fourth being opposed by Germany in particular - as mentioned earlier.

Three main principles inform the EU's approach to Poverty 4. First, the recognition that social exclusion is multi-dimensional requiring a matching approach.
Social care and social work have a part to play but alongside other services such as
housing, social protection and health. Secondly, a partnership approach is

required involving organisations from state, independent and commercial sectors. Thirdly, if these partnerships are to become effective they must include socially excluded people themselves in planning and implementation.

Programmes for eastern and central Europe
As discussed early in this chapter, the EU is one of several supra-state organisations providing substantial financial and technical aid to eastern and central European countries. The broad purpose of aid from these organisations is to assist the development of sound economic and social structures within new democracies.

OUVERTURE, ECOS AND PHARE are the main EU programmes to assist developments in eastern and central Europe, including the establishment of social care and social work organisations and services. OUVERTURE and ECOS support co-operation between local and regional authorities in the EU and central Europe, with projects focusing on regional and local development, the environment and urban planning. ECOS is particularly relevant to social care as it is concerned with social and health policies, including the training of social care staff in the non-EU country.

PHARE originally concentrated assistance on Poland and Hungary but now covers most or all former central European communist countries. Its main function is to support the transformation to market economies in those countries, with an emphasis on western private sector organisations helping new commercial institutions in the recipient countries. PHARE now has a wider remit and is able to assist with reducing unemployment and building up often-rudimentary social welfare sectors. Projects funded by the PHARE programme are selected by the eastern and central European countries according to their countries' priorities.

More recently a new EU programme - LIEN - has been established as part of PHARE, this programme being particularly available to assist social care developments in eastern and central Europe. For example, the writer is director of the European Institute of Social Services at the University of Kent which is a partner in an application with Russian partners for a major training scheme for staff working in child care institutions in several Russian republics. An example of an earlier PHARE-funded project concerning social work was in Poland in 1993 where considerable support was provided for an ambitious programme to increase and modernise social work training.

Tacis is the equivalent programme for ex-Soviet Union states (CIS) (see below, section on education).

Most former communist countries are placing strong emphasis on developing the non-governmental sector in social welfare/social care and using EU programmes with western social care expertise to do so. This is done through Civil Society and Democracy programmes which facilitate positive interchanges between NGOs in the countries concerned.

Freedom of movement of people and services within the EU
The creation of the celebrated Single European Market has implications for social workers in one important respect. The legal Act establishes the right for an individual professional to practise her or his profession in any other member state of the EU, subject to the entry requirements in the other state.

Directives of the European Commission have provided for the mutual recognition of professional qualifications across the European Union, including those of social workers. The requirements are that the professional qualification should involve a minimum of three years' study and training in further or higher education; and that admission to the profession in question should be restricted to practitioners entered on a professional register. These conditions for the recognition of the social work qualification are met in nearly all EU countries, Britain being a notable exception mainly because the title "social worker" in the United Kingdom is not restricted to those with a professional qualification. Most countries have some form of professional register of qualified social workers similar to registers of qualified medical practitioners, but this is not the case in Britain.

Education and Training
The movement of social workers and other social care staff between member states is encouraged in several ways and is increasingly evident. As part of the EU-funded ERASMUS programme social work students are able to undertake part of their professional training in another member state. From 1995 ERASMUS has been superseded by the more extensive SOCRATES programme which includes ERASMUS but now also covers school education, language skills and the promotion of the exchange of information and experience.

The EU's TEMPUS programme is of special relevance to eastern and central European countries. This programme supports co-operation in higher education between EU countries and eastern and central Europe. It forms part of the overall programmes for the economic and social restructuring of the latter countries and is aimed at promoting the quality and supporting the development and renewal of higher education in Albania, Bulgaria, the Czech Republic, Estonia, Hungary, Latvia, Lithuania, Poland, Romania, Russia, the Slovak Republic, Slovenia and

Ukraine. TEMPUS has enabled Schools of Social Work in the European Union to co-operate with their more recently formed counterparts in many of the countries listed above to assist with curriculum development and other aspects of social work education and training. There is limited finance available for these schemes and it is too early to assess the real effectiveness of TEMPUS for the schools involved.

Conclusion

The European Union as a supra-state organisation has played a valuable role in the gradual Europeanisation of social care and social work, with an ever-increasing understanding by social care interests of policies, services and practice in one another's countries. The goal is certainly not to bring about uniformity but rather the celebration of difference and diversity, together with a gradual convergence around good practice in social care work that transcends social, cultural and political differences. It is the active and sensitive support of this exciting process that is one of the major social policy achievements of the European Union in recent years.

References

Cecchini, P. (1988) *The European Challenge 1992 - the benefits of a Single Market*, Aldershot: Wildwood House.

Commission of the European Communities, (1995) *Medium Term Social Action Programme 1995-97*, Communication from the Commission to the Council, the European Parliament and the Committee of the Regions, Brussels.

Deacon, B. (1993) "Social Policy in Central and Eastern Europe" in *Journal of European Social Policy* Vol.3 No.3.

European Commission: Directorate-General for Employment, (1994) Industrial Relations and Social Affairs *European Social Policy: A way forward for the Union* Luxembourg: Office for Official Publications of the European Communities.

Munday, B. (ed) (1989) *The Crisis in Welfare: an international perspective on social services and social work*, Hemel Hempstead: Harvester Wheatsheaf.

Munday, B., Ely, P. (eds) (1996) *Social Care in Europe* Hemel Hempstead: Prentice Hall, Harvester Wheatsheaf.

Swithinbank, A. (1996) "The European Union and Social Care" in Munday and Ely (op.cit.).

Wilson, V. (1966) "People with Disabilities" in Munday and Ely (op.cit.).

Part II: Post-Modern Approaches to the Distribution of Wealth, Welfare and Power

Social Stratification and Differentiation of Incomes in Russia

Tatiana Zaslavskaya

Sociostructural Transformation of the Society

Contemporary Russian society is now in a transitional phase. The entire institutional structure is being transformed, including the relationship of property and power, work and employment, social mobility and income distribution. Élites change their composition, new social groups appear, lower strata go under and join the "social dregs". Economic relations are being criminalised, the sphere of violence is spreading. The system of group interests, modes of behaviour, social interactions is in a state of flux. The general pattern of social stratification and positions of major social groups are changing visibly.

The stratification of the Soviet society in the 1980s was shaped mainly by the position of certain groups within the general system of power and administration which determined the extent of executive rights, the level of decision-making, the economic status, the extent of social networks and the range of informal opportunities. The stability of the Soviet political system contributed to continuity and immutability of the political establishment, led to its encapsulation and isolation from the rest of society. The economic status of various social groups reflected first and foremost the degree to which they were involved in possession, administration and utilisation of public wealth. Prominent here, besides the "nomenclature", were bureaucrats distributing resources, captains of industry controlling the finances and products of their enterprises, people in logistics and trade, as well as some other groups, including black market operators. Altogether they represented not more than 15-20% of the total working population in the country. The remainder were salaried state employees whose sole economic right was to get wages. Variations in their economic status were due primarily to differences in payment for work.

A notable hallmark of the USSR was the fact that wages were not directly linked to the workers' intellectual potential and the nature of their jobs. In most other Soviet bloc countries the public standing of various social groups was determined mostly by their cultural potential: educational level, intellectual complexity of work and functions of management and control. But in the USSR it was the official position that played the major role in social stratification whereas cultural potential numbered sixth among other factors. The salaries reflected the sphere of employment, the power of respective ministries, the wealth and prestige of particular enterprises, rather than the content, complexity and importance of jobs as such.

The Establishment, whose educational and cultural level was not too high, looked askance at the intelligentsia and treated it as a stepdaughter: creative efforts were undervalued and remuneration here was often lower than for manual labour.

Reforms of the last decade have changed the situation. The Communist Party lost its leading role. Concentration of executive power has been diluted, the relations between the centre and the regions have become more equitable. Political leaders are now less stable in their posts as a result of democratisation of political life. Corruption is widespread in state apparatus and the public does not trust it. At the same time, market reforms stimulated economic development and made economy the hub of public life. In these new circumstances economic rather than political factors have decisive roles in determining the status of different social groups.

Today in Russia we see the development of various forms of property other than state-owned: private, co-operative, stock, municipal, public. Consequently, owners of small and large stocks in industry and finance, as well as managers of non-state enterprises, emerge as new social groups. We witness the rebirth of peasantry as a particular class of landowners. Corporate property associated with the fast-growing industrial and financial groups becomes particularly prominent. Differentiation of economic positions is similarly shaped by access (formal or informal) to privatisation, distribution and exchange of state resources and goods. One would expect these factors to lose their role at the time of economic privatisation and maybe it will happen so later. But for now with privatisation under way we see quite the reverse - even indirect involvement in the redistribution of public wealth strongly affects the group's economic status. Officials of economic ministries and local authorities, chief executives and managers in industry and business are doing particularly well in this respect.

Most other groups of Russian society still do not possess any private property or any rights to resources other than their own labour force. As before, their well-being is largely dependent on their work for wages. It does not mean that their economic status remains the same. Firstly, the transition to market relations cancelled any guarantees of stable employment. Secondly, developing mixed economy makes the position of workers in private, state and "intermediate" sectors quite different. Thirdly, in big cities and most advanced spheres of economy there was a growing demand for professionals knowing foreign languages, familiar with computers. It must be noted, though, that in present-day Russian society only that part of its cultural potential is valued that can be put to use "here and now". Fourthly, total abolition of wage regulation by the State and the collapse of trade unions paved the way for widespread administrative abuses: executives raised their incomes by keeping the wages of rank-and-file workers down. Gross pay delays and the practice of compulsory unpaid leaves forced those less well-off below the subsistence level. Finally, poorly developed national labour market and highly unstable regional markets further weakened the links between the quality of work and the wages. All this brings us to the conclusion that despite obvious changes in the social stratification in Russia during the period of reforms its major features have been preserved and in some ways strengthened. One can hardly expect the social stratification pattern inherited from the Soviet past to change overnight. It will take time and enormous effort on the part of democratically minded people to accomplish the task.

Hierarchical Layers of the Russian Society
So, how is the present-day Russian society stratified? What groups make up the strata? How do their social positions differ with respect to each other? In order to give answers to these questions we analysed the data obtained through the survey conducted by the All-Russian Centre of Public Surveys under the title "Economic and Social Changes in Russia". Like most investigations of its kind, the survey represents the bulk of the Russian population, but does not cover the very edges - the élite and the so-called "social bottom". As the survey data for the respondents' families were not full, we focused only on the working population.

To identify different social groups we used nine status variables: occupation, the type of activity, the sphere of employment, the sector of economy, the size of the organisation (number of workers), the respondent's position within the organisation (both subjective and according to job content), educational level, estimated qualification and the level of material well-being. Preliminary ideas about general structure of the contemporary Russian society were based on the above-stated considerations. For each group we had a set of characteristics reflecting, in our opinion, its true nature. To prevent groups based on different characteristics from overlapping, we used the following system of criteria: 1) self-employment in business, 2) top administrative functions, 3) the nature of work (physical or mental), 4) the level of education and qualification, 5) the level of material well-being, 6) the sphere of employment. Fourteen groups emerged according to these characteristics belonging to four layers, each with its distinctive social status - upper, middle, basic, and lower. The resulting pattern of social stratification looks like this:

Layer	Social Groups
Upper	Big and medium entrepreneurs
Middle	Small and semi-entrepreneurs, industrial managers, directors in social sphere, top intelligentsia, workers' élite, military officers
Basic	Rank and file intelligentsia, semi-intelligentsia, trade and services personnel, industrial workers, peasants
Lower	Unqualified workers.

Upper layer comprises only 1-1.5% of the above population of the country, but disposes sizeable resources. It is represented by owners of big and medium-sized companies predominantly in the sphere of trade and banking. They show high economic and social potential. More than four-fifths of them are males, young or middle-aged. The absolute majority have special, two-thirds - higher, education. Normally they rate their professional competence as high. The stated income level is six to seven times the national average, though in reality it must be even higher. Seven-eighths within it are quite rich, the rest are relatively well off. There are more than three positive for each negative estimate of one's own well-being. The morale of the upper layer is high: more than half of them say that "things are not bad" and the rest that "life is not easy, but tolerable". Nobody wants to return to pre-reform state. The hope is rather strong that Russia is heading towards revival and prosperity. The better part of them are convinced that it is people like them who will lead the country out of the present crisis.

Middle layer is the most advanced among the broader layers. It embraces nearly a quarter of the population - those people who have succeeded in adapting quite well to the new economic conditions. The layer consists of small entrepreneurs, semi-entrepreneurs, managers of top and middle levels, business professionals, top intelligentsia, workers, élite and military officers. About one-fifth of them have their own businesses, 10-15% are self-employed, many combine working for wages, with business activity. Thus the prime mechanisms of upward mobility in contemporary Russia are either business activity or administrative functions. High professional qualification promises social advancement only in private and privatised sectors. Middle-aged men represent the bulk of the group. The educational level is rather high, though not as high as of the upper level - three-quarters are with special and among them half with higher education. Professional self-evaluation is very high.

The living standard of the group may be called satisfactory: one-third are comfortably off, more than half relatively secure, but 15% are poor. About one-third are dissatisfied with their income, but they manage to keep the achieved living standard. The morale is more or less stable and rather high. But reforms are greeted less enthusiastically compared with the upper layer. All in all, it can be said that middle class in Russia is in the "embryonic" phase of its development. It is less numerous, has other cultural characteristics, and much lower social prestige than its counterpart in the West. Nevertheless, it plays a leading role in the transformation process and this role is bound to get stronger with time.

The third layer is called **basic** because it embraces two-thirds of the society. People belonging to it occupy salaried jobs with the content pertinent basically to the industrial society. Typically, they are technical jobs requiring moderate levels of qualification, mostly in the state sector of economy. This layer includes rank and file and semi-intelligentsia (40-45%), industrial workers (25-30%), trade and services personnel (20%), as well as peasantry (10%). About three-fifths of them are women predominantly of middle and older age. The average educational level is not very high, but not uniform: two-fifths have basic secondary education, one-third have professional qualifications and one-quarter have higher education. The living standard of this group is low: about half of them live below poverty line and the rest just above it. Negative self-evaluations in this respect are eight to nine times more frequent than positive. Three-quarters say that their incomes lag behind inflation. Three-fifths note the deterioration of their diet and the decline in general quality of their life. All this causes low morale and psychological stress. Nearly half of the people are anxious and depressed, one-third see their situation as desperate and unbearable. The interests are less articulated and the energy is lower than of the other two groups. However, the feelings and behaviour of this deprived layer may be decisive in critical conditions for the destiny of Russia.

Lower layer of Russian society is relatively thin. It represents 6-8% of the working population. But if we take into account the number of tramps not covered by the survey, it may go up to 10-15%. It includes people with scant education and qualifications, doing menial work. Within it women and older persons predominate: there are seven females for three males and the proportion of people over 50 is three times above the average. The living standard of this group is critically low: two-thirds exist under subsistence level and a quarter in utter poverty. The ratio of negative to positive self-evaluations here is 17:1. Nine-tenths say that due to inflation their real incomes are declining. Now they can afford less food than before. Most of them are against reforms.

It should be added that during the period of 1993-5 the share of the upper layer of the population rose from 1 to 1.5% and that of the middle layer from 22 to 27%. At the same time the share of the basic and lower layers fell from 71 to 66% and from 7 to 6% respectively.

Material inequality of different groups and layers is characteristic of the whole system of social disparities in Russia. Besides being significant in itself, it reflects a series of other imbalances: between the town and the country, big cities and small towns, export and "ordinary" branches of economy, entrepreneurship and salaried work, administrative and productive activity, work in public and private sectors, strong and weak companies. Income varies considerably according to prescriptive features (gender, age, origin, health, status), socialisation (education, qualification), personality traits (diligence, competence, daring, etc.). Thus, income differentiation reflects a wide range of economic, social, demographic and other factors.

On the other hand, the living standard, which is closely linked to the income level, determines such expressions of social status as consumption level, life-style, educational opportunities, business potential, career prospects, social connections, etc. In other words, it is formative of social status. Therefore, income distribution and differentiation form the basis of social inequalities. As the problem is of particular importance in present-day Russia, we will analyse its following aspects: 1) trends of real incomes in Russia during the reform period, 2) current differentiation of incomes in Russia compared with other countries, 3) income level in different social strata and its subjective evaluation.

Income Changes and Differentials in Russia

At the start of Perestroika most people in Russia were looking forward to the improvement of their well-being in the near future. In actual fact economic reforms brought about its general decline. Two factors were interacting here - scarcity of goods and inflation. The situation deteriorated dramatically in 1990-1 with the scarcity of foodstuffs and consumer goods becoming total. Liberalisation of prices was allowed to overcome the crisis and to gradually fill the shops with goods, but inflation broke loose. During 1992 consumer prices rose on average 26-fold, while nominal incomes increased only 11-fold. Hence, real incomes fell by two-thirds and savings lost all their value. The situation stabilised in 1993: consumer prices rose at the average rate of 9.6% and nominal incomes rose 11-fold, so that real incomes grew by 12%. Data on the changes in real incomes of the population during the next two years are somewhat contradictory. According to the figures given by the All-Russian Centre of Public Surveys they rose by 16% in 1994 and stayed unchanged in 1995. However, the official statistics showed the decrease of 13% in 1995. In any case, the current level of well-being in Russia is only 50-60% of that in the mid-1980s. Any increases are only "across the board" while for the bulk of the population the living standard is declining. Not surprisingly the percentage of Russians who regard their material situation as "bad" rose from 42 in 1993 to 49 in 1995. Among them those who called it "very bad" showed an increase from 8 to 12%. Positive self-evaluations dropped from 7 to 5%.

The structure of personal incomes is also changing. For instance, in the late 1980s, 72% of all personal gains came from earnings, 14% from social benefits and a further 14% from business activities and as rents. In 1995 figures for these sources of income were 40, 16 and 44% respectively. And we must keep in mind that only about 10% of Russians are seriously involved in business activities.

When we speak about income differentiation in the USSR before Perestroika, we should point out that it was covert. Income differentials for the majority of the population were relatively small and consequently it was easy to accept the traditionally low living standards. Low differentials in nominal monetary incomes were cited by politicians claiming high social homogeneity of the Soviet society, though in reality there were great differences in the well-being of the party nomenclature and the population in general. The trick was quite simple: the level of consumption for higher social layers was not directly linked to their nominal earnings but stemmed from all kinds of benefits and advantages. The mechanism was disguised by providing all citizens with free education and health care, cheap housing, child care and entertainment. Calculation of incomes was made without considering the amount of goods and services received from those "public consumption funds" by members of upper and lower social layers. In this way it was possible to keep up the appearance of relatively "equitable" distribution of personal incomes while in reality there were sharp contrasts in the standards of living between upper and lower strata.

Developing market relations destroyed the precarious equilibrium. The practice of providing valuable goods and services to those in power for free or at reduced rates, if not totally abolished, has been seriously curtailed. The consumer market was filled with attractive imported goods sold only for cash. At the same time, the existing paternalistic system of welfare services began crumbling. The services were getting more and more expensive. Thus, the share of incomes received in kind was decreasing, while the demand for cash earnings was increasing. Yet opportunities for meeting the demand were unequal for different groups of population. Consequently, income polarisation began growing steadily. Surveys show that in the late 1980s the income differential between the topmost and the lowest 10% segments of the population was less than 4.5 times. It rose to 7.8 in 1993 and to 10.5 in autumn of 1995. The official statistics provide a similar picture: 5.5 times in 1991, 11 times in 1993 and 13 times in 1995. The All-Russian Centre of Public Surveys estimated that 40% of all personal incomes in 1994 were concentrated in the hands of 10% of the most prosperous people while the absolute majority of the population had the remaining 60%. The difference between the richest and the poorest groups reached almost 25 times by late 1995. The striking contrast between affluence and poverty is seen by Russians brought up in the tradition of egalitarianism as the triumph of social inequality. Public opinion surveys show that 75% of them consider the existing income differentials to be excessive and more than half of them believe that the state must intervene in order to reduce them.

Illuminating in this respect are the data of a comparative survey of personal income distribution conducted in 1993 in five post-communist countries: Bulgaria, Hungary, Russia, Czech and Slovak Republics. Researchers defined affluence and poverty as relative terms - as marked deviations of incomes from a standard which in each case is set at the average for the country. "The poor" were labelled as those individuals whose *per capita* family income was less than half the national average. "The rich" were considered those whose income was more than double the national average. It was discovered that Russia had the highest differentiation index. The poles of the scale here are more pronounced both in the rift and numerically. For instance, in 1993 the category "poor" applied to 9% of Czechs, 15% of Slovaks and Hungarians, 19% of Bulgarians and 26% of Russians. For comparison: in the UK the index is 20%, in Canada 17%, Germany 8%, Sweden and Holland 3%. There are 8% of relatively "rich" people in Russia, 7% in Bulgaria, 6% in Hungary and Slovakia and 4% in the Czech Republic. The ratio of *per capita* incomes between the "rich" and the "poor" was 6.8 in Slovakia and 8.6 in Russia.

The researchers note that transition towards a market economy is always accompanied by growing inequality. But in Russia, and to a lesser degree in Bulgaria, the deeper differentiation is caused mostly by high inflation and monopolised economy. When the direct state control over the financial activities of the enterprises weakened, those monopolising production (particularly in the sphere of fuel extraction) were able to gain super profits and to distribute them between their employees and some of the government officials. The economic structure of Hungary or former Czechoslovakia is less fit for such manipulations. The State there is more active in controlling the economy and in supporting the poor.

Incomes of Different Social Groups and Layers

Up to this point we have been considering the differentiation of incomes in Russia in general without looking at its links with the social stratification. Now we turn to analysing the incomes and standards of living for different social layers of the population. We will focus on such questions as: a) how big is the difference in real incomes of various groups within Russian society? b) what are their claims, i.e. what monetary compensation for their work and efforts would they judge "fair" or "sufficient"; c) how big is the discrepancy between actual incomes of various social layers and the estimated "fair" level, i.e. the degree to which their social claims are satisfied? To try to answer them we will be using the following indicators:

- the level of basic and additional earnings (BAE)

- the level of *per capita* family income (CFI)

- respondents' estimation of the minimal adequate earnings (MAE)
- estimations of *per capita* living minimum for the family (CLM)
- estimations of *per capita* sufficient income for the family (CSI)
- the ratio of the estimated *per capita* living minimum to the sufficient *per capita* income (CLM:CSI)
- the ratio of actual incomes to the estimated minimal adequate earnings (BAE:MAE)
- the ratio of actual *per capita* family income to the estimated sufficient level (CFI:CSI).

Before analysing the results we must point out that the measure of actual earnings (BAE) used in the survey does not cover all possible incomes. First, the item was specifically targeted at personal incomes rather than business profits. Second, it queried the sum retained after paying taxes. Third, most well-to-do respondents tended to understate their incomes for fear of drawing the attention of criminals, tax inspectors and other law-enforcing organisations. The higher the income level, the more pronounced is the tendency. Fourth, the survey took into account only earnings in monetary form, though some groups receive also additional incomes in kind. For instance, many people in rural communities supply them-selves with food products, servicemen get free meals and uniforms, executives use official cars, bodyguards, recreational facilities and other benefits. All this makes the reported measures somewhat crude.

So, how great is the income differentiation in Russia today? If we take the average incomes of all economically active Russians as 100%, the average income of the upper layer will be 516%, middle 144%, basic 75% and lower 54%. Therefore, the difference between the upper and the lower strata is almost tenfold, between the middle and the lower, approximately threefold. But if we take into account the non-declared part of the incomes, the amount of savings and property, the contrasts in living standards will be much greater. The differences in *per capita* incomes for families belonging to the same layers are less pronounced: between the polar categories it is about seven times. The comparison with the pattern of income differentiation presented above shows that social stratification accounts for the sizeable part of general variance.

The values of barely sufficient remuneration, minimal *per capita* income and "sufficient" *per capita* income suggested by the respondents may be taken as measures of their aspirations concerning well-being, the quality and mode of life.

Nowadays the aspirations are pushed in two opposing directions. On the one hand, the spreading and deepening poverty forces the better part of Russians to curtail their consumption: to deny themselves expensive foodstuffs, services, fashionable clothing, travel, holiday-making, subscription to literary magazines, trunk calls - in other words, many elements of their former way of life. People are getting used to the deteriorating conditions of life, and this adaptation results in lowering the level of income considered as "sufficient". On the other hand, aggressive advertising of western habits of consumption and the glamorous life-style of the "new Russians" push up income expectations, particularly of the young and the prosperous groups.

Such indicators as minimal *per capita* income and sufficient *per capita* income differentiate social layers and groups according to the level of social needs and the type of their goal orientations. The estimated values of sufficient *per capita* income reflect the subjective idea of "normal living". It can be regarded as a non-direct estimation of the living standard sufficient to meet the basic human needs. Behind this indicator lie subjective and diverse ideas of different social groups about "normal living". When older people, dwellers of rural areas and small towns, representatives of the basic and lower layer speak of "sufficient income", they refer to meeting traditional and rather limited needs. For them "normal living" means to "live like before". In contrast most young people, city dwellers, entrepreneurs, highly qualified specialists and business men orient themselves towards modern standards. When they speak of "normal living" they have in mind the western life-style.

During the years 1993-5 the subjective sufficient level of incomes grew faster than the subjective subsistence level: the ratio CSI:CLM was 233% in 1993, 242% in 1994 and 262% in 1995. There are two possible explanations for this. On the one hand, it may reflect the process of familiarisation with the new concept of "subsistence level", of investing it with more appropriate and precise meaning. On the other hand, it may express the claim to a higher living standard, particularly by the thriving groups.

Opinions concerning the *per capita* living minimum are quite uniform: the disparity between the polar layers is only 40%, between the middle and the lower layers it is less than 20%. More-affluent groups seeing it from outside put it relatively higher than those who rely on their own experience. Ideas about "normal" or "sufficient" income are more scattered and that is quite natural. The higher the social status, the more elevated is the estimated value of subsistence level and the perceived difference between minimal and sufficient levels in income. The difference symbolises the social distance separating a group from the poorest segment of the population as seen by the group. Taking the average estimate of the current subsistence level and the current sufficient level of income as 100%, the estimates given by the upper layer are 130 and 182% respectively. The ratio of the latter to the former which characterises the mentioned social distance equals here 139%. For the middle layer the three indices are 111, 120 and 108%, while for the basic and lower layers they are 92, 88 and 95% respectively. We see that both factors (increase in CLM and the difference between CLM and CSI) contribute about equally to the general increase in CSI.

For particular social groups the analysed relations are more variegated. Small entrepreneurs display a high level of claims for "sufficient" incomes while their estimate of minimal income is rather modest. Consequently, the separation between incomes deemed sufficient for themselves and for others here is considerable. It is nearly as big for rank-and-file intelligentsia, though the values themselves are lower for both indicators. It shows that having lesser income claims relative to entrepreneurs they still distance themselves as much from the social bottom. Workers' élite displays a different pattern: its ideas about living minimum are above average but those concerning the sufficient income are close to the average. That means that subjectively they are closer to the poorest segment of the population than many other social groups.

To evaluate the degree to which the claims of different social groups bearing on their personal incomes are satisfied we use two ratios. The first (BAE:MAE) shows the relationship of basic and additional earnings to the respondents' views about minimal earnings needed for their families. The second (CFI:CSI) shows the relationship between the actual *per capita* family income and the estimated sufficient level. The first ratio rose from 0.61 in 1993 to 0.81 in 1995 reflecting two combined trends: the growth of real earnings and some drop in claims for minimal adequate earnings. Nevertheless, its present level leads to the conclusion that the majority of Russians consider their earnings to be not high enough for meeting their basic needs. The difference between poles here is six times. In 1993-5 the actual income level relative to the minimally adequate income was 2.8 times for the upper layer and 1.2 times for the middle layer. However, for the basic layer it was 1.7 times lower and 2.3 times so for the lower layer. The least favourable ratio characterises unqualified workers whose average earnings are less than half their expected minimal income as well as peasants (52%), rank-and-file intelligentsia (54%) and semi-intelligentsia (58%). The highest degree of satisfied income claims distinguished the group of entrepreneurs, though even here it is not high in itself. Semi-entrepreneurs, top intelligentsia and workers' élite are situated somewhere in between with their earnings 8-12% in front of their estimated living minimum.

Turning to the second ratio, we see that actual *per capita* incomes in Russia of late were only one-third of what people see as sufficient earnings. The fact that aspirations go further than the actually existing income level is quite natural. It serves as a motivating factor for higher productivity and qualification. What is critical here, however, is the degree. When the difference between actual earnings and the income required for "normal living" goes over a certain limit, stimulating effect gives way to apathy, alienation from work and then discontentment grows with the possibility of turning into aggression and violence. Such is the situation with the two lower layers of Russian society. As for the upper layer, the dissatisfaction of its representatives with their income is quite normal and stimulating: actual earnings are only 20-25% behind those seen as sufficient and this creates good motivation for further efforts. For the middle layer actual earnings are 2.4 times less than subjectively sufficient level, for the basic layer the difference is 3.3 times, for the lower 4 times. Such a gap between the goal and the reality is far too much for being constructive and stimulating. The result is either resignation or the forms of adaptive behaviour aimed at bare survival (switching to petty business, stealing, criminal activity, etc). Notable is the fact that "sufficient" income levels as they are estimated by people representing the extremes of social scale differ not much - just 2 times, while the inequality in actual earnings is 7- and 10-fold. It proves that egalitarian beliefs are strong and widespread in Russian society. Less qualified workers do not recognise the fact that complex and competent work associated with high responsibility should be encouraged. It also shows that representatives of lower social strata regard the current pattern of income differentiation as unfair. Their claim is to a much bigger piece of the "common pie" than they actually get.

Speaking about the level of income allowing more or less "normal" living most Russians set it at about 20-40% above their earnings in the late 1980s. In our view it does not contradict the fact that for the majority of mass groups the bench-mark of their well-being is the level achieved in the mid-80s on the eve of the reforms. The point is that under the conditions of the market economy, to regain the previous level means much higher real earnings because many goods and services that then were free or very cheap, now have to be purchased for money and the cost is rather high. Therefore, the gap between the actual and aspired incomes of Russian citizens is caused by the former being too low for meeting basic needs rather than by the latter being set too high. There are signs that the living standard in Russia is bound to stabilise at the present minimal level. The tendency is not welcome since it does not stimulate positive economic development in the long run.

Redistributing Wealth and Power
Between the State and Individual Entrepreneurs: Armenia

Marina Kourktchian

This paper is intended to analyse how the total available stock of goods and services was distributed in Soviet society, on both the official and unoffical levels, and to examine how the distribution changed during the transitional period. My main thesis is that during the Soviet period a centralised, highly regulated system of distribution coexisted with a non-regulated, informal, crude and pseudo-market system. During the history of the Soviet system, the secondary mechanism evolved and strengthened, becoming more important in the life of society than the official system. The thesis will be looked at in the Armenian context.

When the transition brought about the complete destruction of the centralised economy, it simultaneously strengthened the unofficial network of social and economic relations - a traditional pattern which is far removed from the western understanding of a free-market model. In other words, the great change in Armenian society was not a smooth, straightforward transition from a centrally regulated economy to a decentralised, free-market economy. It was, instead, an erratic shift from a partly regulated economy to a legalised set of distorted market relationships, modified by a traditional network of non-market relationships.

I shall illustrate this shift by discussing examples of three Armenian social services: public transport by bus, health care, and education.

Transport service

I shall try to describe the real process of distribution in the transport service in Armenia, particularly the bus services, on which I conducted research in 1990 as soon as the new government developed an interest in understanding the conditions for privatisation.

My group carried out the research in all five bus stations in Yerevan, the capital of Armenia. We used a quantitative methodology including a questionnaire for bus drivers, as well as qualitative methodology in the form of a one-week observation in bus stations in combination with in-depth interviews with representatives of different occupations within the bus services.

The following picture was revealed. The official salary of a bus driver was higher than average for the population. But it was considered by him only as a guarantee of social security. He received his main income directly from his services. Passengers had been paying the bus driver for the service directly. But the driver never gave tickets or receipts. The money was collected by the driver without any external control.

On the expenditure side of the process, the driver gave only part of his total receipts to the State. A larger part stayed in his pocket. But at the same time he himself had to pay for all the services for his work. He spent his money for payment in cash for washing the bus, for servicing and repairing it, for obtaining replacement parts and even for getting a better route - i.e. a more profitable one. Drivers who did not want to be involved in this process would not be able to work at all. I want to repeat the observation that all the people to whom this income was allocated in cash were state-salaried employees. As a result, the bus driver's total income, after expenses, was about two to three times the size of his official state salary. This did not secure a rich life for him, but an average standard of living in real terms - average, that is, when compared with the real standard of living achieved by others who also had unofficial, supplementary incomes.

Our research thus revealed that the wage had lost its function as payment for work done and had come to serve only as a guarantee of social security. The work itself was paid for by private interests, beyond state control. And these conditions applied to all occupational groups within the bus services.

The idea of privatisation was wholly undesirable for all the employees of the bus services, because for them it meant only the loss of a guaranteed minimum income without adding any new sources of benefit or the possibility of higher achievement.

The proposal of privatisation died at the very beginning when it became obvious that there was no interest in a radical change in the ownership of the services, neither at the administrative level nor among the lower-level employees.

The main changes which have happened in this area during the past five years of transition are the following:

- Because of the enormous rate of inflation in the country, the state salary of the workers has grossly devalued. It has become so small in comparison with prices that it has lost its significance, even as an anti-poverty guarantee.

- The official prices for using the buses have been increased, but by less than the inflation rate. Because it is unable to increase salaries, the State has to keep down the price of such a basic need as transport.

- The prices for servicing the buses themselves - that is, for keeping them in running condition - have been increased in line with inflation.

Looking at this picture as a whole, it would seem that the bus driver could not survive, as his salary has only a symbolic meaning. The actual sum of money that he is collecting as he drives a given route has much less value, and at the same time he must meet enormously increased expenses for looking after his bus. And there is, indeed, a crisis in official bus services: the number of buses running on the planned routes has severely decreased.

But informal relations have exposed themselves in a new way. After working only a short time on an officially planned route with a state-regulated price for the service, a typical bus driver has changed his route to one more suitable for himself. He is now likely to use his bus - the same bus - for his private business, charging a price for the service established by himself. Usually it is about four to five times the official price.

In consequence, the town now has two kinds of bus service. On the one hand, there are buses running along officially announced routes with low prices. On the other hand, there are "private" buses, five times more expensive, running mostly in crowded places. Apart from the price of the ticket, the difference for users is that they can wait an unlimited time for an officially running bus, while there is no difficulty in catching a "private" bus. The main problems with the "private" buses are that they are expensive for many people, and they run only on the profitable routes to a limited number of destinations.

"Private" in this case means privately used state property with uncontrolled market:state relations and unregulated distribution of income. "Taxes" derived from this "private" business are not formally gathered in and redistributed in a state budget, but redistributed through "private" pockets at all levels of administration. To be a state employee as a bus driver today means, first, to get access to a bus; and, secondly, the opportunity for purposive involvement in the institutional structure.

The question of whether these practices are legal or illegal seems to me somewhat rhetorical.

The educational system:

I now want to distinguish between legal and illegal work performed within the educational system. The educational system in all Soviet republics had the following structure:

- Schools for general education, from seven to seventeen years of age;
- Specialised secondary schools for those who wanted to acquire specific occupational skills. These offered two- to four-year courses and would be available to pupils who had completed eight years' study in a general educational school;
- Higher education establishments offering five-year courses.

Below higher education, the educational system was based on comprehensive school lines without selection and without streaming. Selection started only with higher education, although at that stage it became very competitive. Applicants, who could be anyone with a general school or specialised school certificate, had the right to choose only one establishment of higher education, and had to pass four relevant examinations. Every department had its own set of examinations. The number of students receiving admittance every year for each department was strictly limited. Only those who were able to obtain the best examination marks were automatically admitted. Virtually every student who obtained a certificate of general education (which meant 80-90% of those who finished school) attempted to enter a higher educational establishment. Tertiary education carried with it much higher expectations than merely gaining entry to a profession (for instance, it was the only way to avoid the compulsory three years in the army). This extremely large number of applications resulted in very strong competition for higher education.

The competition, in turn, made it possible for the universities to increase the level of knowledge required to enter and, therefore, to create a wide gap between the demands of schools and those of higher education establishments. Only highly skilled people were able to overcome this gap independently. Normally almost everyone took private tuition with a lecturer from a higher education establishment for one or two years before making a formal application to the establishment.

It was a very widespread practice for lecturers to teach at home if their field of expertise happened to correspond to an examination subject. The approximate number of pupils at a single home lecture sometimes reached 20-25 or even more. Such coaching was, nevertheless, expensive, and parents had to save money for several years in order to pay for this intensive training.

As a result, secondary schools lost their prestige and became simply a place to obtain a certificate rather than knowledge. In-depth knowledge was obtained through private classes, again beyond any state control. Lecturers who for various reasons were not involved in private practice used to work in two or more places. It was not very difficult to do this, because of weak controls over the performance of state employees. So the quality of work remained a question of personal conscience for everyone.

What has changed during the five years of the transition?

First of all, the practice of "private" tutorials remains unchanged. But there are some important changes elsewhere in the system of higher education in Armenia. I want to focus on two of them which constitute innovations.

a. Innovation is to be found in the means by which the government has extricated itself from a complicated dilemma. It sought to preserve the positive image of free education, while keeping control of this ideologically and politically important institution. But at the same time it has managed to free itself from the obligation to pay the main part of the necessary expenditure.

In five years, the government has approximately doubled the number of students. Applicants who have received low marks, but agree to pay for their education, are now permitted to enter higher education establishments. The number of students in each entering class has therefore increased by a factor of two.

Only half the students now receive their education free (but in absolute numbers there are as many of them as there were before), while the other half have to pay for theirs. The fee-paying students have the same status, the same responsibilities and the same rights as the state-supported students.

This massive expansion has not been reflected in the salary of the teachers because teacher salaries are calculated according to the time they spend teaching in a classroom and have very little relation to the number of students in each group. The Soviet tradition of higher education is based mostly on dealing with groups and includes little provision for personal contact with any student on a one-to-one basis. So the new rules have not changed the size of the salary, but only the source of it: the payments received from the fee-paying half of the student population covers the main portion of the teacher's salary. And, of course, the new system also depends on one of the two groups of students paying for the education of the other group.

As a result:

● The system of higher education has not changed its status and remains totally under government control. There is no tangible change either in the hierarchical structure of management, or in the style of dealing with academic staff and students.

● The government has transferred the main financial burden from itself to the users. It is not difficult to see that this mixture of free and fee-paying education has nothing in common with private education. Instead of competition between institutions, and a variety of choice for the user, it produces only an overload of the establishments.

I consider this to be an example of the government itself using the informal tradition of direct pay-in-cash to solve its own problem.

b. But at the same time some private higher educational establishments have been founded. These are organised by teachers in the state-controlled establishments, many of whom are now working for both institutions in parallel. The new establishments are fee-charging, with virtually unlimited freedom for their managers. But what is most interesting in the new arrangements is that, while these private establishments are officially permitted, their certificates of graduation, granted to students upon completion of their courses, are not officially recognised as certificates of higher education.

Effectively, therefore, the newly created "private" establishments cannot enter into competition with the state-controlled establishments. But what they can do is to supply possibilities for teachers to increase their low state salary by several magnitudes.

The Health Service
Officially the only agency of provision for health care was the State. Like Britain's National Health Service, it was intended to be free at the point of use, and to provide an arena in which the idea of equality was expected to reveal itself in its full value. Free drugs were supplied in the hospitals and for the treatment of chronic illnesses at home. In all other cases prices were very low and access to drugs was guaranteed even for the very poor.

The actual practice differed somewhat from the theory. Although payment for treatment was officially discouraged, it was made on a regular basis to doctors and nurses in ordinary state hospitals. The Soviet system of health-care provision was based on a strong professional and administrative domination of the hospitals. It was possible to get free service, but it was very unreliable and to a great extent depended on the personal morality of doctors. Unfortunately the Hippocratic Oath did not always work.

A very specific concept of morality was formed in this field. High moral standards did not mean providing a free service, with equal treatment for everyone obtaining a state salary, but instead morality came to mean the set of principles forming a code by which to justify who should be paid, and how much, in order to ensure the well-being of the patients.

The following case will serve to illustrate this process. It is taken from the record of an interview with the wife of a patient who had received treatment in a hospital over a period of one month. The women was aged 62, and an engineer. Her husband was aged 68, a pensioner. The interview was carried out in 1988.

"The preliminary diagnosis of my husband was cancer and he had to go to the hospital for final diagnosis and possibly some treatment. It was the biggest specialised hospital in Armenia. We were lucky to see a very competent, attentive doctor.

The diagnosis was confirmed, and my husband had to stay in hospital for chemotherapy.

When this course of treatment was over and he could return home we started to work out how much we should pay to our doctor. I asked my friends and acquaintances who might have some impression of the usual price of this kind of treatment, and my husband spoke with other patients in the hospital, who were more experienced in this matter. Soon, the generally accepted sum became clear.

The day when he was due to leave the hospital, I put the money in an envelope and went to the doctor. After some consultation about future treatment, I expressed my gratitude and asked her to accept the envelope as a manifestation of it. But she flatly refused to take it, saying that she had never taken money from people like us, engineers, whose only source of income was the state salary. 'I am not an angel', she said, 'and I have a family I am responsible for. I do need to take money from some of my patients, but I know from whom. There are some patients from whom I can receive money without feeling guilty. You are not in this group.'

I was really pleased to meet so respectable and conscientious a doctor. My husband had on several occasions experienced hospitals for other reasons and it was only the second time that a doctor had refused to take money. This time we have spent very little money in the hospital: only some money that my husband gave to a hospital orderly to change his bedclothes, and to nurses for treatment procedures."

The story of this woman is a highly typical one for the pre-transitional period in the health service. It was in general a fee-paying service, but with exceptions and very informal. The cost of services was unclear, and mostly a matter of the discretion of patients and their relatives. On occasion, the crudity of a cash payment would be ameliorated by offering a gift of comparable value rather than an envelope containing a wad of banknotes. And it was usually manageable for the vast majority.

The main change which has taken place after five years of transition is the clarification of the prices. Now there is no necessity to discover a price by asking around. Doctors and nurses willingly tell you what it is before the treatment begins. Some hospitals and medical centres have a published list of prices for different services.

Some prices, however, especially those for surgical procedures, are payable in hard currency (United States dollars or Deutschmarks) and are thus not affordable for many people.

There is a new problem with drugs and medical dressings. Because there is a shortage of these commodities in the hospitals, patients themselves often have to buy them somewhere outside and bring them with them into hospital.

During an investigation I conducted in October 1994 about new legislation on health services, I was told by a spokesperson for the Ministry of Health of Armenia that there is no such thing as private medical care in Armenia, and there is no legal permission for the private practice of medicine (with the small exception of some practitioners of stomatology).

It became clear that the entire institution of "private" health services with fee-paying regulation, and published lists of prices, is operating without any connection to the State, beyond its control, and, thus, yielding it no benefit.

Social Work and the Second Economy
Before the "Great Transition", Armenian society – like all the other countries of the Soviet Union - was unfamiliar with such an area of governmental responsibility as "social work". The context of social work did not sit easily within the ideology of authoritarian socialism.

Primarily this was because the self-image of the regime was such that it could not tolerate a demand for such a profession. Not only under Stalin's megalomania, but throughout its 70-year history, Soviet society declared itself to be just. In the USSR, the official view was that the problems of poverty, unemployment and unhappiness had all been solved.

There was also a deeper, or structural, reason for the absence of a social work profession. According to the strict model of socialism asserted by the Soviet ideology, policy operated in a society formed by collectives, both in theory and in practice. This assumption was reinforced culturally, by a value system which also gave priority to the group whenever there seemed to be a need for focused attention and support. In consequence, individuals were not considered to be important units within the system.

The practice of social work began in Armenia soon after the break-up of the Soviet Union, which itself reflected a deep crisis within that whole society. It came about in unpromising, but needy, circumstances. Even before the political collapse of Communism at the end of the 1990s, Armenia had suffered a devastating natural disaster in 1988. A major earthquake destroyed a third of the country. Both the physical impact and the psychological horror have had lasting effects. Soon after its declaration of independence in 1991 Armenia found itself involved in an ethnic conflict with its neighbouring state of Azerbaijan. The warfare resulted in an economic blockade of Armenia, which in turn led first to the collapse of the economy and second to the disintegration and wholesale non-functioning of most social institutions.

The new government was trying to make policy and implement it. It was immediately obvious that it had neither the resources nor the experience required. What that meant for the ordinary people of Armenia was the complete absence of an internal safety net and social support. Their only hope was for external help: international aid, more precisely western aid, in the form both of humanitarian support and constructive investment.

In this catastrophic situation, the concept of social work practice was one of western contributions offered in response to the pronounced social needs of post-Soviet Armenia. In the early 1990s, it put down two roots into Armenian society: an academic one, which helped to create a body of social work professionals in the country, and an institutional one, in the form of central government involvement in the creation and maintenance of social work practice.

The academic influence began in 1992 when the first of a series of groups of teachers from the Yerevan State University travelled to London for a year of training at the London School of Economics and Political Science. On their return, they established a course to provide training for professional social workers in Armenia.

This strategy is a long-term one, the practical results of which can be discussed only in a few years' time. But nevertheless the task of devising a social work training programme did require the Armenian group of academics responsible for it to discuss, and produce viable answers to, a series of fundamental questions. These included: what would the Armenian model of social work look like? How far did western ideas correspond with the local system of values? Which elements of the western experience of social work could immediately be discarded as inappropriate, and which principles or practices would need to be examined with care in case they clashed with the local cultural traditions? And what status could be established for the unprecedented profession of social work?

Of all the questions confronted by the academics as they tried to assemble the theory which would guide Armenian practice in social work, one of the most difficult was: how could the newly developing institution of social work be prevented from being distorted by informal relationships? If legislative restraint were to be imposed upon social workers, would that succeed in keeping them separate from the second economy operations? For example, it was suspected, with a high probability and deep concern, that a social worker in a hospital could easily be turned into a facilitator, or financial broker, of the informal monetary deals between doctors and patients.

An early example of the tangible contradiction between authentic social work practice and the existence of an extended second economy occurred in 1992. On the advice of foreign consultants, an executive branch of the Armenian Government, the Ministry of Labour and Social Security, adopted social work as a device for the alleviation of poverty.

After consultations with western experts, a network of social services was established all over Armenia. It was proposed that it would be the task of the services first to identify the poorest families, and then to provide assistance. It was also proposed, initially, that the staff members operating the services at the local level should be granted considerable discretionary power in making the crucial decisions about who would be eligible to receive benefit. But it was quickly realised that this would encourage a tendency towards an undesirable development of the services by involving its staff in the informal distribution process of the second economy. To ward off this danger, successive versions of the plan for the structure of social services reduced the powers granted to the staff in the local offices, step by step.

Within a short period after its initial design, the whole system was effectively transferred from decentralised local responsibility to the surveillance of a centralised bureaucratic body which is required to follow detailed instructions worked out in the Ministry. This set of instructions establishes eleven categories of claimant considered to be worthy of benefit. These include, for example, pensioners living alone, the disabled, and families with more than three children. Local social service staff have no powers to deviate from these instructions, even if a solitary pensioner is well provided for, or a disabled person lives in a supportive family without any particular need. More disturbingly, the social worker is equally without power when a family is in deep poverty but did not belong to any of the categories listed.

To illustrate the problem created by this system, the following example is taken from an interview conducted, in July 1995, with the manager of the Social Service

Office in Yerevan. The respondent was a man of 34, married with two children. His working experience was three years (i.e. he had served from the time when the service was introduced).

" When I was recruited, I expected to work with people, to help them, to be proud of what I am doing. Now I am very disappointed. I have no right to do something independently. Very often I have to refuse benefit to people who are obviously starving, and to provide support to those who are not in need. This simplified list of social categories is not adequate to our complex social reality."

Question - Do you think that if the local services were to be given responsibility to identify those in poverty and decide eligibility for benefit, the system would work properly ?

" Only if our official salary would be considerably increased. Look, with only my official salary my family is living in poverty itself. How can I think about other families and ignore my own? I believe that nobody would blame me if I would look for the possibility of supporting my own family."

This conversation was very typical of most of the 40 employees of the social services interviewed for the study reported here. The situation described by the respondent is an example of the manner in which the first attempt to implement social work practice in Armenia was frustrated by the need to guard against the intrusion of the second economy. Effectively, the perceived need for close supervision of local services has meant that local service staff, who were conceived of initially as social workers, have effectively become clerical staff.

The second economy exists, and it is socially tolerated. It does provide a comprehensible scheme for the distribution of the society's resources - however far its distribution may deviate from any recognisable conception of social justice. But it produces also a profound dilemma: how to find the right model of social work which can be implanted in the social reality of Armenia without causing damage to the main ideas and values of social work. The dilemma, so far, remains unresolved.

Summary
The main changes which have occurred during the five years of transition after 1989 are the wholesale collapse at the official level of any regulation, and the freeing of the unofficial style of relations. Without looking at post-Soviet society from this perspective, it is impossible to understand how people can and do survive when the average salary paid by the State is $3.00 a month, and prices are not much lower than western ones. Dealing with the State makes sense for citizens today mainly as a means of access to resources, property and the institutional structure.

From one part of the social system to another, the informal approach to the conduct of business relations takes on different forms. The differences are, however, less significant than the similarities: in all cases the informal relationships lack any formal link with the official institutions of government; they operate without any framework of regulatory legislation; and in all kinds of deals, from negotiating the electricity supply to a factory to securing a surgical prosthesis after a road accident, the payment must be handled directly, often face-to-face, and nearly always in cash.

Does the newly established supremacy of the informal economy constitute a step along the road towards a free market? Possibly, but if it does then the journey will be an exceptionally long one. So far, the contribution of the informal economy to the economics of transition has been to push the State into deeper and deeper crisis.

References

Asland, A. (1990) "How Small is the Soviet Economy?", pp13-61 in Rowen, H. S. & Wolf C.(eds) *The Impoverished Superpower*, San Francisco, CA: ICS Press.

Etzioni, A. (1988) *The Moral Dimension: Toward a New Economics*, New York: Free Press.

Grossman, G. (1977) "The Second Economy of the USSR *Problems of Communism* 26, 5, pp25-40.

Kaminski, A. Z. (1989)"Coercion, Corruption and Reform: State and Society in the Soviet-Type Socialist Regime", J*ournal of Theoretical Politics* 1, 1, pp77-102.

Katsenelinboigen, A. (1977) "Coloured Markets in the Soviet Union", *Soviet Studies* 29, 1, pp62-85.

Rose, R. (1985) "Getting By in Three Economies: The Resources of the Official, Unofficial and Domestic Economies", pp103-141 in Lane, J. E. (ed), *State and Market*, London: Sage.

Rose, R. (1992) "Toward a Civil Economy?", *Journal of Democracy* 3, 2, pp13-26,.

Rose, R. (1992) "Divisions and Contradictions in Economies in Transition". Glasgow: Centre for the Study of Public Policy, University of Strathclyde.

Rose, R., Haerpfer. C. (1994) "Mass Response to Transformation in Post-Communist Society", *Europe-Asia Studies* 46, 1, pp3-28.

Sik, E. (1992) "From the Second Economy to the Informal Economy", *Journal of Public Policy* 12, 2 pp153-175,

Winiecki, J (1988) *The Distorted World of Soviet-Type Economics*, London: Routledge.

Introducing New Professions:
The Case of Russian Social Work

Alexander Solovyov

Social work is a relatively young occupation. It first emerged as a particular field of activity at the end of the last century. Since then it has significantly strengthened its position and proved to be an important part of modern social organisation. Still its status is far from being fully established and a lively public debate is going on about its scope, goals and prospects.

Taking the development of the social work profession as the focus, we will start with the general characteristics of professions. Then we will consider the rise of professions as an historical process. After that we will turn to evaluating the current professional status of social work. Finally, we will outline the development of social work in Britain and the United States where it has a comparatively long history and well-established traditions, as well as in Russia where it only now begins to assert itself as an autonomous profession.

What is a Profession?
The terms "profession" and "occupation" are close but not completely equivalent. Normally the first term is used in a more restricted sense: professions are a particular class of occupations. As all occupations, professions can be regarded as elements of social organisation based upon division of labour according to technological specialisation. Professionalisation represents a characteristic feature of modern societies with highly differentiated and co-ordinated internal structures.

There have been many attempts to define the concept. Millerson (1964) reviewed the work of 21 authors who had tried to extract essential elements of the true profession. He found that in all 33 attributes were regarded as essential, but no single attribute was accepted by all the authors.

Let us take a couple of examples. Greenwood (1965) gives the following definition: "A profession is an organised group which is constantly interacting with the society that forms its matrix, which performs its social functions through a network of formal and informal relationships, and which created its own subculture requiring adjustments to it as a prerequisite for career success." This definition is broad and indicates general attributes common not only to all professions, but even to most occupations. A more specific formula is suggested by Rueschemeyer (1964): "The professions are service- or community-oriented occupations applying a systematic body of knowledge to problems which are highly relevant to central values of the society." This definition pinpoints attributes differentiating professions from other occupations.

Starting with broad definition, Greenwood (1965) then embarks on a more detailed analysis and singles out five distinctive attributes:

- systematic theory
- authority
- community sanctions
- ethical code
- a culture.

Johnson (1972) gives the following list of most frequently mentioned traits (core elements):

- skill based on theoretical knowledge
- the provision of training and education
- testing the competence of members
- organisation
- adherence to a professional code of conduct
- altruistic service.

A systematic theory is considered to be the key element on which a profession hinges. It shapes many other features. For instance, university education, required for practising professions, is a direct consequence of a very broad knowledge base and complex skills involved. To attain professional competence a novice must go through a lengthy period of formal education in an academic setting, while on-the-job training through apprenticeship is usually sufficient for most skill-based occupations. As Jackson (1970:6) puts it: "A trained mind is given precedence to technical competence which it is assumed can be readily picked up once the formal education process is completed."

Professional knowledge is esoteric in the sense that it is not readily accessible to laymen. This creates a social distance between the practitioner and the client. The greater the social distance, the greater the exposure to possible exploitation and the need for social control (Johnson, 1972). But as there is nobody outside the profession competent enough to evaluate such matters, peer control becomes a major type of direction over professional activity. Non-professional occupations are more open to public control - e.g. through mass media - and to bureaucratic interference.

Another sign of professional autonomy is the principle of confidentiality. It is the expression of a special kind of relationship between the professional and the client. The latter trusts the former and is ready to communicate to him/her information of a very personal nature. The professional assumes the role of a friendly and empathic listener. And society acknowledges the special character of this relationship, granting the practitioner the right to represent the client's interests and a considerable margin of discretion.

The principle of confidentiality forms part of a regulative code of professional behaviour. Prescribing specific forms of behaviour towards clients, colleagues and the general public, the code sets a standard of professionalism and serves as a safeguard against abuses of professional power. As Greenwood (1965:516) points out: "Through its ethical code the profession's commitment to the social welfare becomes a matter of public record, thereby insuring for itself the continued confidence of the community. Without such confidence the profession could not retain its monopoly".

Among other principles of professional ethics regulating the client:practitioner relationships are universalism and disinterestedness. The first obliges the practitioner to treat his/her clients impartially and equally regardless of their age, gender, race and social position. The second means that the idea of service to the clients must be paramount among the motives behind the professional conduct. (See Shanin's paper in this volume above.) Not only should it outweigh other benefits of the job (material or otherwise) but in many cases it calls for personal sacrifices. The medical profession provides a wealth of telling examples.

Another set of principles governs the relationships between colleagues within the profession. They demand of each member co-operative, equalitarian and supportive behaviour towards its peers. They also imply professional self-discipline and mutual interdependence. Ideally, each representative of a profession strives towards the highest possible level of services and competence using the experience and resources of his/her colleagues. On the other hand, s/he is eager to disseminate any advances in theory and practice to colleagues through personal contacts, professional journals, workshops and conferences.

Written and unwritten norms, values and symbols, together with various institutional settings, educational and research centres and professional associations, form a distinctive professional culture. To the uninitiated the workings of the system are for the most part incomprehensible. Professional jargon complicates this state of things even further. A novice is faced with a huge task of absorbing all the elements of the professional culture. It takes years both during formal education and after its completion. The whole process is called "professional socialisation". Having gone through it, the individual is accepted as a true member of the professional community by his peers. Personal commitment to the cause is another product of this lengthy process. To the professional person the work becomes an important part of his or her life. When speaking about professions we refer to a career which is essentially a calling.

The Rise of Professions as an Historical Proces

The analysis so far has focused on the characteristics of the fully fledged professions which distinguish them from other occupations. Such an approach is known as the "trait model". The model describes a particular type of occupational control and a high social status achieved by certain professional groups. But it tends to overlook the fact that the present status and the specific organisation of these occupations have emerged as a result of a long process of evolution and struggle. To make the picture comprehensive, the trait model should be complemented by a functional analysis concerned with the developmental aspect and the stages of this historical process.

The functional model (Carr-Saunders, 1955; Goode, 1969) presents a continuum along which various occupations can be positioned. The established professions are placed on one pole of the continuum - the high degree of professionalisation. Between them and non-professional occupations are located the forms of occupational organisation which may be termed "semi-professional". The term means that they display certain affinity with genuine professions, but at the same time lack some of the essential features listed above. Social work in its present state is qualified by most researchers as a semi-profession.

Professionalisation is conceived as a process through which an occupation moves towards acquiring a full professional status. Wilensky (1964) marks the following stages of the process:

- the emergence of a full-time occupation
- the establishment of a training school
- the founding of a professional association
- political agitation directed towards the protection of the association by law
- the adoption of a formal code.

Greenwood (1965) points out that an occupation striving towards professional status seeks to prove that: a) the performance of the occupational skills requires special education; b) those who possess this education deliver a superior service; c) the human need being served is of sufficient social importance to justify the superior performance.

Traditional professions succeeded in convincing the general public that all the above - mentioned assertions are true with regard to them. Social work was less successful in this despite the attempts to raise the professional status of the occupation. The aspiration is understandable. But an impartial analysis shows that it reflects more the ideal state of affairs than the actual realities.

It must be noted that there are alternative ways of regarding the nature of professions. A critical approach (Johnson, 1972; Bailey and Brake, 1975) emphasises the monopolistic character of professional institutions, their self-interest and preoccupation with status. It concentrated on negative features of professionalism - privilege and exclusion.

Curiously enough, criticism of this kind originated both from the political Left and Right. Some Marxist critics pictured professions as instruments of class dominance and oppression. Liberal critics saw professions as alliances preventing the achievement of a really free market of services.

In a way, this so called "power approach" is a useful counterbalance to the idealised picture on which we dwelt earlier. It highlights some real problems and conflicts that exist in the relationships of a profession to its clients, other occupational groups and society at large. But in its extreme form it goes too far in criticising professionalism.

Freidson (1994) gives a comprehensive analysis of different approaches and emphasises positive aspects of the professional model: it is based on the democratic notion that people are capable of controlling themselves by collective means, that they can be committed to their challenging work rather than alienated from it, and that it provides a milieu which encourages intellectual innovation and disinterested service. He concludes that "a monopoly held by an occupation whose members are committed to the integrity of a craft that is of value to others is a more desirable and less destructive solution to an important social problem than is a free play of unbridled material interest or the reduction of all work to formally specified procedures" (p181).

The Professional Status of Social Work

There are several objective factors that prevent social work from reaching high professional status. The most prominent among them are:

- great inner diversity
- rather weak knowledge base
- strong bureaucratic control.

The diversity stems from the fact that social workers operate in a number of different settings performing a wide range of functions and pursuing varied goals. The result is that social work becomes a very special type of activity depending upon the office and agency in which it is practised. Boundaries between various helping activities are often blurred and this further complicates the matter.

Substantial diversity exists even at the level of general goal-setting. The overarching aim of social work - promotion of human well-being - can be pursued by different means: by facilitating adjustment of individuals to existing circumstances or by attempting to change economic and social environments. The first approach is generally called therapeutic or clinical. The terms "direct practice" and "personal services" are also used to distinguish this approach. The key method under this model of practice is casework. The opposite pole is represented by social planning, community organisation, and social reform. This strand was very strong at the inception of social work as public endeavour, but in the 1970s it re-emerged in the form of radical social work (Bailey and Brake, 1975). The double focus is already present in social work taken in its entirety, but as the two approaches often seem incompatible, the controversy between reform and rehabilitation is sometimes referred to as the basic dilemma of social work (Toren, 1972).

It was indicated earlier that a substantial body of knowledge constitutes the heart of a profession. The knowledge base of social work is multifaceted (Ramon, 1991) and derived from a number of sources: developmental and social psychology, sociology, and cultural anthropology. The parent disciplines themselves are in the process of active development. Thus, the knowledge base is not stable and solid enough. In addition, part of the knowledge is about social framework in which professional activity takes place. This part of knowledge is more factual than conceptual in character. Moreover, the social reality itself is susceptible to change and therefore this part of professional knowledge is even more fluid and tied to specific circumstances.

It was already mentioned that social workers operate in a variety of settings. Relatively few of them function as independent practitioners - mostly as family counsellors. Some work for specialised private agencies. But the majority serve as employees in different public institutions (schools, hospitals, correction establishments and public assistance agencies) and thus are subject to administrative control limiting their professional freedom.

Analysing the position of professionals within a bureaucratic organisation, Scott (1969) defines the key concepts as follows: "the term 'professional' refers to a person who by virtue of long training is qualified to perform specialised activities autonomously - relatively free from external supervision or regulation, while 'bureaucrat' refers to a person performing specialised but more routine activities within a hierarchical structure. The authority of knowledge and the authority of administrative hierarchy are basically incompatible, and this creates tension between the two sets of principles."

There are some additional factors contributing to a relatively low professional status of social work (Garvin and Tropman, 1992):

- it is a predominantly female profession
- since social work, by and large, serves the least prestigious members of the community, its own prestige is adversely affected
- social workers very often articulate unpopular points of view (e.g., an accepting attitude towards deviancy)
- social workers deal with familiar problems, and that narrows the distance between the professional and lay knowledge
- only a small percentage of social workers possess full educational qualifications
- the function of social work is not regarded as indispensable to the maintenance of the ongoing life of a society.

We spent some time considering factors which prevent social work from reaching high professional status. It is often assumed that achieving full professionalism is a good thing since it brings certain rewards (material and moral) to the members of the occupational group. But if we take a broader perspective and see an occupation in its global mission - serving particular societal needs rather than as a clique pursuing their egoistic interests – another facet of the problem becomes apparent: a tendency towards "deprofessionalisation" reflects some intrinsic features of social work as a caring occupation, since excessive professionalisation is liable to cause the loss of its basic humanitarian values.

Seen in this light, some of the apparent "weaknesses" of social work as a profession turn out to be expressions of its specific mission and its specific place among other caring professions. Take the knowledge base, for example. It is indeed eclectic and not solid enough due to the multiplicity of tasks that social workers perform and settings in which they are employed. Some may see it as a drawback. But the dominant tendency now is to regard shared values rather than the knowledge used or methods employed as a true basis of professional unity.

One of the most basic values in social work asserts the worth and dignity of every human being. This belief claims the right of each person to decent living and respect. Another value stresses the importance of personal growth and self-realisation. It calls for creation of such an environment in which everyone is able to develop his or her potential to the full. But since people are social beings and depend on each other for meeting their fundamental needs, everyone has a responsibility to help others realise themselves in the same way. Still another value proclaims the right of individuals to be different from each other. Taken in its entirety, the system of such beliefs constitutes professional ideology which serves as a core of professional culture.

Opponents of excessive professionalisation point to the historical fact that social work started as a voluntary activity in the form of a charity movement. Even today the voluntary sector plays an important role in providing social services. The problem is to find the right balance between statutory and voluntary organisations, between public and private sectors, between highly trained and support personnel. To try to achieve full professionalisation in this respect would be both practically untenable and contrary to the spirit of the endeavour.

An Outline of Social Work History in Britain and the US

Social work in Britain started in the nineteenth century as a philanthropic movement. The Charity Organisation Society (COS) was founded in 1869. It aimed at rationalising benevolence and organising "scientific" philanthropy. Initially the work was performed by volunteers striving to alleviate poverty in society.

But soon it was acknowledged that people who were to deal with the complex problems of poverty and family life required special training. Out of this early practice developed the concept of social work as a skilled process of giving help. In 1903 the COS started the School of Sociology in London. In 1912 the school was amalgamated with the social science department of the London School of Economics.

The whole ideology behind the activities of the COS was strongly individualistic and viewed the problem of poverty as caused by personal failure. It took for granted the class structure of Victorian England and its stability.

By the turn of the century, the COS came increasingly under attack for its failure to take into account social causes of poverty and for its opposition to developing state schemes for social welfare . Therefore, during the first two decades of our century alternative conceptions of social work, more in tune with the social thinking of the time, began developing. The concept of charity was giving way to that of social service based on the idea of citizenship and social rights. But, on the whole, the development of social work in Britain was rather slow due to its initial close association with the charity movement (Yelloly, 1980).

Social work practice in the United States started later than in the United Kingdom and initially relied heavily on the early British experience. But in the 1920s and 1930s it was growing rapidly in several fields: family and child welfare, medical, psychiatric and school social work. The American Association of Social Workers was established in 1921. Around the same time several other associations were formed to reflect a variety of specific interests and professional concerns. The first professional organisation in the United Kingdom – the British Federation of Social Workers – was founded in 1935.

The major stress at that time was on method and setting. The approach tended to emphasise differences among the fields and thus contributed to greater fragmentation in practice as a whole. The early failure to make clear distinction between social welfare and social work, between agency and profession, led to further confusion. The situation called for clarifying the conceptual foundation of the profession, for finding a common base underlying the different forms of social work practice, for drawing boundaries between social work and other professions and within the profession itsel

After the Second World War social work in Britain began expanding very rapidly. The general political climate in the country was favourable to the process. The establishment of the welfare state led to the creation of many new social services. That, in turn, produced the demand for trained staff and gave fresh impetus to the growth of social work education. The field of social work became more diversified and more specialised. The élite group was represented by psychiatric social workers employed mostly in hospitals and child guidance clinics.

Psychoanalysis became the predominant theoretical orientation. In practice the emphasis was on individual help with inner emotional problems, and here many similarities between social casework and psychoanalysis were apparent. The so-called intensive casework became in fact synonymous with psychotherapy.

The consecutive development, broadly speaking, represented an attempt to overcome the bias of the method-and-skill model of social work, a shift of attention from personal to social factors, from private sorrows to public issues. Criticising the casework approach, however, we must recognise its historical role as an effort to produce a competent practitioner, as a drive to professionalism (Bartlett, 1970).

In 1955 the existing professional organisations in the United States merged into the National Association of Social Workers (NASW) which has served since that time as the central body for the profession. Three years prior to the formation of NASW, the Council of Social Work Education was founded. It is an affiliation of schools of social work that sets standards for the teaching of social work at university level. The Council's journal "Education for Social Work" along with NASW's journal "Social Work" are among the key professional publications in the United States.

In the 1970s both social work services and social work education in Britain expanded very rapidly. In 1971 the statutory Central Council for Education and Training in Social Work (CCETSW) superseded the three previously existing separate bodies. It concentrated on bringing over 120 courses to a common minimum standard and introduced the certificate of qualification in social work (CQSW) for all courses which it recognised.

In the early 1980s, due to the deteriorating political and economic environment both were contracting and some social work courses had closed. The period saw a trend towards "marketisation" of social services and a greater emphasis on community care. Among new themes which got prominence at the time were child abuse, anti-discriminatory practice, advocacy, user participation and empowerment.

The same period in the United States can be characterised as paradoxical (Garvin and Tropman, 1992) because of conflicting streams and countervailing pressures. But on the whole it was a period when retraditionalisation of American society became a major trend. In the area of social policy, negativism towards the poor and disadvantaged began to surface. Social support has been replaced by suspicion and scarcity. But simultaneously a new interest in voluntary agencies has arisen. On the other hand, the number of practitioners employed by private for-profit organisations was growing rapidly.

Overall, the history of social work in Britain and the United States shows a steady growth accompanied by competing tendencies of differentiation and integration. Another process can also be traced - the back and forth swinging between two sets of values: commitment to equity (providing people with what they deserve based on the contributions they make) and commitment to adequacy (providing people with the needed minimums). It reflects the fact that the profession operates within the broader framework of social policy and its cyclical fluctuations.

The History and Current State of Social Work in Russia
The tradition of care for and assistance to the needy has deep roots in Russian society. It goes back to the communal life of the Russian peasantry which until quite recently constituted the bulk of the population and to deeply ingrained Christian beliefs.

Institutionalised social care started in the late eighteenth century both on the state and community levels. In the nineteenth century several charity organisations came into existence, among them the Royal Philanthropic Society. At the turn of the century a new trend emerged - a shift from voluntary to professional help. Specialised training courses were introduced in the institutions of higher education for women, organised at the time.

Initially, as in the West, social work in Russia was performed mostly by women from well-to-do families inspired by liberal and humanistic ideals. Among voluntary organisations involved in social work, a prominent role was played by the Red Cross and various Church groups. Thus, up to 1917 the development of social services in Russia mirrored in many respects the process in Britain and the United States.

Turbulent political events of the early twentieth century (the First World War, the Bolshevik revolution, the Civil War) generated intense and widespread human problems. The pitch of general suffering rose so high that for many millions of people it was a sheer struggle for survival. In that critical situation the new Soviet state put all spheres of public life under its control. By regulating the distribution of resources it eventually managed to resolve the crisis, to provide a minimal subsistence level for the huge population, to create a fairly efficient system of public health care and education.

Capitalising on the achievements, official propaganda was quick to proclaim that under socialism all key problems of human existence had been radically solved. Existing social problems like alcohol abuse were played down and called "remnants of the capitalist past". Such ideological tenets oriented social services towards improving well-being of the people by containing "social ills" and by providing material assistance to the most disadvantaged groups of the population. The very term "social work" was not in use. Elements of social work were divided between several state departments: the Ministry of Internal Affairs, the Ministries of Education and Health, and the Ministry of Social Welfare. No special training for social workers existed. The whole system functioned as a highly compartmentalised and bureaucratically run network of social control and state provisions.

The situation changed dramatically ten years ago with the beginning of "perestroika". Democratisation and "glasnost" followed, and the mass media got a free hand to highlight the social problems of the nation. The resulting picture was rather gloomy, and that produced a psychological shock. It must be borne in mind that under Communism many types of official statistics constituted classified information. When data on crime and substance misuse were eventually published they did look alarming.

The break-up of the Soviet Union and the collapse of the state-run economy led to dire social consequences: the living standard of the general population has fallen sharply, the "shock therapy" resulted in material hardships for millions of Russians, the number of vulnerable people rose dramatically. The period witnessed the emergence of such phenomena as unemployment, homelessness, and a wave of refugees for which no safety networks existed.

However, the uneasy times gave fresh impetus to the development of social work in the country and prompted its recognition as an essential element in the structure of modern society. New agencies, both statutory and non-governmental, sprang into being. The voluntary sector was revitalised with such tasks as the distribution of massive western aid. More people were drawn into the activity. The need for qualified personnel was strongly felt at all levels of services. Managerial skills acquired particular importance in the transitional period from a state-run to a market economy. Consequently, social work education became top priority. Social work as a distinct profession was officially recognised in Russia in 1991. About the same time two professional organisations were formed: the Association of Social Pedagogues and Social Workers and the Association of Social Services. Social work education was introduced at university level. A professional journal was launched.

At the moment, the overarching goal for the profession is to improve the quality of life for the most vulnerable groups of the population. Material aid should be supplemented by psychosocial support. Personal services are to become the key element of the system. It is necessary to co-ordinate the activities of various sectors, including statutory and non-governmental agencies, and to expand the network to cover all parts of the country.

In building new social support networks and developing social work education we rely on the experience of our western colleagues which provides us with useful models and techniques. Translation of professional literature helps to fill the gap in this area. Direct contacts between practitioners and educators greatly facilitate the growth of the new profession in Russia. Still the question arises as to whether mere imitation will be productive. Undoubtedly, many problems are universal and so their approved solutions can be borrowed. On the other hand, the current situation in Russia has many specific features which must be taken into account. We must be very sensitive to them and critical in adopting approaches generated elsewhere.

Conclusions

1. Professions are occupations which specialise in delivering complex individualised services directed at satisfying fundamental human needs.

2. Professionalisation is seen as the growth and inner differentiation of traditional professions as well as the emergence of new ones is a process characteristic of the structural transformation of modern society.

3. Social work is one of the new professions striving to gain full professional status. Still there are objective factors which stand in the way of this development. So the present state of the occupation is better described as semi-professional.

4. Britain and the United States were among the countries where social work first established itself as a full-time occupation. The consecutive advance of the profession in both countries proceeded along basically similar lines with reciprocal influences.

5. Social work in Russia had its precursors in the form of charity organisations and welfare provisions. But as an officially recognised profession it came into being only recently - at the beginning of the 1990s.

6. Trying to boost the development of the new profession in Russia its members are drawing heavily on the western experience. At the same time they have to take into account historical traditions and current socio-political factors.

References

Bailey, R., Brake, M. (eds.) (1975) *Radical Social Work*. London: Arnold.

Bartlett, H.M. (1970) *The Common Base of Social Work* Practice.Washington: NASW.

Carr-Saunders, A. M. (1955) M*etropolitan Conditions and Traditional Professional Relationships. In: The Metropolis in Modern Life*. Ed. by Fisher, R. M. Garden City: Doubleday, pp279-287.

Freidson, E. (1994) *Professionalism Reborn: Theory, Prophecy, and Policy.* Cambridge, Polity Press.

Garvin, Ch. D., Tropman J.C. (1992) *Social Work in Contemporary Society*. Englewood Cliffs: Prentice Hall.

Goode, W. J. (1969) *The Theoretical Limits to Professionalization. In: The Semi-Professions and Their Organisation.* Ed. by Etzioni, A.N.Y.: Free Press, pp.266-313.

Greenwood, E. (1965) *Attributes of a Profession. In: Social Welfare Institutions: A Sociological Reader.* Ed. by M.N. Zald. N.Y.: Wiley, pp.509-523.

Jackson, J. A. (ed.) (1970) *Professions and Professionalization*: Cambridge University Press.

Johnson, T. J. (1972) *Professions and Power.* L.: Macmillan.

Lorenz, W. (1994) *Social Work in Changing Europe.* L.-NY.: Routledge.

Millerson, G. (1964) *The Qualifying Associations: A Study in Professionalisation.* L.: Routledge.

Panov, A. (1995) Social Work in Russia: Problems and Perspectives *NISW International News*, No.3, pp2-3.

Ramon, S. (1991) "Principles and Conceptual Knowledge". In: *Beyond Community Care: Normalisation and Integration Work.* Ed. by Ramon, S. London: Macmillan, pp.6-34.

Richan, W., Mendelsohn, A. (1973) *Social Work: The Unloved Profession.* N.Y.: New Viewpoints.

Rueschemeyer, D. (1964) Doctors and Lawyers: A Comment on the Theory of the Professions Canadian *Review of Sociology and Anthropolog*, No.1, pp.17-30.

Scott, W. R. (1964) "Professional Employee in a Bureaucratic Structure: Social Work". In: *The Semi-Professionals and Their Organisation.* Ed. by Etzioni, A.N.Y.: Free House, pp.82-140.

Toren, N. (1972) *Social Work: The Case of a Semi-Profession.* Beverly Hills/London: Sage.

Wilensky, H. L. (1964) "The Professionalization for Everyone" *American Journal of Sociology*, vol.70, pp137-158.

Woodroofe, K. (1968) *From Charity to Social Work: In England and the United States* London: Routledge and Kegan Paul.

Yelloly, M. (1980) *Social Work Theory and Psychoanalysis* N.Y.: Van Nostrand.

The Emergence and Development of the Non-Profit Sector in Hungary

Katalin Lévai

Historical Overview

Non-profit organisations had been an integral part of Hungarian society and had a significant economic and political role before the Second World War. Some 14,000 associations were registered in 1932. As a consequence of the communist take-over, almost all associations and all foundations were abolished in 1949. The regulation of associations was rather liberal until 1956, but became increasingly centralised during the 1970s and the 1980s. A law introduced in 1970 made it compulsory to report to the authorities even the intention of forming an association. As for foundations, even the legal form was abolished in 1949, and the institution was not revitalised until 1987 as a consequence of the efforts of prominent Hungarians - like George Soros - to establish foundation-like institutions.

In 1981 a new regulation gave the authorities the power to prohibit the formation of any association considered to be a "danger to the socialist and political system". Despite these legal constraints, during these decades the number of registered associations increased and reached a relatively high figure (6,000 to 8,000). This contradiction suggests the interesting conclusion that the authorities did not use their powers against the newly established associations.

It would appear that even long before the changes there were tangible differences among the different kinds of associations. In the first place, the large, so-called "national organisations" – like the Patriotic People's Front – were created by laws or government decrees and played a significant political role. Secondly, there were numerous other national and also party-controlled organisations – like the Women's Council, or the Nature Conservation Association – which had less political and social influence. Thirdly, the rest of the associations were smaller and local: 80% of the total consisted of local sports, cultural, hobby and firemen's associations. It was not until 1990 that the proportion of these types of associations fell from 80% to 70%. Clearly these associations were kept under strict control so they could not become really self-motivated. On the other hand these "pseudo-organisations" played a significant role in the revival of the non-profit sector after 1989 - especially in the smaller towns - as the successors of the former party-state organisations and have proved to be more viable than many of the newly established ones.

This legally and officially recognised formal organisational structure was complemented – both outside and inside – by a constantly growing number of oppositional and alternative non-profit organisations. These were set up mostly by concerned professionals, activists of the democratic opposition or the Churches. Before the changes, civil society was a predominantly illegal, loosely organised movement-like entity resisting and challenging the above-mentioned formal structures imposed on the society, where the persons involved undertook a political as well as personal risk. This perception of the civil society is fundamentally different from the rather generic definition used after the political changes for the sphere of non-profit foundations and informal associations which complement the business and government sectors in various economic and social fields. It is therefore not correct to say that there was no history or basis for the development of this sector in Hungary and that it emerged from scratch after 1989. On the other hand, civil society before that time used to be the "small circles of freedom". They included high schools and friendly societies, even though they did not appear in institutional forms. Activities in the "second economy" such as private home-building, showed similarly the features of the non-profit sector, but without an institutional framework.

During the course of the 1980s these informal structures and civil initiatives played an increasingly important and active role, especially in the field of social policy. This phenomenon reflected the significant deficiencies of the 1980s in fields relating to family life, child care and education. The activists of these initiatives had serious debates in the early 1980s with those wanting to maintain the state monopoly of social policy. The supporters of the change towards a "mixed system" argued that it could create an opportunity for social ventures, draw large numbers of people into various social activities and promote the integrity of residential communities. Thus there was an increasing desire for a mixed system of state and non-state related social services, but poverty was still a taboo subject in a socialist country like Hungary. The first non-state-related initiatives of the 1980s were fairly different from each other and pursued the following objectives:

a.   The organisations for the voluntary safeguarding of interests - such as the Fund for the Support of the Poor (Szeta), the Social Workers' Association and the Association of People with Large Families – were of political importance. They broke away from the prevailing political paradigm in which social groups were not allowed to protect their own interests since the omnipotent state did it for them. The Fund for the Support of the Poor (Szeta) was the group in Hungary oriented towards social problems to address the phenomenon of poverty. Szeta, a non-registered, primarily political rather than a social initiative, was set up by a group of intellectuals in Budapest in 1979 to help the poor and needy. This help consisted partly of cash payments and clothing exchanges.

b. The voluntary Church-related social services and institutions (e.g. Rescuing Drunkards, Baptist Section of Neglected Youth) have become more and more promoted within the various Churches after decades of suppression.

c. The group of voluntary federations and associations – such as the Association of the Physically Handicapped and Anti-alcoholic Clubs – represented the most dynamically expanding part of the emerging civil society. They addressed partly the same problems (drug abuse) as the organisations mentioned above and partly different ones (AIDS).

d. The partly-non-profit ventures, such as Lares and Minerva, intended to provide services to the general population. Their objectives were quite similar to those of the Church institutes, but they worked without an institutional base and state subventions. Lares Human Service Co-operative was the first post-communist non-governmental human services organisation in Hungary, using the institution created by the1981 Venture Act. Lares and other "social ventures" endeavoured to become non-profit organisations, but the appropriate legal and institutional framework was missing. These organisations aimed to perform free services if funding could be ensured from other sources. The Lares-type ventures were unique institutions: they intended to combine the advantages of a state institution and the small-scale venture system. They were good examples of the slow process whereby the State first tolerated, then accepted and later promoted the non-state-related organisations.

e. The profit-oriented ventures were not tolerated before the end of the 1980s.

Consequently autonomy did exist in a restricted form before the changes as well although these endeavours for autonomy were controlled by the State party mechanism.

The rapid expansion after 1989
Restrictions on all kinds of associations were lifted with the 1989 Associations Act that declared the right of association to be a fundamental and inalienable constitutional freedom. Since the political changes, civil society has built up its institutional structure and now represents a positive contribution to the development of the society.

The Hungarian non-profit sector has shown a dynamic growth in the last five or six years. The number of non-profit organisations has substantially increased in the past few years: from 9,000 in 1989 to over 31,000 at the end of 1992. The number of these organisations is still growing, even if at a slower pace in 1994 and 1995 than earlier. The number of foundations in particular grew very sharply, showing a 450% growth in 1989-1990.

"Returning to the natural trend" is one of the possible reasons for this expansion, which happens when a society gets rid of imposed structures. On the one hand many informal activities which existed earlier have acquired an institutional form. On the other hand, as noted above, the historical roots and latent initiatives have always been present in the Hungarian society. Many of the new associations are only successors of organisations that were abolished after 1945. It is likely that the increased social mobility stimulates individual willingness for interest representation.

A feature of this growth has been the mushrooming of small NGOs with very similar activities and a low inclination for co-operation. The sudden opportunity to act absolutely independently worked against forming coalitions and rather resulted in competition among these small organisations. In this "euphoria of freedom" concerned people tried to achieve something by themselves, irrespective of others' efforts similar to theirs.

On the other hand, it was a general belief during the changes that these new institutions of the so fervently hoped for 'mixed system" would be able to replace the State in many fields. The widely recognised disastrous condition of social, health and other services has also inspired many to undertake a role in a foundation or association.

At the same time many foundations were used for tax evasion purposes after the introduction of tax exemption rules between 1990 and 1992. Foundations serving the public good were exempt and could accept tax-deductible donations without any restrictions. The foundations became an attractive form for service activities. The result of these liberal provisions was that many profit-oriented ventures used this non-profit form. For example the first cable television companies were established as foundations, thus avoiding tax payments for two years.

The types of activities of foundations and associations vary widely. While the highest percentage of associations are still in the traditional fields of sports and hobbies, a remarkable increase can be observed in the number of interest representation groups (employer and employee organisations). One of the peculiarities of the Hungarian sector, stemming from its historical context, is the relatively high proportion of cultural and religious associations. On the other hand, the activity of foundations is focused on the fields of education and culture as well as social services. However, the social activities of these organisations are more dominant than could be concluded from the statistics.

While the sector has shown an unbelievable growth statistically, the revival of civil society is not going to be a triumphal march. The prime mover of the changes is individual activity, but the available financial resources are extremely limited. Hence most of the new NGOs are dependent on support from the central government and local authorities. Governmental funding is still the prevailing source of income for the sector, constituting more than 50% of their total incomes. According to the budget, government support for non-profit organisations, overwhelmingly for foundations, grew by 534% between 1990 and 1993. This amount consists of the direct donations from government funds and the normative support for social, health and educational organisations. Foundations get support through the government's different organs; associations may apply for funding to a parliamentary committee and the distribution of the grants is voted by parliament.

The central government and local authorities may set up so-called public foundations, which became a very popular form of providing services from central resources for certain groups of the society. Many local government agencies have set up public foundations to help run the public schools and hospitals. The level of funding of other NGOs depends largely on their relationship with local government.

Approximately one-fourth of the non-profit sector's incomes are derived from the business sector. Unfortunately there are no data concerning the proportion of private enterprises in this support. However, businesses do not cultivate the culture of philanthropy and social responsibility in Hungary. The multinational companies are the most active sponsors, but they prefer larger NGOs with attractive PR potential (cultural and sports events, etc.). The difficulties of NGOs in finding sponsorship from businesses explains why the State is still the "greatest sponsor".

There are only a few grant-giving foundations in Hungary. The biggest one is the Soros Foundation, set up in 1984. The Autonómia Foundation for self-reliance supports mainly gypsy farming and enterprises.

About one-fifth of the total financial support and time for charitable purposes have been donated by individuals to Hungarian non-profit organisations. Most of their giving is to Churches, followed by foundations in the fields of social services, education and culture. The amount of support from individuals suggests that the foundations' efforts are appreciated by the society.

Co-operation Between the Local Authorities and the Non-profit Sector

In recent years growing attention has been given to the possibilities and new forms of co-operation between the State and non-State sectors. In both western and eastern Europe a shift can be observed in the monopoly held by the State on the representation of public interest. Governments are less and less able and willing to provide for the satisfaction of public needs, while the changes that have occurred in social structures - for example, the change in the composition of families, the rapid ageing of the population, the spread of unemployment - require extraordinary financial and human resources. Many respected researchers explain the steadily growing appearance of non-profit factors, especially in the fields of social and health care, by the failure of the State to shoulder tasks, while others attribute the phenomenon to market failures. Without wishing to adopt a position on this issue, this essay presents a short analysis of the first findings of one and a half years of research

This research was conducted among top social policy experts of local authorities in big cities (72 persons) and staff members, generally in top positions, of non-profit organisations (51 persons). The research was based on a survey by self-administered questionnaire and targeted interviews. The main aim was to find an answer to the questions of how the State and the non-State factors see the likelihood of co-operation between the two sectors in the social field; the advantages they attribute to co-operation and the obstacles they face in co-operation. Since analysis of the findings has not yet been completed, this article is based on the partial results.

The first question, formulated in general terms, was: 'Do you consider it important for co-operation to develop between the local authorities and non-profit institutions in the area of handling social problems?

The answer of the experts working in the non-profit sphere – with four exceptions – was an unequivocal "yes". More than half of those working for local authorities answered "yes" to this question, close to a quarter were uncertain, while the remainder of the respondents tended rather to express concerns that had arisen in the course of co-operation rather than the need for it. The uncertain answers and those rejecting co-operation will be discussed later.

The second question was: 'Where do you see the meaning and the practical benefit of such co-operation?

The answers received from the local authority workers were divided as follows, drawing attention to the practical benefit and importance of information coming from non-profit organisations. The local authority experts stressed that the different foundations and associations transmit information, both on the work of institutions operating in the given area and on the clients or certain groups of clients, which greatly facilitates their work since they are unable to obtain such information at all or only through considerable extra work. The information received helps them to target their assistance more effectively (in most cases they were referring to aid) to those in need, and also to establish contact with non-profit organisations they did not even know existed despite the fact that they work in the care system of the same settlement. They considered that information received in time helps them to do more effective work, to save time and energy. A number of them considered it important to mention that the information can be of enormous value, but that the exchange of information arose only through good personal relations among workers of the different institutions and not through automatic processes.

"We strive to give humane and effective help. But we do not have time to become acquainted with the situation of each client. At such times it is very welcome if colleagues working in the association or foundations report on their own experiences. They have built up a great many personal relations and know the field well." (Expert working in the social department of a country local authority.)

"The biggest problem of home care for the elderly is that we are not able to ensure a twenty-four-hour service for elderly people who would require it. This is not so much a matter of funds as of lack of personnel. The district family welfare centre organised a social policy round-table; one of the participants was a colleague from the Lutheran charity service who complained that they have no funds but they could mobilise many enthusiastic helpers. This led to an agreement with them on providing care for a few elderly persons, which has been working well. We provide the financing and they give the people." (Head of the social department of a Budapest district local authority.)

Stressing shortcomings in the services due to overburdening of the local authority workers and underfinancing of institutions and which hoped to fill these gaps through co-operation with the third sector, this group took for granted the need to reduce public expenditures and also noted that the market factors did not have an interest in the production of public benefits, so the only possibility open is the non-profit sector. They intended an important role for the third sector mainly in the area of personal services, particularly emphasising the role of mental hygiene and advice, something for which the administration of official affairs left them no time, and which they do not regard as tasks falling within the competence of public administration.

"Everyone now knows that public expenditures have reached their final limit. Even so we observe with surprise that many people in our society are

falling behind, despite the fact that this happens not only in other societies comparable to ours but in much wealthier ones. The local authority cannot deal effectively with these people falling behind in the way that the foundations, for example, specialising in this can." (Deputy head of the social department of the local authority of a large town in eastern Hungary

"In the present economic recession there is obviously a need to reduce public expenditures in this sector where they do not represent productive and job-creating investments. The central budget restrictions and austerity measures are being felt very keenly. We could reach the point where a great part of the social, educational and cultural problems cease to represent a public task and withdraw entirely to the third sector or the private sector. We have not yet reached that stage, but it is a fact that the non-profit organisations can help a lot in these areas. I have in mind the club for the disabled or the self-help groups for the unemployed, all of which are the result of local non-profit initiatives." (Deputy mayor of the local authority of a country town.)

Considering it advantageous to create competition among the different non-profit factors to raise the standard of services, the local authorities call for tenders to provide different public services and then sign a contract with the winning bidder. Naturally, not all contracts signed represent a competitive situation, although a growing number of local authorities are striving to create one. They regard this as important because in their opinion competition forces the participants to operate efficiently and favours those who provide good quality service at acceptable prices. However, signing an outside contract is a complicated method because announcing tenders and controlling the contracts require great expertise. In recent years many problems arose from the fact that some local authorities considered that their own participation in the co-operation ended when they signed the contract and they did not follow what happened subsequently in the area of service concerned. This practice is now changing and it can be seen that local authorities are increasingly striving to sign contracts which give them the role of professional controller and enable them to monitor the programme.

"Where there is competition, the results are better and the institutions have a greater awareness of the cost implications of their activity. The services are of a higher standard if the service providers have to compete because they keep prices low in that case. No institutions like competition and although we are not aiming for throat-cutting competition, I can say from experience that since we have been advertising contracts all organisations are making an effort to submit fair applications and to keep their prices

down because they know that the cost factor is one of the most important considerations. A club set up in a cellar and used to train young drug addicts is working excellently because it has a good leader, good staff and requires a minimum of infrastructure. Obviously, it is simpler for us to support them than an organisation that wants to start out from scratch and expects every-thing from us." (Staff member in a leading position in the social department of the local authority in a Budapest district.)

"Whether a local authority supports a non-profit organisation depends to a great extent on the local conditions, the level of economic development of the county or settlement, and of course, on the relationship they have formed with the local authority. Generally speaking, it can be found that more and more local authorities and local authority institutions are setting up their own foundations to maintain schools, care homes and hospitals. These are part state, part non-profit organisations which are in strong competition with the non-profit service providers. But this is a healthy competition." (Chairman of the social committee of a local authority in a town in northern Hungary.)

The answers received to the same question from staff members of non-profit organisations have been divided into the following categories:

A.   Answers which stressed the dismantling and financial difficulties of the State tasks as the most important constraining factor encouraging co-operation among the different sectors. If the local authority is incapable of meeting local social needs at a suitable level, then it is in its basic interest, too, to find allies. Some of the respondents also considered it important to note that the non-profit factors should not be regarded as the causes of cuts in the local authority's budget, but as partners who are bringing help to an overburdened institution in a difficult financial situation. The majority of interviewees considered that the relationship can only serve the interests of clients if it is based on partnership

"The notion of the providential state is waning and it is becoming increas-ingly obvious that the local authorities cannot cope with the tasks. The need has arisen for a highly structured, complex system in which the local and regional organisations enjoy broad autonomy and different forms of self-administration are also made possible. There is a need for co-existence of the structures operating at different levels. It is not only the non-profit organisations that are making a very strong demand for state funds: the state institutions also need the help of the non-profit organisations. And I place the emphasis on this mutuality." (A non-profit expert who is a member or head of several non-profit organisations.)

"The withdrawal of the state is a well known phenomenon. The growth in the significance of the profit-oriented private sector is important, but it is quite certain that the market is not always the best solution because it is either not interested or not capable of producing goods serving the public interest. This leaves the third sector as the most appropriate alternative." (Head of a Hungarian-American non-profit organisation.)

"There are certain areas which not only the local authorities but occasionally also the business sphere is prepared to support because it could bring publicity, or because the outlay is recovered by the firm. I have in mind foundations supporting children or children's hospitals, cultural and popular family or sports events. In the fields of caring service, education or, for example, care of the disabled, the non-profit organisations are very creative in trying all kinds of self-financing methods such as fund-raising events and markets, but the proceeds of these ensure only a part of the sources. At all events, they can have a very important effect in reducing costs." (One of the heads of a non-profit organisation providing caring service.)

B.   Here the spendthrift, wasteful and bureaucratic state management of funds was contrasted with the cheaper, more-cost-conscious financial management of the non-profit organisations. They considered that a non-profit institution provides certain services more cheaply, better and more quickly than the local authority and so even for economic reasons alone it is worth entering into a contract with it. The respondents stressed that many local authorities are still guided by the traditional bureaucratic approach, concentrating on inputs rather than on the results. But if an institution is financed on the basis of inputs, there is very little incentive to improve the performance of workers in the institution. In contrast, workers in non-profit institutions are paid more on the basis of performance and results and so they make every effort to work more effectively.

"The big, formal and institutionalised organisations are obliged to work with a big bureaucracy and that always costs more to maintain than the foundations and associations where it is a vital interest to use the limited funds as efficiently as possible. The smaller organisations also have a greater awareness of the complexity of the problems and concerns of their clients than the public authority is capable of achieving. This is why they work with great commitment and very low costs principally in the caring services, in mental hygiene assistance, in an advisory role or in caring for the elderly." (Staff member of a Budapest welfare foundation.)

*"We don't give money, we provide services. But these services can be
obtained only from us, and while I know they cannot replace the money
people need, at least it gives them the feeling that they too count, they belong
somewhere and can talk about their problems."* (Staff member of a family
guidance service in a country town, operating in foundation form.)

C.   Here the focus was mainly on creativity, the use of innovative solutions and
the readiness to experiment. The local authorities should be open to the non-profit
institutions because they are more likely to receive proposals for the innovation of
services from them than from the bureaucracy since these institutions are presum-
ably better acquainted with the demands and expectations of the clientele than are
the employees of the local authority. And besides being more in line with the
wishes of clients than are the traditional bureaucratic solutions, innovations can
also mean economic advantages.

*"Fortunately, the local authority proved to be a good partner in the question
of the school social workers. Earlier, all problems that arose with the
children had to be dealt with by the teachers even though everyone knew
that this was not their job. Now we have set up a system whereby the local
authority finances the employment of eight independent school social
workers in the district from the public work fund but entrusts their professional supervision to the staff of the foundation."* (Staff member of a
Budapest family guidance centre financed partly by a foundation and partly
by the state.)

*"We took the idea of involving parents in the life of the kindergarten and
educating the children from Americans. Since there are lots of unemployed
parents here, this occupation was especially important for them and it also
helped them to begin to feel almost as though they were owners. The local
authority contributes to the cost of further training for the kindergarten
teachers.   This is needed for them to learn the special development
program."* (Staff member of a foundation family welfare centre.)

D.   Non-profit factors can play a role of intermediary between the local
authority and the clients. They are guided by the intention of conciliation and not
the aggravation of conflicts. They function as the barometers of public needs,
reflecting the problems and tensions that arise in local society. They represent a
level of mediation between the clients and public administration which is capable
of creating a link between individuals and the State. If the local authority allows
scope in its work for this special role of the non-profit organisations it can avoid

many pitfalls and much unpleasantness, and can come into contact with a 'more consolidated' clientele, better socialised for dealing with bureaucracy.

"We strive for mutual understanding with the clients and the employees of the local authority, avoiding conflicts. We try to keep our distance from the political and economic spheres, from the Mafias where the 'holders are keepers' rule applies. We won a grant for the development of local communities and our first step was to convene a social round-table. At least people will know who faces whom." (Head of an association in a country town dealing with interest protection.)

"A new approach to the relationship between representative democracy and direct democracy can emerge from the relations between the associations and local society on one hand and the local authorities on the other. This only works if nobody strives for monopoly positions or to restore the earlier state of affairs." (The representative of a non-profit organisation giving legal advice.)

E.   Finally, it is worth mentioning the handful of respondents who drew attention to the possibility of voluntary work, in this way stressing the importance of help from the voluntary sector. However, they too agreed that the involvement of voluntary workers in providing social services has not yet become the general practice in Hungary, but could be important as a possibility and future strategy.

"Voluntary work is not yet very fashionable in Hungary, but our foundation can build on the help of volunteers to an enormous extent. Large numbers of volunteers are working in home care for the elderly, but they are also beginning to appear in the organisations of the disabled. The trainee social workers regularly do voluntary social work, which we call developing social sensitivity." (Head of a Budapest foundation.)

The third question was: "In your experience, what are the problems and difficulties that can arise in the course of co-operation?"

The greatest danger was perceived in dealing with 'amateurs' who may be enormously enthusiastic and well intentioned but who have little expertise. Although they recognised that there is a great need of the former, they consider that it cannot be a substitute for expertise. The respondents also emphasised that they know little about the actual operation of the non-profit institutions; they do not know them and so in their opinion the mistrust of them is justified.

"The whole field of foundations is dreadfully confused. They have an enormous sense of mission but their financial system is entirely opaque and, in fact, no rules at all apply to them. Practically anyone can set up a foundation today and then count on receiving the same capitation as a central budget-financed institution and also make use of other sources. Who can control their actual activity?" (Deputy mayor of the local authority of a country town.)

Drawing attention to the danger of corruption it is difficult to keep trace of how much the non-profit organisations spend for what purposes; their financial operation lacks transparency. Because of the unclear legal regulation there are broad possibilities for profiteering and abuses. The respondents look mainly to the elaboration of suitable legal instruments and guarantees for reduction of the possibility of corruption.

"The funds of the foundations are not restricted by target figures for the various items; their annual budget is completely fluid. The tax regulations are still too liberal with them and as long as the law fails to clarify the tax concessions, the definition of public benefit, the conditions of accountability, there is no guarantee of honest operation." (Head of the social department of a Budapest local authority.)

"It has happened more than once that they submit a number of applications and win grants for the same activity, and despite this they complain that they have no funds. It is high time a law was passed to make the foundations accountable." (Expert of a local authority in a country town.)

Linking the frequency of *ad hoc* decisions and ill-prepared experiments with the uncertain and generally weak financial situation of the non-profit organisations. In the opinion of the respondents, decisions of this type do more harm than good for both the users of the services and the prestige of the social profession. A few respondents attributed this practice in general to the irresponsible and ill-considered attitude of the non-profit organisations.

"There are many loopholes in the legislation and the non-profit organisations are quick to take advantage of them. While the activity of the foundations enjoyed tax exemption on the grounds of public benefit and donations were tax-deductible, they undertook all kinds of services. But when certain restrictions came into force, they suddenly withdrew and abandoned their earlier activity. Of course, it was the consumers who suffered most from these steps." (Staff member of the local authority in a country town.)

"More than one foundation is incapable of creating the financial basis required for its activity over the long term but despite this starts big undertakings, like establishing a kindergarten for disabled children. When the money runs out and they receive no more support, they send the children away. In my opinion this is irresponsible behaviour." (Member of the social committee of the local authority in a country town.)

More than two-thirds of replies from the non-profit experts stressed that the continuous struggle for funds not only consumes a great part of their energies but also has a negative influence on maintaining their operation over the long term. They attributed the unevenness and uncertainties appearing in the services they provide for the improvement of their situation mainly to the constraint of lack of funds, and looked to more-responsible financial policy on the part of the state and to the proposed non-profit act.

"Speaking generally, it can be said that social responsibility, a sense of responsibility for the wider community also expressed in material support is not yet a part of Hungarian enterprise and business culture. The majority of non-profit organisations are struggling to cope with constant financial problems and this also influences the standard of the services they provide. The State and business institutions should give more help to this sector: they are the big capital owners and they have the possibility to do this." (Head of a Budapest foundation.)

"There is very little precise data on the supports received by the foundations. It is a fact that in practice we feel the effects of the stricter measures, the growing tax burdens much more than the State supports." (A non-profit expert living in a country town

Others in this group saw that one of the main obstacles to long-term co-operation lies in the fact that the local authority decisions needed for co-operation are strongly dependent on individuals. When a change occurs in a post in the local authority, earlier agreements can be cancelled from one day to the next. In this connection a number of respondents mentioned how difficult it is to persuade the local authorities to enter into a written contract or to give a legal guarantee valid for a period of several years.

"Before the local government elections we signed an agreement on co-operation which gave our foundation training and technical assistance as a basic support. Then came the elections, the decision-makers were replaced and the new ones would not even talk to us." (Staff member of a social service foundation in a country town.)

"For months we bombarded the deputy mayor to sign a written contract with us giving us the right of decision in the allocation of social housing. Even after countless attempts we were unable to obtain this." (A Budapest family welfare officer.)

Still others viewed official bureaucracy as the chief enemy of co-operation. In their opinion, the majority of local authorities still do not want to understand what co-operation with the non-profit organisations could mean, and have a tendency to underestimate the significance of the non-governmental organisations. It is difficult to make local authorities understand what their intentions are, they are often forced to conceal the experimental nature of their undertakings because "bureaucracies don't like experimenting." They are frequently obliged to agree to compromises that are very difficult for them to accept, since they bargain from a much weaker financial position. Nevertheless, they generally accept these compromises for the sake of representing the interests of a special group.

"They often deal with us as though we were clients too, which of course is true in a way because we are making requests of them too." (Head of a Budapest foundation.)

"We wanted to set up a job-creating undertaking for young Romas, with the support of the local authority. It was a long while before we finally convinced them that such an undertaking is worthwhile. The fact that in the end we were able to help only three people was very largely because we received only one-third of the support originally promised." (Head of an interest representation association in a country town.)

Some expressed the fear of some of the non-profit organisations that their autonomy would suffer in the co-operation. They cited their methods and style of work which differ greatly from those of the bureaucracy; they are often forced to make these bureaucratic for the sake of acceptability. In order to represent the interests of their clients they are often forced into situations in which they function in almost the same way as a bureaucracy and not like a service. In this way they subordinate their concept of social work and consequently their whole activity to the will of the economically stronger partner. They wish to accept professional control only from local authorities which are well acquainted with the non-profit sphere and familiar with the new working methods.

"It is a characteristic of the non-profit organisation that it resists both exclusive economic interests and the institutionalised attitude. It applies its own style and approach in social work and often also acts as a model and a model transmitter. It strives to develop examples in the field of social

*services. In co-operation it would like to realise its own ideas, but unfortu-
nately this is not always possible. There are situations where it is forced into
conjurer's tricks to get itself accepted by the bureaucracy."* (Head of a
Budapest foundation.)

The following main conclusions can be drawn from the answers given to the
questions.

A contradictory, yet strong, mutual dependency between an institutionalised
structure and a structure now entering the phase of institutionalisation and professionalisation appears to be emerging between the local authorities and the
non-profit organisations. It is not easy for organisations at different levels of institutionalisation to accept and understand the logic of each other's operation, even if
there are hard economic arguments in favour of co-operation. Despite this, the con-
frontation between the State and non-State organisations appears to be easing due,
in my opinion, largely to the change of attitude on the part of local authorities ready
to renew themselves. The interviews also confirmed that, from the outset, the non-
profit organisations show greater readiness for co-operation than the local
authorities since this is their fundamental interest and in many cases serves their
survival, while the local authorities have only slowly opened towards the non-
profit sector. This is probably because co-operation requires a radical re-evaluation
of the State's view of its role which is a very slow and difficult process. A local
authority which really wishes to serve its citizens has to recognise the limits of its
competence and see that it has a need for the non-profit organisations since they
efficiently complement its own work. But for them to be able to recognise this, the
non-profit organisations must demonstrate that they are on a high standard, both
professionally and as regards their institutionalisation.

Since by far the greatest part of the budget of the non-profit organisations still
comes from the local authorities, it cannot be said that a fully equal relationship
can arise between the non-profit organisations and the local authorities. A number
of them mentioned that they are unable to step out of the role of supplicants.
During the past three years the tax regulations applying to non-profit organisations
have been made stricter, the range of tax-deductible supports has been reduced.
The justification given on the part of the State for these restrictive measures was
the desire to prevent the earlier abuses and impede corruption. As the answers also
demonstrated that the majority of non-profit organisations objected to these
measures, seeing them as increasing their dependency and defencelessness in face
of the State. One thing on which both partners agreed, however, was that, for democratic institutional functioning to develop, providing a suitable frame in which
contracts could be signed, there is a need for comprehensive legal regulation.

The problem of the underfinanced state of institutions cannot be evaded. While the lack of funds afflicts the whole sector, at the level of institutions it appears to varying extent and with differing emphases. Many of the respondents from the non-profit organisations stressed that they (also) look to a more responsible State social policy for the improvement of their situation. On the side of the local authorities, many people interpret this as avoiding responsibility and the continued existence of faith placed in the miracle-working State. This whole problem strongly influences the thinking of specialists in both the local authorities and the non-profit organisations, which is not at all surprising given that where centralisation was strong, the State was regarded as the principal defender of the public interest. It would be fortunate if, in the future, the social factors were to avoid endless debates conducted on the cause of the financial crises and, instead, they were all to make the best of what they have; if the State were to give real content to the practice of social justice and social solidarity and the protection of certain basic social values and thus really become an instrument of public good; and if the non-profit sector, playing its role of intermediary and attention-drawer, were to help shape a better relationship between the citizens and the government. This could lead to a new model of government in which it would not only be a matter of ensuring public services but of combined efforts by the different sectors – State, non-profit, private – in the interest of satisfying the community needs on a higher level. The development of such a partnership among all those participating in social services has become important for a growing number of institutions.

It emerges quite clearly from the investigation to date that a growing number of institutions have recognised the need for innovative solutions in order to overcome the almost constant shortage of funds. In theory, the smaller organisations which are closer to the consumer have a greater readiness to introduce innovations than the big institutions, but the findings so far have not confirmed this hypothesis. The local authorities included in the survey show the same degree of willingness to introduce innovative solutions as the non-profit organisations. The problem was not so much the shaping of new solutions as the rejection of old, ingrained mechanisms. This could be the cause of the certain degree of negative attitude on the part of a few local authorities to "experimenting" by the non-profit organisations. The participants are still in the very early stages of a process of mutual learning, the sharing of creative ideas and learning various civil techniques. However, the modernisation of the social service system requires the extensive application of these techniques since it is under great pressure to solve social problems with the least possible expenditure of funds. At the same time this also implies a blurring of the borderlines between the non-profit, private and State spheres and that growing numbers of private and non-profit service providers will take part in the provision of public services, as we can see in the practice of many other countries. While the withdrawal of the State and the dismantling of it have become a part of our everyday social rhetoric, at the local level signs of precisely the opposite can also be found: most of the local authorities are making enormous efforts to improve the services, pursuing a strong and active local policy. It is not so much commitment and the will to innovate that are lacking from their approach as trust and understanding towards the other sectors.

There can be no doubt that no one is enthusiastic about having to perform under severe constraints, but these can only be thrown off through joint efforts. Recognition of this can lead to the shaping of a new and more effective local welfare policy.

References

Biro, A., Levai, K. (1994) *Reflections on Civil Society* Esely.

Bullain, N. (1995) *The Nonprofit Sector in Hungary*, Via Europe, Summer Issue.

Ferge, Z. (1996) *The Role of the State*. Kritika,

Gyulavari, T. (1996) *Innovative Local Policy*. Esely.

Hegyesi, G. (1993) *The Development of Civil Society*. Szociologia.

Kochanowicz, J. *New Solidarities? Market Change and Social Cohesion in a Historical Perspective*. Esely.

Kolarska-Bobinska, L (1996) *The Changing Face of Civil Society in Eastern Europe*. Conference Paper, Budapest, 1993.

Kovács, P., Lévai, K. (1995) *Towards a New Social Contract* Népszabadság, November

Kuti, E. (ed) (1993) *The Nonprofit Sector in Hungary*. Nonprofit Research Group, Budapest.

Lévai, K. (1996) "Co-operation between the Local Authorities and the Nonprofit Sector", in: *Innovative Local Authorities*. Local Society Research Group, Budapest.

Nonprofit Organizations in Hungary. (1995) Office of Central Statistics, Budapest.

Seres, L. (1995) *Missing in Action*. Magyar Narancs, February..

Talyigas, K. (1995) The Increasing Role of Self Organisation in Hungary. Esely Fuzetek,.

Vajda, A. (1995) *Foundations, Associations and Governmental Institutions*. Active Society Foundation.

Vobruba, G (1996) *Shifts in the Welfare Services*. Esely.

Advocacy as a Policy and Practice Issue

David Brandon

Advocacy is the most important element in the link between social work and social policy. Hopefully, the social worker listens carefully and sympathetically to the voice of distressed service-users and helps to amplify their sadness and anger so that those who have power to bring about necessary changes in social security and many other relevant systems can hear. At least in theory, social work intervention turns into social policy.

So it is surprising that the term has appeared so rarely in social work and social policy texts until the last five years, in stark contrast to the other major professional element of counselling. For example, in the important Barclay Report the term is missing from the index although the main text comments: "Social workers would be failing in their duty if they did not speak out in the light of their personal knowledge and the evidence amassed from contact with such [poor and disadvantaged] people, challenging . . . policy decisions or the way resources are allocated" (1982,110).

A UN document on social work states: "Human rights are inseparable from social work theory, values and ethics, and practice. Rights corresponding to human needs have to be upheld and fostered and to embody the justification and motivation for social work action. Advocacy of such rights must, therefore, be an integral part of social work, even if in countries living under authoritarian regimes such advocacy can have serious consequences for social work professionals" (1994, 5). How easy it is to write those words; how hard to practise them.

Most social work commentators view advocacy as a core function. In an early text, Day (1972) sees social workers as "advocates for the socially deprived". Siporin argues that the social worker is "a spokesman for the needy in our society, particularly for the poor and disadvantaged. . . More recently, this has been referred to as the social worker's *advocacy* role, although with some confusion about its place in an adversary process, and with some neglect about the need for balance between social obligations and the rights of both social workers and clients" (Siporin, 1975). Case advocacy is defined as "partisan intervention on behalf of an individual client or identified client group with one or more secondary institutions to secure or enhance a needed service, resource or entitlement" (McGowan, 1987).

It is perceived as an important role by the practitioners. In a study in the United States, almost 90% of social workers reported involvement in advocacy as part of their job, but fewer than 1% considered themselves full-time advocates. Most advocacy was on behalf of individuals internal to the organisation they worked for; any collective advocacy was done as volunteers. The author concludes: "The National Association of Social Workers should explore ways to support and understand social work advocacy, and schools of social work should rededicate themselves to teaching and practising and studying this core activity" (Ezell, 1994).

There are two distinctly different advocacy roles – *direct advocacy*, with which this chapter is primarily concerned, and *indirect advocacy* – in supporting self-advocacy groups for people with disabilities. For example, the blossoming Disability Movement has been largely rejecting of individual social casework, seeing it as overtly oppressive. Some innovative social workers have turned their backs on the traditional approaches and developed intervention based more squarely on advocacy - helping people to speak out. d"Aboville worked with people who had spinal cord injuries to develop self-help and to pressurise for better supports (d"Aboville, 1993)

Conflicts?

It seems clear from the increasing numbers of articles in the professional Press that the advocacy bandwagon is really quickening. This relates, in part, to the substantial changes in the care-in-community field in the United Kingdom and increasing emphasis on user participation in services. It is perceived as a new and expanding area, in some ways, ready for colonisation. However, most service professionals face an essential and fundamental clash of vested interests. They have core professional obligations but also conflicting responsibilities which arise from roles as agents of their employing bodies - social services, voluntary organisations or health authorities. It still says "Broadshire Social Services" or "NHS Trust" or whatever on their monthly pay-cheque.

Gathercole outlines five different sorts of potential conflict (Butler, 1988):

Organisational:
service survival interests are often seen as more important than user interests. Scandal must be avoided, even at the cost of continuing neglect, abuse or exploitation.

Professional:
staff may discourage promotion of users' interests which may challenge the good name of the profession.

Managerial:
interests of managers may differ from what grass roots staff see as the interests of users,

e.g.
bonuses paid to health service managers for resettling people from hospitals.

Personal:
even if serving only one person, one's own personal needs, e.g. for rest, etc., may be a source of conflict.

Competition:
service workers have competing demands on their time from other residents

---

Service professionals may try hard to represent individual users" interests in various settings like case conferences or ward rounds but, at the same time, are salaried from the service agency, often seen as the major source of oppression. That basic conflict also exists, usually in a more subtle form, in the non-governmental agencies. Ironically, they are often perceived as the voice of the consumer although they can be bastions of paternalism. Certainly they may advocate both individually and collectively, but their money comes more and more from mechanisms like joint financing for direct service provision, bringing them increasingly in conflict with vital advocacy functions. Increasingly they are major service providers.

These conflicts often involve professional blind spots. Wolfensberger (1972) stresses: ". . . many benevolent, humanistic clinicians see themselves as servants of the public, offering themselves and their services in a non-controlling fashion. They see their clients as free agents, free to reject the offered services. Their self-concept – in part due to the indoctrination received during training – is frequently compatible with action perceived as controlling, directing or dictating client behaviour. Yet here it is where so many human service workers deceive themselves, because their roles are not only almost always societally sanctioned, but in an endless array of encounters between server and the served, the server is the interpreter of, and agent for, the intents of society, and wields a truly amazing amount of power and control, even if he [sic] may not consciously perceive himself as so doing . . . Indeed, it is not too much to say that who will be rich or poor, healthy or sick, bright or dumb, honest or crooked – and even born or unborn – depends in many cases, and to a significant extent, upon the decision of human managers."

Rose (1990) comments on these conflicting pressures: "Social work has been embedded in a structural contradiction since its professional origins. The nature of this contradiction arises from the social historical fact that the profession receives both its legitimation and primary funding from the capitalist state, the same structural base that creates the poverty and abuses of its clients. The profession has been able to avoid or deny its internal contradiction through the adaptation or development of individual defect explanatory paradigms to guide its practice. Whether the guiding model has been taken from psychiatry, psychodynamic theory, ego psychology, behaviourism, or even more recent progressive psychosocial concepts, the result has been the same – systematic exclusion of the social reality of capitalist structures, ideological forms and processes shaping daily life and individual subjective experience." In order to be effective advocates, we need to adopt views that are essentially projective and structuralist. We have to see the issues as embedded in social and economic structures as well as in the individual lives of our clients/patients.

Multifaceted professional roles can result in some splendid examples of confusion: ". . . an elderly woman was extremely puzzled by her social worker's refusal to act as an advocate on her behalf in her dealing with the housing department and health professionals. The social worker felt she should be encouraged to undertake these negotiations herself as she did not want to encourage dependency, but had not shared the rationale for her actions. Instead she imposed an ideal of independence . . . which was not open to negotiation" (Clarke, 1989). On one level, the client was being pressurised into self-advocacy by being denied the advocacy role of the professional service worker! On another, we are simply observing the simple reframing of old-fashioned paternalism. Anyway, the local government Ombudsman found in the client's favour, commenting that very little had been explained to her.

The conflicts are not always so clear cut. There is sometimes no clear choice between conflict or its absence but more of a very long continuum. Many battles fought by nurses and social workers are *not* against the interests of the services provided by their employing agency. Social workers often represent the interests of clients battling against the monsters of social security, in which their employers are, at worst, only indirectly involved. "A few months ago, Michael was finding life very tough. His benefit income of £61 a week was just not enough to pay his phone bill, buy a new gas fire, replace worn-out clothes and provide him with enough to eat. He had survived on benefit income for years and was not in debt, but things were piling up. He was very worried about his money and had asked for his telephone to be disconnected. He had stopped going to MIND events because he had no spending money and he felt ashamed of his uncut hair and poor clothing."

"When he was contacted by a mental health social worker, his loss of weight, burns from his unsafe gas fire and money worries had begun to concern his friends and relatives. Three months after this contact with the worker, Michael's income had more than doubled. This was because of the support he had received, which resulted in a successful claim for Disability Living allowance" (Davis, 1993).

The Police and Criminal Evidence Act 1984 provides a further example of minimal conflict. It includes safeguards for some vulnerable persons held in police custody. The relevant guidance involves some social workers and nurses in an advocacy role: "In the case of persons who are mentally ill or mentally handicapped, it may, in certain circumstances, be more satisfactory for all concerned if the 'appropriate adult' is someone who has experience of training in their care rather than a relative lacking in such qualifications" (Skelt, 1988).

Many care professionals are extremely nervous and resistant to external advocacy systems. They resent any possible outside and inside interference and become extremely defensive and hostile. They are afraid to be found out, doing good sub-standard work. They may have much or nothing to hide and can develop a siege mentality.

Some professionals see advocacy as territory over which they have major control. Hayward sees the claiming of unique powers of advocacy as a sort or proactive strike against possible intruders. "It is natural for mental health professionals in hospitals and residential establishments to deny the need for advocacy. Staff frequently feel they are the only advocates. This frequently leads to the well-intentioned but suffocating paternalism that pervades public services" (Hayward, 1992)". Outsiders are potentially hostile invaders who overtly or covertly want to undermine their position.

The Family Rights Group comments relevantly: "a serious flaw in some social workers" thinking . . . is that once they have taken a decision that they consider to be in the best interests of their client, anyone opposing that judgement is deemed to be acting contrary to the best interests of the client" (Barclay, 1982). On a more structural level, Lipsky comments about the myth of street level bureaucrats, including social workers: "it assumes only that policy and people who implement it are well intentioned and that their work constitutes a net social benefit (Lipsky, 1980)". If you believe that you'll believe anything.

Part of this overall struggle between service professionals and mainly profession-al advocates lies in the battle for influence and power; part comes from deep philosophical differences. Just consider these in a psychiatric context: "There is one view that a man should be protected from those who could care for him, for all are prone to abuse him. The other view suggests that patient care deals with the whole person and requires direct intervention in aspects of his life" (Wolfensberger, 1977).

Service professionals, like nurses, doctors and social workers, suffer from a huge problem of vested interest. They are most frequently employed by the services complained against. Although they cannot be pure advocates, they must still have an important advocacy role. Wolfensberger outlines the different barriers to advocacy but still writes: "Everything that has been said so far . . . does not deny that a staff member of a service agency might not be an advocate. However, in order to be an advocate, such a worker would usually have to act outside the scope of his/her agency and work role, and/or reject rather than implement its society–mandated policies - with all the risks pertaining to that" (Wolfensberger, 1977).

Advocates are so very scarce, who else is going to speak out on a daily basis for the relatively powerless, except the service people? In those subterranean areas of services like prisons and special hospitals, who else is going to point out their deficiencies? There is a very considerable danger that the newly developing independent advocacy systems will seem to take away core responsibilities from the relevant professionals. They will feel that the advocacy is being done by independent others.

Whistleblowers
The real heroes of internal advocacy are whistleblowers (Bean, 1986). They can exert pressure from inside to improve often scandalous situations. "An individual must have the right to blow the whistle on his organisation . . . rather than be forced to condone illegality . . . oppression of the disadvantaged . . ." (Chu, 1974). Titmuss pointed out that "criticism from without of professional conduct and standards of work tends to be increasingly resented the more highly these groups are organised" (Titmuss, 1958). Attacks coming from within are seen as disloyal, particularly if made public.

Organisations defend themselves stoutly against people who are seen as saboteurs. For example, a British Medical Journal editorial entitled grimly "The Rise of Stalinism in the National Health Service" comments on the "reign of terror" in the services. Professionals are often subject to gagging clauses in their employment contracts and there is a wholesale persecution of whistleblowers (Smith, 1994). Research on whistleblowers is clear in identifying reasons for taking action. This was because of "research distorted or rendered useless by inducements: levels of staffing and facilities so low as to threaten to nullify customary standards of care, impending closure of units or beds, the abuse or neglect of patients by colleagues who fall below professional expectations, theft and fraud". Professionals with serious concerns would be frustrated at every step by internal procedures (Hunt, 1995).

Training?
It seems peculiar that although many professionals claim advocacy as an important core function, none outside the legal profession consider it worthwhile to provide effective training. There is very little discussion of advocacy skills in the various textbooks, even though, for example, the process of welfare rights work - an important aspect of advocacy - is well documented. "Given that advocacy is part of the social work task, it is depressing that there is so little training or literature available to help social work staff develop effective advocacy skills" (Bateman, 1991). As one example of what this might involve, Bateman

suggests that principled advocacy involved with more formal systems like social
security benefits has six stages (Bateman, 1995):

the presentation of the problem:
where the problem requiring advocacy is presented or discovered by the
advocate

information-gathering: gathering relevant information and obtaining
instructions from the client

legal research: comparing the facts with legal, policy or procedural sources

interpretation and feedback to the client: analysing the facts and legal
sources and forming a judgement about the nature of the problem

active negotiation and advocacy: undertaking the necessary negotiations
and/or preliminary advocacy with the other side

litigation: use of formal appeals and other mechanisms to achieve
objectives

He suggests a thorough and detailed training programme for social workers and
others. Currently there are no formal programmes in the relevant professional
courses in the United Kingdom and very few elsewhere.

Rose wants social workers in mental health to turn completely away from therapeutic models – seen as part of the problem – to advocacy models, part of the
solution. ". . . typical clinical models of social work inadvertently reproduce the
feeling of powerlessness, the experience of oneself as inadequate, incompetent or
crazy, even when adaptation to client roles may promote immediate or short term
relief and the appearance of growth" (Rose, 1990, 48-9).

He argues for three major elements in professional work with service users: contextualisation, empowerment, and collectivity. "Focusing on *contextualisation,* on
bringing to consciousness both the unique experience of the individual and the
social base for the individual's experience, also means that attention must be
primarily given to the structural factors which impose dependency . . . *empowerment* means a process of dialogue through which the client is continuously
supported to produce the range of possibilities that he/she sees as appropriate to
his/her needs; that the client is the centre for all decisions that affect her/his life . . .
collectivity means that the focus on the social basis of identity and experience is
designed to reduce isolation and the terror of experiencing oneself as uniquely
defective and stagnant.

Consequences

It is important to continue raising the considerable issues of role conflict and lack of independence within the various professions, especially where they are directly employed by service providers. Various relevant articles still express little awareness of the dilemmas that service professionals ordinarily face. For example, recently McMahon (1993) examined the role of school psychologists as child advocates without analysing any of these conflicts.

As noted earlier, despite the problems of lack of independence, care professionals *must* continue to provide the major advocacy role. That raises difficult problems about the serious cost to individuals in a culture where some services are so autocratic. Beresford (1994) cautions: "Can professionals be advocates? Yes, but when they have power over individual service users, or responsibilities other than to speak for the person, then there is a conflict of interest, and the person will need an independent advocate. But at all times service workers need to have some awareness of, and try to protect, the service user's interests (however imperfectly they do this, given conflicts of interest) and not just leave this to the advocate.

There are *four major consequences* coming from social work advocacy

Raising consciousness

Freire (1972) wrote powerfully of the "fear of freedom", ". . . a fear which may equally well lead them to desire the role of oppressor or bind them to the role of oppressed, should be examined". He was arguing for a much greater awareness of the nature of oppression; of the infinite possibilities of freedom and the fear that accompanies it. Hundreds of thousands of individuals are largely unaware of being oppressed – they are socially and economically marginalised, live in huge institutions, eat poor food, live in poverty, are often physically and sexually abused. They need to be awakened rather than simply stigmatised.

Social workers need to see themselves as potential oppressors. "In general, the power drive is given freest rein when it can appear under the cloak of objective and moral rectitude. People are the most cruel when they can use cruelty to enforce the 'good' " (Guggenbuhl-Craig, 1971). We must maintain contact with our deep - shadow side otherwise we shall become so destructive in work with others.

Developing advocacy skills and appropriate structures

In citizen advocacy, the Management Boards present serious problems because they tend to be white and able-bodied. They are "owned" by the dominant and most oppressive group. It is crucial that disabled people take over the whole process themselves as an effective check on the imperialistic ambitions of the various professionals.

Advocacy remains essentially fragile and vulnerable and needs considerable protection. It is carried on the backs of a comparatively few individuals who are continually under attack. They make criticism of structures and systems and mostly get back personal abuse. Wolfensberger reminds us: "Why is advocacy vulnerable? The answer lies partly in the 'cosmic reality' of entropy. Good thinks are apt to get worse, not better. A second part of the answer is the enmity of the moral nature of advocacy. All sorts of dynamics push moral endeavour away and devalue certain people. Hence, most welfare service bureaucracies discriminate, and victimise people, with government sanction via funding and legal structures, despite the presence of good people who work within them. These services control the lives of vulnerable people" (Wolfensberger, 1990).

Opening doors so that services are more participative

It is useless if we develop effective advocacy systems and the services remain or become even more defensive than at present. The doors must be opened even wider so that many more people may share in the overall policy making. The personal costs of the various whistleblowers are an eloquent testimony to the excessive defensiveness of the different institutions. We have a few wounds and scars ourselves. We need to develop systems which are much more responsive to service users and their allies and hopefully involve less-emotional costs.

One element in any fresh openness must lie in the more effective handling of complaints; offering people easier and more effective means to redress wrongs. Most local and health authorities seemingly have excellent procedures. However, in reality complainants are frequently made to feel guilty, even as if they are on trial. Sometimes it feels like Storming the Bastille. They are combating deeply ingrained patterns of territoriality; they are outsiders awakening the aggressive desires of those besieged inside to repel all boarders.

Establishing clear rights and redress
The Americans have established a comprehensive disability Act and many Europeans with disabilities, especially the British, want to follow suit. So far, this pressure has not succeeded other than becoming a major unifying force. The new disability Act just going on to the Statute Book is largely unacceptable to the disability lobby because it has no teeth. It permits a whole range of desirable elements like access to public buildings but provides little money and few means of enforcement.

"The patients' rights movement shows that the direct action of a relatively powerless group can have significant effects on overall social policy, even if its success in part depends upon the support of more powerful groups intent on co-option. . . While sympathetic professionals might prefer a more polite form of strategy, it is probably necessary to have the sharp level of criticism and action provided by the patients' movement as a complement to mainstream reform. . . The fact that patients' rights issues are often pressed by a powerless group takes the direction of reform somewhat out of the hands of policy makers and higher level professionals" (Brown, 1985). It is this powerful combination of disabled outsiders and inside professionals which is so very effective.

Social Policy
Nearly 40 years ago, Richard Titmuss wrote: "All collectively provided services are deliberately designed to meet certain socially recognised 'needs'; they are manifestations, first of society's will to survive as an organic whole and, secondly, of the expressed wish of all the people to assist the survival of some people" (Titmuss, 1958, 39). People with disabilities, increasingly through the advocacy movements, are trying to play a major role in the construction and management of those services. Much of that energy, as we have seen, is directed necessarily towards the issues of rights – especially in emulating the American disability rights legislation.

Most marginalised people are excluded from the very ordinary elements in daily living available to a great many of us. They live in poor environments, have hardly any money, poor transport arrangements and extremely low status. They know the real meaning of poverty, powerlessness and inequity. They have precious few genuine opportunities. Processes of inclusion and the reduction of stigma enable people with disabilities to take part in the definitions of what constitutes normality from which they have been traditionally excluded (Flaker, 1994).

Establishing rights through advocacy can be part of a considerable change. It can help restrict the megalomaniac ambitions of the wealthy and powerful. Donnison comments: "Rights must be equally and effectively available to all citizens if they are not to become another source of inequality – another means of excluding the powerless from full citizenship. Legal rights which are not associated with any equalising shift in distribution of incomes and opportunities should be treated with scepticism" (Donnison, 1991 p.85).

The gradual growth of advocacy systems takes away much power from professionals and also from the voluntary organisations. They challenge the essential assumed right of staff and organisations like Barnardo's and Mencap to speak out on their behalf and demand a redefinition of the whole nature of professionalism. They are ready and willing to speak out for themselves and challenge what they increasingly see as the self-seeking paternalism of others. They can considerably increase the strength of the lobby – the extent of unelected influence – and erode the influence of democratically elected bodies.

The current government policies are based on enabling rather than enforcing. For example, the recent Disability Rights Act 1995 enables authorities to provide a whole range of services but makes mandatory hardly any and contains no sanctions to encourage compliance. It is difficult to see how such permissive strategies can have much impact on real discrimination against people with disabilities. Likewise, cost cutting is an underlying principle of most current European governments. Advocacy is not going to be funded properly in such a climate.

Conclusion

It would be tragic if the whole advocacy movement became just another aspect of the professionalisation of ordinary human life, including disability; that it became another service with all its many products taken out of the control of people with disabilities. Seabrook comments wryly and wisely, as usual: "The presence of armies of advisers, counsellors and therapists at the scene of every human and social catastrophe is just another example of the professionalising of grief, the expropriation and processing of human emotions, after the model of any other industry, like canning fish or adding value to semi-finished goods from the factory. It brings forth a new division of labour, which gives an impression of a society advancing, caring; whereas the truth is that much of this consists of what is largely privatised economic activity masquerading as something else; and that something else is part of the priceless capacity of human beings to create and offer things to each other freely" (Seabrook, 1994).

Advocacy is a part of a much wider participation movement in which social workers have a crucial part to play. They can be facilitators in enabling those who have been marginalised – those who are sick, poor, disabled – to play their proper part in formulating social policy. There are very positive signs in the self-advocacy movement and in advocacy by social workers that we are at the beginning of the birth of a very powerful inclusive social movement.

Donnison wisely comments that "people cannot question the assumptions of the dominant groups in their society all by themselves. To formulate new ways of doing things and set them in motion they need the support of other people who share their perception of the world and help them challenge the conventional wisdom. . ." (Donnison, 1991). Advocacy is in the forefront of that challenge and social work provides some of the impetus for its expansion.

References

Barclay Report: (1982) *Social Workers – their roles and tasks. National Institute for Social Work*, p110.

Bateman, N. Legal Lessons. *Social Work Today*: 1 August 1991.

Bateman, N. (1995) *Advocacy Skills*. London, Arena, p140.

Bean, P. (1986) *Mental Disorder and Legal Control*. Cambridge, Cambridge University Press.

Beresford, P. (1994) "Advocacy" in *Speaking Out for Advocacy – a report of the National Conference*, London, Labyrinth.

Brown, P. (ed) (1985) *Mental Health Care and Social Policy*. Routledge, p207

Butler, K. (1988) *Citizen Advocacy – a powerful partnership*. London, National Citizen Advocacy, p13

Chu, F. D., & Trotter, S. (1974) *The Madness Establishment*. Washington D. C, Ralph Nader Study Group on the National Institute of Mental Health, Grossman.

Clarke, M. (1989) Patient/Client Advocates *Journal of Advanced Nursing*, 14 pp513-14)

d"Aboville, E. (1993) Social Work in an Organisation of Disabled People in Oliver, M. (ed) Social Work: Disabled people and disabling environments. Jessica Kingsley, pp64-85).

Davis, A. (1993) *Claiming Success*. London, Open MIND, December.

Day, P. (1972) *Communication in Social Work*. Oxford, Pergamon Press, pp92-3.

Donnison, D. (1991) *A Radical Agenda*. Rivers, Oram Press, p193.

Ezell, E. (1994) Advocacy Practice of Social Workers' Families in society: *The Journal of Contemporary Human Services*. Families International, pp36-46.

Flaker, V. (1994) *On the Values of Normalisation*, Care in Place. December pp25-30.

Freire, P. (1972) *Pedagogy of the Oppressed*. Harmondsworth, Penguin Education, p23.

Guggenbuhl-Craig, (1971) *A Power in the Helping Professions*, New York, Spring Publications, USA, p10.

Hayward, R. (1992) Developing an Advocacy Service for People with Mental Health Problems in Bradford, Bradford, Report of the conference held at the Community Arts Centre on 9 November.

Hunt, G. (1995) *Whistleblowing in the Health Service*. London, Edward Arnold, p20.

Lipsky, M. (1980) *Street level Bureaucracy - Dilemmas of the individual in Public Services*. Beverly Hills, Sage.

McGowan, B. G. (1987) "Advocacy" in the *Encyclopaedia of Social Work*, 18th edition, National Association of Social Workers, p92.

McMahon, T. J. (1993) On the Concept of Child Advocacy: a review of the theory and methodology, *School Psychology Review*, vol 22 no 4,pp744-55.

Rose, S. Advocacy/Empowerment: an approach to clinical practice for Social Work, *Journal of Sociology and Social Welfare*, vol 17, June 1990, pp 41-51.

Seabrook, J. Vested Disinterests, *New Statesman & Society*, 20 May 1994, p 14

Siporin, M. (1975) *Introduction to Social Work Practice*. New York, Collier MacMillan.

Skelt, A. Held in Police Custody, *Nursing Times*, vol 84, no 4, 1988, pp50-52.

Smith, R. "The Rise of Stalinism in the NHS" (editorial) *British Medical Journal,* 16 December 1994.

Titmuss, R. (1958) *Essays on the Welfare State*. London, Allen & Unwin, p127.

United Nations (1994) "Human Rights and Social Work" Centre for Human Rights, UN, Geneva and New York,p5.

Wolfensberger, W. (1972) *The Principle of Normalisation in Human Services*. Toronto, NIMR.

Wolfensberger, W. (1977) *A Multi-component advocacy/protection Scheme.* CAMR.

Wolfensberger, W. (1990) Citizen Advocacy Principles and Perversions, World Citizen Advocacy Congress: Lincoln, Nebraska, 6 October.

Part III: Changing Cultures of Care

Changing Cultures of Care: Underlying Ideologies, Policies and Practices in Post-Communist and Post-Fordist Societies: The Two Germanies

Prue Chamberlyne

The international context of rapid and fundamental social change brings new attention to the nature and resources of the informal sphere of family relationships, that unrecognised, unpaid area of servicing which lies beyond formal welfare arrangements. All welfare systems rest on and presuppose this "private" area of social functioning, which is generally deemed as "women's work". It is a sphere which is deeply rooted in the historical, gendered division of labour, and in the location of production "outside" and reproduction "inside" the home. It is the submerged seven-eighths of the "welfare iceberg".

The reasons for new attention to "the social" and "the informal" vary in different political systems as well as in different kinds of discourse. This chapter first considers ways in which the informal sphere has entered public debate in the contrasting cases of "post-communist" and "post-fordist" societies in eastern and western Europe. The second part of the chapter draws on a specific research project which focused on home-caring situations in eastern and western Germany, in order to contrast ideologies, policies and practices of the informal sphere in those two societies. The final section discusses the implications of the research findings for broader policy development in eastern and western Europe.

Post-Communist and Post-Fordist Societies

In order to facilitate the entry of women into the labour force, state socialist societies carried an explicit ideology of providing services to unburden the private domestic sphere. The socialist ideal of emancipating women through drawing them out of the private into the public sphere of production remained prominent in political rhetoric and in public representations of women. Service provision varied considerably in central and eastern European countries, reflecting not only economic patterns but underlying cultural values, which could bear heavily on the casting of women's roles, Polish catholicism being a case in point. In general, however, women's employment was higher, and childcare, youth and residential provisions were more comprehensive than in the West. Their dismantling through marketisation and neo-liberalism thus produces anxious questions: Will families, and principally women, in post-communist societies resume the traditional family functions which are presupposed by liberal theory? And can the particular forms of wider informal social infrastructures which support such domestic functioning in west European societies be established in post-communist countries?

Writing about East Germany in 1991, Claus Offe predicted that the ship of incoming Federal welfare organisations would run aground in the shallowness of social and cultural infrastructures (Offe 1991, 79). By such infrastructures he meant the web of political organisations, pressure groups, associations and voluntary organisations, which typically centre on the neighbourhood and community in western societies, which are often referred to as "civil society", and which mediate between the individual and the State, and between the private and the public spheres. But while many western commentators habitually condemned the absence of civil society in "totalitarian" state socialist societies (Keane 1988), a rival view has long pointed to forms of political participation which remained undetected by the instruments of western political science. These forms of political participation included legal and workplace structures and public petitions, which had no direct parallel in the West, but also the extensive "informal networks" which were crucial to the informal economy, to the circulation of consumption goods, and to exchanges of advice and information. According to Hankiss, these infrastructures amounted to a "second society" (Lefort 1986, Nelson 1980, Hankiss 1990, Chamberlayne 1990).

In the context of the collapse of the state socialist regimes, there continues a stream of literature which points to these informal social infrastructures as an explanation of both the durability of the state socialist regimes, and of longstanding internal processes of social change which culminated in the eventual and sudden downfall. Counterculture as incipient opposition and as an arena of meaningful social engagement, and the informal economy as a site of individual enterprise, mutual self-help and compensation for the dysfunctions of the system, particularly in the area of consumption, offer a strong and convincing challenge to theories of "totalitarianism" (Hankiss 1990, Watson 1993, Szalai 1995, Wallace 1995, Pollack 1995). In the context of this literature a major policy issue becomes whether such infrastructures can survive the ravages of liberalism, whether they can be grafted into new forms of social organisation.

For ironically it is perhaps western societies which have more drastically destroyed the social infrastructures which, according to celebrants of western "civil society", are needed as supports to the private sphere of reproduction. Not that most western social policy had a coherent policy towards social infrastructures in the informal sphere. Ever greater individualisation has brought social disintegration, and this has been reinforced by individualising strategies within welfare policy itself. The importance of social policy for political legitimation also led to governments overemphasising state roles – the post-war period saw little attention to the strengthening of informal infrastructures (Evers and

Nowotny 1987, Rosanvallon 1988). The "Janus-headed" system of welfare in the Federal Republic of Germany might seem an exception here (Leibfried and Ostner 1991). Its social insurance system, based on employment records, is as individualising as elsewhere. But its "service sector", run through a plurality of welfare organisations, is based on the principle of subsidiarity, which is oriented to the informal sphere. It will be argued here, however, that the premises of the federal system of subsidiarity are out of step with changing social realities.

"Post-Fordism"in western Europe provides a very different context for debate about informal social structures from post-communism, and yet there are commonalities in rising unemployment and reductions in public services. In western Europe, post-World War Two "Fordism" comprised a social contract of full employment rewarded by the "social wage", a comprehensive package of welfare provision which compensated for the alienated division between mental and manual labour. There were of course considerable variations among west European societies. By and large "welfare stateism" was reached later in southern than in northern welfare systems, and social democracy, catholicism and liberalism lead to differences in ideologies of the family, women's rights and the informal sphere. However, all these welfare arrangements were premised on the nuclear family structure, and the underlying "sexual contract" whereby domestic responsibilities, which are unpaid, are allocated to women (Pateman 1988). Within those parameters, however, there were significant differences in state ideologies and policies concerning the informal sphere. Whereas social catholicism explicitly prioritised family policy and traditional gender roles, Scandinavian social democracy emphasised women's rights, and liberal Britain, even in its postwar period of social democracy, maintained a high degree of insistence on family privacy (Chamberlayne 1993, Lewis 1992).

By the 1980s and 1990s all western political systems were affected by processes which may be generically termed "post-Fordist". The shift away from "standard" patterns of working life and earnings and the end of full employment seriously eroded the contribution base of social insurance systems, while the dependency ratio of non-working to working population increased. Global competition between European "welfare state" societies and Japanese and US economies forced further reductions in social spending. Moreover, changes in gender patterns and family forms undermined the nuclear family structure which was also written into west European social insurance systems.

According to post-modernist theory, post-Fordism brought major cultural changes too, the enhancing of individualisation, personal choice and autonomy.

131

Employment required more flexibility of skills and of personal qualities, and men began to invest more effort and interest in their emotional and domestic lives. Women, whose skills in mediating human relations and in negotiating with welfare systems became more highly valued in a "service-based" economy, found themselves catapulted from the periphery to the centre of society (Giddens 1991, Balbo 1987, 214). According to Beck, it is in this new industrial revolution of the late twentieth century that women's democratic right to equality may at last be realised (Beck 1992). Feminists, by contrast, lay claim to forcing the area of social reproduction and the informal sphere onto political agendas through women's movements and through political struggle. In this view it is women who have relentlessly exposed the roots of gender inequality in the domestic sphere and its reinforcement in welfare systems, who have insisted that "the personal is political" (Sassoon 1987, Pascall 1986, Gordon 1989).

For Beck, however, the growing independence of women arouses anxiety. In a society based on formal equality and individual autonomy, what will be the well-springs of the ineffable love and care upon which human society has depended? Where will humans be without "the identity-forming power of stable human relationships" (Beck 1992, 114)? Western social policy experts pose the problem more broadly. Will modern women continue to provide the bulk of family and household care which has traditionally underpinned the welfare state? How can the gap be closed between the reduced availability of women for unpaid home-caring, and increased demand for such care in an ageing society with reduced social spending? The impact of reduced public provisions is plain to see. Drastic increases in levels of social breakdown such as child abuse, child poverty, divorce, rising mortality, occur in the countries which have made extreme reversals in social redistribution, such as Britain and Russia. Gender issues are at stake here too, and they echo loudly in western societies. In some policy circles, including those of the European Union, such gender dilemmas have reached public agendas. How can the canons of gender equality and social citizenship be applied to the informal sphere? How can men be persuaded to take their full share of domestic responsibility?

But all these arguments tend to be conducted in rather abstract terms of ideology and policy, rather than of practice and experience. For the neglect of the informal sphere in public policy has been paralleled in social research. While there has been a growing appeal to the importance of the informal sphere, barely any primary comparative research has been conducted. Yet ideologies and policies may be removed from actual practices; real knowledge of how the informal sphere does operate in particular situations is a prerequisite of effective policy.

East and West Germany Compared

Some light on experience and practice in the informal sphere may be drawn from
the *Cultures of Care* project, a comparative study of home-caring in two cities in
East Germany and West German. The interviews were conducted in 1992-3, and
thus, in the East German case, spanned experiences from well before the collapse
of the Wall through the early stages of unification.

East and West Germany, despite their relatively brief 40-year separation, represent
extreme examples of eastern and western welfare systems. East Germany carried
through the state socialist project of facilitating women's employment more fully
than other eastern bloc countries, with better and more extensive child care
services. West Germany, by contrast, lagged furthest behind among western
political systems in its facilitation of women's work. It was perhaps the one west
European society in which the combining of home and employment roles
remained extremely problematic, resulting in polarisation between "housewives",
who were privileged in the welfare system, and whose roles were formally desig-
nated in the system of "subsidiarity", and career women, many of whom opted to
remain childless (Ostner 1995, Chamberlayne 1995).

Using biographical-interpretative methods (Rosenthal 1993, Chamberlayne,
forthcoming), the research compared caring situations and carer strategies in the
context of the two societies of East Germany and West Germany. The method
treats carers as active and moral agents, with unconscious as well as conscious
motivations. By focusing on interrelationships between the personal and the
social, and particularly between the private and the public, the study reveals how
individual lives are "lived through" particular social systems, while at the same
time different systems are "lived out" in particular biographies.

Comparisons between the case studies showed graphically ways in which caring
biographies and caring strategies were framed by the particular social conditions
of the respective societies. A combination of structural and cultural factors
exerted a marked "pull into the home" in caring situations in West Germany,
compared with a clear "push out of the home" in East German society.

"Structural factors" in West Germany included the way in which services are
organised into the home, a wide range of professionals visiting the home to
provide a service, which, in the GDR, would have been provided in clinics, day
centres or residential homes.

A second structural factor concerned housing. A large proportion of the carers in
our study were making plans to move house. But whereas the West Germans were
moving to gain more space, so that the domiciliary services could more easily be

accommodated, the East Germans were moving house to improve access to external services, such as schools or crèches. Dwellings in West Germany are in any case larger and post-war housing subsidies encouraged the inclusion of separate flats in family houses. Thus several of the carers in our study lived in next to their parents or in-laws. In East Germany, flats were small. Multi-generational living therefore involved accommodating the bed-ridden mother in the living room, or in the carer's own bedroom, or a week-time arrangement in which four generations lived in a three-roomed flat.

A third structural factor concerned the pattern of women's employment. This was critical in influencing carers' identities. Over 90% of women of employment age in East Germany worked, as did most of the East German carers in our sample. Even those who had retired or become full-time carers maintained strong work identities and/or became involved in outside activities, such as disability campaigning. This "outer-connectedness" was a strong feature of East German caring situations.

The fourth and fifth factors were predominantly cultural and concerned partnerships and involvement in extrafamilial social networks. Whether East German men in general took a greater responsibility for household tasks is a matter of dispute; it may be that the pattern of dual earner households promotes a greater sharing of domestic tasks. Partners of the East German carers in our study were certainly more directly involved in caring tasks than their West German counterparts. Two couples, for example, who were dissatisfied with the medical treatment of their disabled children, jointly carried out over a number of years alternative therapies which involved several hours of training each day. Although both couples worked, and were "tied" to the home for the training, this did not result in a loss of outer-connectedness. Both couples learnt of the techniques through social networks, and both maintained such contacts.

Just one of the East German cases was exceptional to the pattern of outer-orientedness, an older man, who since the 1950s had cared for his epileptic wife, refusing services and advice. By maintaining his own taxi business, keeping his wife in the fortress of his own home, even taking on a traditional "woman's" role, he held out against the basic tenets of state socialism. This was perhaps a classic case of the exception proving the rule.

In contrast to the dominant pattern of outer-orientedness among the East German carers, carers in West Germany were remarkably home-oriented. They were mostly housewives, without any aspiration to work, and generally speaking they had remarkably few social contacts in the outside world. The study shows that the "traditional", extended family situation, with close relatives nearby, several children in the family, and possibly a family business, could be extremely isolating for a woman carer, especially if she submitted to family expectations or internalised the traditional values of family self-sufficiency, which entailed herself taking sole responsibility for caring. The traditionally gendered division of labour precluded partner support in immediate caring. West German partners were likely to be working long hours of overtime, on the assembly line, or in the family business, and other female family members might well not have the experience or skill to deal with a tenuous or undignified medical condition, or the behaviour of an autistic child. And "belief" in the self-sufficiency of the extended family, which might well have been upheld through collaboration between siblings in one generation, could clash with new patterns of fragmentation in the next generation of that family.

By definition, all carers in western societies have multiple connections with the outside world through the welfare and medical professionals with whom they are in contact. Indeed, it is through mediating and negotiating welfare systems, as well as family relationships, that women have gained the skills which are so eminently transferable in "service society" (Balbo 1987). This study suggests that many West German carers are exceptions to this "modern" pattern. For despite connections with outside professionals, the carers in our study were notably passive in relation to the services, some actually refusing services, others merely subject to outside interventions.

The study thus showed a marked correlation between home-orientedness and passivity towards, even refusal to accept, outside services. This mode of caring we termed "traditional", in contrast to a "modern" mode in which a greater degree of outer-connectedness correlated with a more active negotiating, even campaigning relationship with services. (See diagram overleaf)

Time perspectives were also a crucial dimension in carers' identities. "Traditional" carers had lost their sense of connection with the past or the future, whereas "modern" carers maintained past, multiple identities, and made tentative but confident projections into the future. Traditional carers tended to have integrated caring into an existing or latent identity, as a housewife, "good mother", or "good wife". Their passivity and lack of preparation for the future spelled impending crisis, since the person they cared for was often in a rapidly deteriorating condition. Modern carers, by contrast, showed a greater capacity for adaptability and change. Caring had often brought a major personal development for them, they had "blossomed" in the situation, gaining new expertise and self-assertiveness in the face of authority, new decisiveness in the face of difficulty .

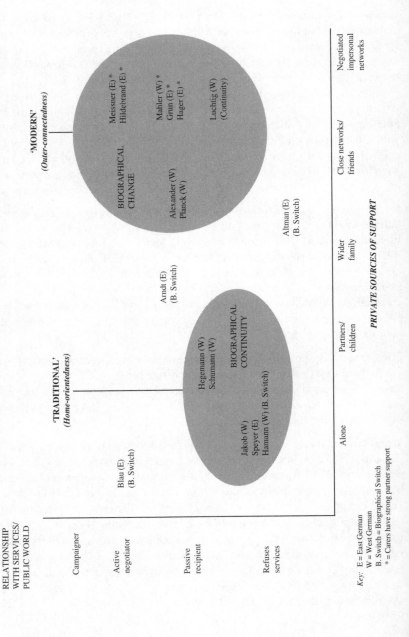

'TRADITIONAL' AND 'MODERN' MODES OF CARING

Not all West German carers became "trapped" in the home and in a single caring identity. As the diagram shows, in half the cases which we analysed in depth carers had achieved a more "modern" outer-connectedness with extrafamilial networks and related to services as active negotiators. These carers tended to belong to loosely structured families, or to occupy marginalised positions in their families. They were also supported by active groups of friends and neighbours, who boosted their confidence in their social actions and in their confrontations with officialdom. One carer, who felt her whole life had been spent in servitude to her domineering mother, had only in recent years propelled herself into an outside arena of music and crafts. Her mother's frailty constantly imperilled this laboriously achieved balance between public and private worlds. The "modern" west German cases had therefore "freed" themselves from more traditional family structures and ideologies.

Just one of these West German caring situations was "modern" in the "alternative" sense. By "alternative" is meant the social milieu of the "new class" of educated social professionals which has figured prominently in studies of West German society, and in politics, for example in the rise of the Green Party in the 1980s (Vester 1994). This was a couple, both trained social workers, who, despite extensive family links, were more oriented to wider social networks. They were about to set up home with a friend who was a single mother, they had fostered children as well as their own, and planned to adopt more. This transcending of public and private boundaries characterised many aspects of their lives.

Ideology, Policy and Practice
From the presentation of these cases it is clear that carer situations and carer strategies are shaped and structured by the welfare and social systems of which they are part. The structurally and ideologically "home-based" orientation of West German subsidiarity, with its formal designation of caring as a family responsibility, finds clear expression in the "traditional" mode of caring. Similarly, the more collectively oriented system of state socialism finds expression in the greater outer-orientedness of the "modern" mode of caring, which is adopted by the majority of East German carers in our study.

However, it is also clear that systems do not dictate behaviour, even when they exert particular, even extreme, pressures. It is also clear that "systems" themselves are not homogeneous, consistent entities. State policy develops over time, intersected by wider economic and demographic patterns and changes, and may become internally contradictory. Both professionals and service users develop their own collective and individual responses, forming new cultural variations. So although individual lives are "lived through" particular social systems, and social systems are "lived out" in individual lives, there are also constant processes of social change

In West Germany, family policy of the 1950s and 1960s consciously sought to restore the patriarchal family form, in counterposition to the destruction of family privacy by both Nazism and Communism, and indeed as a main plank in the forming of a political identity distinct from both National Socialism and state socialism (Bast and Ostner 1992; Moeller 1989). Welfare policy in the Federal Republic in the long post-war era of Christian Democracy under Adenauer was strongly marked by social catholicism, with its central tenet of subsidiarity. Resistance to the oppressiveness of the traditional nuclear family form played a large part in fuelling the cultural revolution of 1968 and the development of "alternative" life-styles. In the 1970s family policy in West Germany, reflecting these broad political changes, shifted to emphasise the rights of individual family members, especially children and women. Individual self-development through mutual self-help and collective action as well as through more personalised counselling and educational techniques became the basis of the new profession of "social pedagogy", which achieved a higher status than the more traditional social work training. In the 1980s social policy returned to the theme of greater recognition of home roles (Münch 1990). Feminists, who in that decade achieved great prominence on the political stage, were divided, as for example between "mothers" and "careerists", with 26% opting for voluntary child-lessness (Ostner 1993, 106). Feminist research flourished, much of it exploring female subjectivities and further politicising the private sphere. To the "non-traditional" influences in West German welfare might be added the widespread use of "Zivis" in ancillary welfare roles: young men who chose to work in community services as an alternative to military conscription. Many Zivis went on to enter traditionally female welfare professions, and many households were introduced by Zivis to young men performing typically female tasks.

Thus, while "traditionalism" in family life remained structurally and culturally rooted in West German society, there were marked countervailing forces. Examples appeared in our study, particularly among the "modern" cases, in the guise of community workers who build women's self-help neighbourhood groups, which become quite militant in fighting officials, or in the social milieus which provided extrafamilial forms of support. There were also marked class differences in relationships with professionals in West Germany. Middle class carers tended to receive intensive and proactive advice from professionals, whereas support for working class women came more from lower-level domiciliary professionals and community organisers.

Caring situations and carer strategies of carers in *East Germany* revealed a similar mix of elements of official ideology and policy, and of "system effects", cultural forms which had developed in response to officialdom. Official policy favoured residential provision for severely dependent people, and the definition of women as "working mothers" exerted pressure *against* rather than *for* full-time caring. We have noted one older, male carer who built a fortress in the private sphere in defiance of the system. In fact, however, most East German carers worked, and even those who had been made redundant following unification were retraining. Moreover, the few women in this study who did become full-time carers remained active in the outside world, they did not "retreat" into the private sphere.

The "activity" in the outside world was largely pitted against the system rather than in line with official policy, however. Indeed, the common western depiction of East German life as standardised, and marked by conformity and passivity, was not borne out by our study. As we have seen, East German carers were not only more outward oriented than their western counterparts, they were more likely to be negotiators and campaigners, and to have a capacity for personal change and adaptability. Cynical official attitudes, and low standards of service, which deteriorated even more from staffing gaps due to the exodus of population in 1989, pushed people into fighting for alternative treatments. And the informal networks of moral and practical help which permeated East German society, which had been initially encouraged for political reasons but had acquired their own dynamic, provided channels through which alternative services and treatments could be accessed (Pollack 1995).

Hofmann (1991) characterises networks among those involved in disability, as among those involved with frail elderly people and those in alternative youth cultures, as a "quiet" movement, not very visible or formalised and certainly not recognised in the West, but a significant component in the outburst of independent initiatives in 1989-90. Part of his argument is that those reliant on the most neglectful services of the State were most aware of the limitations of the socialist State, most disabused of its claims to satisfy human need, most subject to its callousness. Official policy towards the non-productive disabled was disturbing to many professionals, and many went out of their way to be helpful.

Conclusion
Western literature on caring treats the modernisation of women's roles, through increased employment and independence, as a "problem" leading to a "caring deficit". This is echoed in the new literature on "communitarianism", in which traditional family values are invoked to remedy the alleged "parenting deficit"

(Campbell 1995). In contrast to this celebration of "the traditional", the *Cultures of Care* project found "traditional" caring situations more problematical than "modern" ones.

With its focus on carer situations and carer strategies, the project did not attempt to evaluate the quality of the relationship between carer and cared-for. However, it suggested that "traditional" forms of caring in the extended family were more likely to be in crisis, with carers locked in caring identities without repertories for the future, and shouldering an undue burden without partner or outside support. It seems unlikely that these situations were "better" for the cared-for person. By contrast, the more "modern" mode of caring was characterised by a wider set of identities and repertories, more active engagement with the outside world, more negotiation for services, the acquisition of new personal and social skills. Sources of support were diverse in this mode of caring, although involvement in networks was often facilitated and sustained by partner support, especially in East Germany.

The results of this study are disquieting, and not only for Germany. For the welfare systems of the former West and East Germanies have a significance beyond themselves, representing extreme poles in European welfare systems. And while, from the vantage point of informal caring, the more traditionalising and crisis-inducing system is in the ascendancy, the more modernising system is being destroyed for the sake of 'free' market economy ideology.

The West German system is based on subsidiarity, a concept which is gaining authority in European politics. It appeals to liberals, who fear a strong central state, to conservatives who want to retraditionalise the family reliance on a lower level, even to social democrats who are struggling with resource constraints, who can use it in support of a discourse of decentralisation and pluralisation. West German subsidiarity, as this relates specifically to caring, has particular structural and ideological roots, which might not apply in other societies. It is therefore important to decide whether subsidiarity could be implemented in ways which would facilitate "modern" ways of caring, avoid "entrapment" in the private sphere, and instead promote outer-connectedness, activate wider social networks, generate personal development and transferable skills, promote men's full sharing in caring tasks, ensure that other identities and repertories beyond caring are sustained and developed in caring situations. It can indeed be argued that "subsidiarity" need not presuppose traditional family forms. In West Germany in the 1980s, for example, there was discussion of recasting it as "new subsidiarity" to embrace social initia-tives in "alternative" milieus. Studies have shown, however, how the large, traditional welfare organisations succeeded in marginalising these initiatives

(Grunow 1986). This does not disprove the case; subsidiarity is not bound to one mould.

Within the context of social transformation in central and eastern Europe, the German case is extreme, since the takeover of East Germany by Federal systems was a more sudden and comprehensive process of "liberalisation" than elsewhere. In other central and eastern European countries there might be more chance of grafting new structures onto old, as was recommended by some social policy specialists in the case of East Germany (Backhaus-Maul and Olk 1992, 117). Even in the case of East Germany, at least some features of the more collective infrastructures may endure, and "East German culture" may survive. Clare Wallace (1995) suggests that mutual intergenerational support or "social capital" remains an important resource in the new Czech Republic, and Julia Szalai (1995) points to the longstanding and continuing modernising tendencies of women's influence in the sphere of social reproduction in Hungary. Women may seem to have "disappeared" from "politics", but they exerted a decisive influence in the fall of the State socialist regime in Hungary, and they play a large part in the myriad non-elected social policy commissions which have sprung up. They are using their accumulated knowledge in mobilising seemingly 'sleeping' potentials of local communities" (1995, 20).

The conclusion of this chapter is, therefore, that there is much dynamism and scope for social imagination in the informal sphere, at an individual level and at a collective level, and that policy makers would do well to pay it more attention, in all modern societies.

Notes concerning Diagram ('Traditional' and 'Modern' Modes of Caring)
The diagram is based on three axes. The vertical axis concerns carers' relationships with services and the public world, and ranges from refusal of services to campaigning for them. The horizontal axis concerns private or informal sources of support, ranging from a lack of any, where a carer carries the responsibility alone, through support from partner, wider family and friends to impersonal networks. The third dimension concerns biographical continuity, switch and change, i.e. the way caring is integrated into the carer's life. Two main clusters emerge. Those who are pulled into the home, who refuse services or are passive towards them, and who incorporate caring into an existing life pattern we have termed "traditional" carers. The second group, who are more active negotiators or campaigners regarding services, have stronger connections outside the home and have made significant adaptations in their lives through caring, are termed "modern" carers. It is notable that those who are most actively connected outside the home also have strong partner support. A third, smaller group are the East German switch cases who are new to caring and still torn between different identities.

The project, which was conducted with Annette King as Research Officer, was funded by the ESRC in 1992-4 (R000 23 3921).

Fifty carers were interviewed, 25 in each city and most of them were interviewed twice. Sixteen cases were analysed in depth, using the methods of case construction as development by Gabriele Rosenthal (1992). These are the cases which figure in the diagram, to which many of the remarks refer. The "switch" cases in the diagram tended to be in new caring situations, and still to be torn between competing identities. Here again it is noticeable that the East German switch cases are much more strongly outwardly-oriented than the West German case. In Vester's scheme of social milieus in West Germany, the upper class alternative milieu only comprises 2% of the population in 1992, having dropped from 4% in 1982 (Vester 1994,37). Of course, our small scale qualitative study does not even attempt to be statistically representative, though we sought a broad social range in our selection of cases.

Bibliography

Backhaus-Maul, H and Okl, T. (1992) 'Intermediare Organisationen als Gegenstand sozialwissenschaftlicher Forschung'. In *Sozialpolitik im Prozess der deutschen Vereinigung* (ed. W. Schmahl). Frankfurt/M: Campus

Balbo, L. (1987) 'Family, Women and the State: Notes Towards a Typology of Family Roles and Public Intervention'. In *Changing Boundaries of the Political* (ed. C.S. Maier). Cambridge: Cambridge University Press.

Beck, U. (1992) *Risk Society. Towards a New Modernity*. London: Sage.

Campbell, B. (1995) Old Fogies and Angry Young Men. *Soundings*, I:1, 47-64.

Chamberlyne, P. (1990) *Neighbourhood and Tenant Participation in the GDR. Social Policy in the New Eastern Europe* (eds. B. Daecon and J. Szalai). Aldershot: Avebury.

Chamberlyne. P, (1993) *Models of Welfare and Informal Care. In Informal care in Europe* (ed. J. Twigg). Proceedings of a conference held in York. York: Social Policy Research Unit.

Chamberlyne, P, (1994) Women and Social Policy in Germany. In *Social Policy in Germany* (eds. J. Clasen and R. Freeman). London: Harvester Wheatsheaf.

Chamberlyne, P. (1995) Gender and the Private Sphere: A Touchstone of Misunderstanding between Eastern and Western Germany? *Social Politics*, 2:1, 25-36.

Chamberlyne, P. & King, A. (forthcoming) Biographical Approaches in Comparative Work: the Cultures of Care Project. In *Cross-National Research Methods in the Social Sciences* (eds. L. Hantrais and S. Mangen). London: Pinter.

Evers, A. & Nowotny, H. (1987) (eds) *The Changing Face of Welfare*. Aldershot: Gower.

Giddens, A. (1991) *Modernity and Self-Identity, Self and Society in the Late Modern Age*. Cambridge; Polity.

Grunow, D. (1986) De-bureaucratisation and the self-help movement: towards a restructuring of the welfare state in the FRG? In *Comparing Welfare States and their futures* (ed.E.Oyen) Aldershot: Gower

Hankiss, E. (1990) *East European Alternatives*. Oxford: Oxford University Press.

Heidenheimer, A. *et al.* (1983) (eds) *Comparative Public Policy: The Politics of Public Choice in Europe and America*, Second Edition. London: Macmillan.

Hoffman, M. (1991) *Aufbruch im Warteland-Ostdeutsche soziale Bewegungen im Wandel*. Bamberg: Palette Verlag.

Keane, J. (1988) (ed.) *Civil Society and the State: New European Perspectives*. London: Verso.

Lefort. C. (1986) *The Political Forms of Modern Society: Bureaucracy, Democracy and Totalitarianism*. Oxford: Polity.

Leibfried, S. & Ostner, I. (1991) 'The particularism of West German Welfare Capitalism'. In *The Sociology of Social Security* (eds. M.Adler, C.Bell, J. Clasen, A. Sinfield). Edinburgh : Edinburgh University Press.

Moeller, R. (1989) Reconstructing the Family in Reconstruction Germany. *Feminist Studies* 15:1, 137-169.

Munch, U. (1990) *Familienpolitik in der BRD*. Freiburg: Lambertus Verlag.

Nelson, D. (1980) *Local Politics in Communist Countries*. Kentucky: Lexington.

Offe, C. (1991) Die Deursche Vereinigung als 'Naturliches Experiment'. In *Experiment Vereinigung:ein sozialer Grossversuch* (eds. B. Giesen and C. Leggewie). Berlin: Rotbuch.

Ostner, I. (1993) Slow Motion: Women, Work and the Family in Germany. In Women and Social Policies in *Europe: Work, Family and the State* (ed J.Lewis). Aldershot: Gower.

Pascall, L. G. (1986) *Social Policy: A Feminist Analysis*. London: Tavistock.

Pateman, C. (1988) *The Sexual Contract*. London: Polity.

Pateman, C. (1989) *The Disorder of Women*. London: Polity.

Pollack, D. (1992) Zwischen alten Verhaltensdispositionen und neuen Anforderungsprofilen-Bemerkungen zu den mentalitatsspezifischen Voraussetzungen des Operierens von Interessenverbanden und Organisationen in den neuen Bundeslandern. *Probleme der Einheit*, 12:2. Halbband.

Pollack, D. *Kirche in der Organisationsgesellschaft: zum Wandel der gesellschaftlichen Lage der evangelischen kirche in der DDR*. Stuttgart: Kohlhammer.

Rosanvallon, P. (1988) 'The Decline of Social Visibility'. In *Civil Society and the State* (ed. J. Keane). London: Verso.

Rosenthal, G. & Baron, D. (1992) A Biographical Case Study of a Victimizer's Daughter's Strategy: Pseudo-idnetification with the Victims of the Holocaust. *Journal of Narrative Life-History*, 2:2, 105-127.

Rosenthal, G. (1993) 'Reconstruction of life stories: principles of selection in generating stories for narrative biographical interviews'. In *The Narrative Study of Lives* (eds. R. Josselson and A. Lieblich). London. Sage.

Sassoon, A. (1987) *Women and the State: the Shifting Boundaries between Public and Private*. London: Hutchinson.

Szalai. J. (1995) *Women and Democratisation: Some Notes on Recent Changes in Hungary*. Paper delivered at the European Sociological Association Conference: Budapest

Titterton, M. (1992) Managing Threats to Welfare: The Search for a new Paradigm of Welfare. *Journal of Social Policy*, 21: 1 , 1-23.

Vester, M. (1994) 'Solidaritat im Spagat. Umbruche und sozialer Wandel in Ost- und Westdeutschland'. In *Aufbruche-Anstosse* (ed. H-W Meyer). Koln. Bund Verlag.

Wallace, C. (1990) Family Dependencies in Poland. *Journal of European Social Policy*, 5:2, 97-110.

Watson, P. (1993) Eastern Europe's Silent revolution: Gender. *Sociology*, 27:3, 471-487.

Approaches to Deinstitutionalisation: Western and Eastern Europe, Social Policy, Social Work and Related Disciplines

Shulamit Ramon

In this chapter an attempt is made to look at:

- the meaning of deinstitutionalisation;

- the way it has been treated in western and in eastern Europe.

- responses and initiatives by the main stakeholders to deinstitution-alisation: politicians, the media, professionals, users, carers, the "general public".

- approaches to deinstitutionalisation in social policy, social work, psychiatry and sociology.

Institutionalisation and Deinstitutionalisation in Western Europe

It took Europe 300 years to build its institutional network for people suffering from a variety of disabling conditions. The institutions were aimed at providing

- asylum for vulnerable people

- containment of deviancy

- re-education of the residents.

The pre-1945 period

People were brought into institutions for a variety of disabilities. Nevertheless, these establishments developed several unifying features:

- most institutions were built in the countryside, thus meeting two requirements: segregation and the provision of a calming landscape

- for most of the time, people went in against their wishes

- until the end of the Second World War most residents tended to remain in the institution long after the disappearance of the reason that brought them there in the first place

- the management made all of the decisions concerning everyday life, dictating every petty detail in the day, in addition to professional interventions

- in the early period residents worked in a variety of domestic jobs. Yet later most residents were not allowed to do much by way of looking after themselves and the place in which they lived, due to assumed inability to do so and on grounds that this would consist in exploitation or distancing them from their sick role. Only in some instances, and especially since the second half of the twentieth century, work was encouraged as part of therapy (occupational therapy, industrial work units).

These unifying, all encompassing features led Goffman to coin the concept of the *total institution* (Goffman, 1961).

Alternative models co-existed, such as

- fostering people with disabilities by ordinary families, such as in the Belgian town of Geel, began in the eighteenth century (Roosens, 1979)

- lodging in a large village, as in Dur-sur-Arun and Ainey-le-Chateau since 1901 (Jodelet, 1991).

These two emblematic examples highlighted that people with disabilities such as learning difficulties and mental illness could lead a predominantly ordinary life with its everyday pleasures and burdens, even if they were isolated socially, occupied an inferior social position, and were not allowed to decide whether they wished to live there or not.

Qualitatively, their lives were richer than those of the residents in the best total institutions, when quality is measured by degree of choice, freedom, presence in the community, personal competence, and varied relationships with other people, including non-disabled people.

It also stands to reason that the cost of maintaining these people in the fostering and lodging schemes was considerably lower than in a total institution, as they usually earned their keep by their own work.

While these possibilities remained as living examples, they were not followed elsewhere.

Given that alternatives to total institutions existed, we do need to understand the reasons behind the move to total institutions instead of letting people stay where they were with support, or moving them to a fostering lodging environment which was less totalistic in its control over their everyday lives.

Furthermore, we also need to understand why – until the middle of the twentieth century – the institutional regime went from being less totalistic to being more so.

At the early stage of creating institutions it was believed that people with a disability were in part responsible for their situation and therefore a mixture of motives was attributed to their a-social behaviour. Thus in the English Poor Law the poor were perceived as both unfortunate and intentionally not doing enough to improve their own conditions. To make them work for their keep seemed therefore appropriate in terms of fostering personal responsibility.

With the advance of the illness model into our understanding of disabilities and vulnerabilities, sufferers became absolved of intentionally becoming disabled. It was further assumed that therefore they are also unable to take any responsibility for their lives. The qualitative jump from having a disability to being perceived as DISABLED in any aspect of living has been explained by Goffman when he analysed the generalised effect of stigma, whereby an identifying detail becomes a master status (Goffman, 1963).

The jump was encouraged by the separation between the states of illness and health in relation to acute illness as fostered by western medicine, and the development of large institutions – general hospitals - where the best of medicine was supposed to be practised. Thus the move to total institutions was also linked to seeing medicine as a science, to assumptions of what is science, and where to practise its achievements.

As Foucault has illustrated, the move to the "clinical gaze" included a tendency to viewing people as objects of scientific enquiry and work (Foucault, 1973).

I would like to propose that the sight of permanent disability became intolerable as it indicated the failure of medicine (and of *science* and of *progress*), and not only of the fear that people with disabilities were deviant, infringing a variety of taken-for-granted but unspoken rules of social and personal conduct. Thus it is the chronicity and incurability of their state which could not be tolerated.

As institutions go, some places were better than others. Some directors, doctors, and unqualified workers were more considerate than others, and therefore the regime in such places was more friendly and caring. However, we have few descriptions of everyday life in institutions from the pre-twentieth century period, and even fewer provided by residents rather than professionals. It is only from 1970 that an interest in finding out what the residents have to say about their place of living emerges. It made perfect logic to assume that people unable to take any responsibility for their lives would be unable to give a reliable account of it. Only when the assumptions concerning personal ability and responsibility change in the direction of believing that disability *per se* does not take away personal ability and responsibility is it time to become interested in what residents have to say about their environment.

We need to understand why and how this shift in perception and belief came about, culminating in the view that total institutions are neither benevolent nor economically viable solutions.

The post-war period: 1945-1970
As proposed by Rose (1985) and by myself (1985) the ideological shift began during the Second World War, when

- people who were definitely not labelled as ill, disabled or deviant required professional psychosocial help *en mass* due to pressure arising from the war situation. This dented the assumed relationship between needing help and being different from the majority, as the majority itself required such help

- the personal dignity and respect for others which German people with disabilities - and some of the staff - have displayed while taken to their death by their fellow Germans during the infamous Eutonesia project stood as evidence of their humanity (Perske,1972)

- physically wounded, and psychologically traumatised, soldiers were in fact the first to be offered a less-than-totatlistic institutional environment as the setting for therapeutic intervention and recovery in the form of the THERAPEUTIC COMMUNITY during the war (Jones, 1952). In that environment they were encouraged to take active responsibility for themselves and for everyday life in the setting. The staff working in the community were encouraged in turn to stop wearing hospital uniforms, to be ready to accept open criticisms of their activities coming from the patients in communal meetings and to be available to residents not only during set times for individualised meetings but throughout their work shift. All of this amounted not only to a tacit acceptance that people with a disability nevertheless had some abilities left, including that of decision-making about their own lives, but also to reducing somewhat the power imbalance between residents and staff

- everyday life events and roles became imbued with psychological meaning, to an extent pathologising the normal and normalising what was thereto considered pathological. This is exemplified in the way motherhood became considered and mothers were treated (Bowlby, 1951). While not shifting the weight of stigma attributed to anyone with a diagnosed disability, this helped to blur somewhat the rigid edge of the differences between "normal" and "abnormal" people

- A strong push towards rehabilitation of people with disabilities was in evidence since the war, which led to convincingly positive results and a reconsideration of what was possible to revert at least to the level of reasonable everyday functioning across the board of different types of disabilities

- Drugs which repressed psychotic symptoms more quickly than was possible before and with side-effects which the psychiatrists – rather than the recipients – were ready to tolerate became available

- hospital wards were overcrowded; the rate of newly built hospitals was perceived to be insufficient to meet the need for hospital beds.

All of this has meant that sending people with long-term disabilities to an institution for life became questioned by some prominent professionals, by politicians, some informal carers, and journalists. Descriptions of poor institutional living and the scandals which erupted occasionally (Robb, 1967 and Cochrane, 1991) made it all the more desirable to re-examine the inevitability of institutional living as the only viable solution for this group of people.

The re-examination has led to experimentation with a variety of attempts to humanise the institutional environment, with alternative ways of living outside the total institution, and the establishment of professional multidisciplinary teams based outside hospitals. Usually all of this took place without attempting to find out what people with disabilities and their relatives or friends wanted and without new legislation.

Thus the desirability of the new alternatives and their enforceability *vis-à-is* institutional solutions remained doubtful.

The post 1970 period

During this period we witnessed the first attempts to close down institutions in the US and in Italy (Scull, 1978; Brown, 1985; Mauri, 1986; Ramon, 1990).

While in the US these focused on a variety of institutions and disabilities, in Italy the main target was psychiatric hospitals. The American move was engineered by Right-wing politicians, supported by some professionals interested in cost-cutting. The Italian change was spearheaded by mental health Left-wing professionals who have managed to get wide-ranging public support for a policy of integrating people with mental illness into their communities.

These differences are reflected also in the ways in which the closures were conducted, the degree to which patients and workers were partners to the change process, and the end products.

American closures were characterised by being predominantly administrative in orientation and non-participatory in terms of staff, patients, relatives and the wider community. Attention was paid to where people will live and who will look after them, selling of assets and making staff redundant while community mental health centres had already been in place since the mid-1960s.

Scant attention was paid to the *process* of closure, how people would live and spend their time out of the hospital, how they would become integrated, or what would happen to the unemployed workers, and to how to prevent the hospitalisation of a new generation of people suffering from mental distress.

Instead, the Italians focused on changing the hospital from within *first* and with it the way patients saw themselves and were seen by others, as well as the way the staff perceived their responsibilities and abilities. Staff were not made redundant, but moved eventually with service users – the new name which the Italians have coined for patients (utenti) – to work in community-based services. A lot of attention was given to how people lived, what they did during the day, what they contributed to other people with whom they lived, the small and big gestures of integration (Basaglia, 1968; Mosher and Burti 1989).

There was no direct American legislation concerning hospital closure, though there was to establish community mental health centres in 1963 (Brown, 1985). The Italians did legislate the closure by terminating building new hospitals and new admissions, and by establishing mental health community teams in 1978 (Mosher, 1982).

It would therefore seem that the Americans went for *dehospitalisation* while the Italians were interested in *deinstitutionalisation*.

A much quieter, less publicised, but more-in-depth change took place in relation to people with learning difficulties across western Europe. As more - and earlier - work by community-based teams was done with children in this category and their parents, they were either not sent to institutions any more or remained in the community much longer than before, until the end of compulsory education, studying in special day-schools. Parents took greater interest and initiatives in setting up enriching settings for their children, with the support of key professionals. Local authorities were ready to financially support such initiatives instead of insisting that all of it should be done by them. The majority of these children have never entered an institution, but instead either remained with their parents or went to live in small group homes after receiving some form of vocational training and remaining attached to sheltered work schemes.

This resulted in serious questioning of the need to maintain institutions for this group, and in raising the possibility that most of the adults living in institutions did not need to remain there.

The timing of these questions coincided with the ascendancy of the NORMAL-ISATION, or SOCIAL ROLE VALORISATION approach (Nirje, 1969; Wolfensberger, 1983; Ramon, 1991).

Developed in the Scandinavian countries in the 1950s, reaching the US in the 1960s and the rest of western Europe in the 1980s, the approach is based on the assumptions that institutional living is undesirable for people with any disability and that almost all people with long-term disability can - and should - live in the community, leading an ordinary life as much as possible and with varying degrees of individualised support (Nirje, 1969).

The Danish and the Swedish professionals who have developed the approach have been able to put them into practice, clearly demonstrating that such ideas are realistic, more satisfactory for people with learning difficulties and their families, and for the professionals working with them, with most of the community solutions being cheaper than institutional placements.

Similar changes have taken place by now in other European countries, especially in Britain, Italy and the Netherlands.

Doubts remain about:

- the degree of integration in the community

- whether emotionally it may be more difficult for someone with mild learning difficulty to face up to what they are unable to achieve unlike their peers without learning difficulties than for someone left in an institution unaware of possibilities existing outside the institution in the first place

- the regime in some of the community placements may still be institutional and paternalistic.

As an offshoot of the Social Role Valorisation approach, but also of the movement towards greater empowerment of people with learning difficulties and mental distress (Brandon, 1995) we have also seen the development of self-advocacy, education, and lobbying organisations of people with learning difficulties, one of the most heartening developments in this field to have occurred.

A parallel move has also taken place among people with physical disabilities, who benefited from the push towards rehabilitation more than any other group of people with disabilities, as this trend meant that wherever possible the effect of the disability was arrested if not reversed in many cases, and that the development of mechanical aids eased also the degree of functional disability to perform a given task. Yet many of those with a visible disability – such as blindness or paralysis – continued to be sent to special boarding schools or smaller institutions, until the 1980s (Oliver, 1990; Vernon, 1996).

The disability movement has by now put forward the argument that the main problem with disability has to do with social attitudes towards it and towards people with a disability than in the functional constraints created by the disabling condition. In making this claim they do not argue that these constraints do not exist, but that they can be lived with if society would be more accepting of their right to lead a life like everybody else, by virtue of being people.

The movement is calling therefore for legislation which will outlaw any discrimination of people because of disability and for improving access to public facilities which continue to prevent people with physical disability from using them, such as public transport, cinemas, museums, theatres, public libraries, schools and universities, and restaurants in all European countries.

It would therefore seem that deinstitutionalisation is a necessary and important, yet insufficient, condition to ensure the reintegration into ordinary life of people with disabilities.

Such a wide-ranging change included also a large number of stakeholders, such as national and local politicians, service users and their relatives, professionals, and often the media

The backlash

Throughout the development of attempts to deinstitutionalise there have been groups opposing this position. The opposition consists of:

- Those who continue to be afraid of living with disabled people.

- Those concerned with their own loss of power as a result of losing the power base of the institution.

- Those concerned with insufficient and inadequate support in the community when institutions cease to be the main setting of disabled people. They include feminists who argued that the bulk of informal care falls on women, who will be prevented from getting on with their lives in the name of caring for relatives (Graham, 1993). Within this group there is a sub-group which believes that a minority of disabled people require specialised residential settings as the best option for their lives.

- Those proud of the achievements of a segregated group who do not want it to lose what has been achieved, in a similar way that any minority group would resist attempts not to allow it to preserve its culture (Sacks, 1992). This position is to be found especially among deaf people.

The variations in the reasons for the opposition are so wide that each reason necessitates a different response, even though some of the reasons are interrelated. For example, those afraid of loss of power:

- never acknowledge that such a threat is at the root of their opposition

- would usually express their reactions as due to the inadequacy of non-institutional solutions

- exaggerate the number of people who may need residential solution or the length of such a solution

- just claim that "they [the disabled] are unpredictable" and therefore cannot be trusted, as if the unpredictability is unrelated to how people are treated by professionals and by society in general.

Any observer of the recession-ridden European economies ruled by radical right wing governments would be quick to point to the insufficiency and inadequacy of the investment in services for people with disabilities. Is this a good enough reason to let them rot in institutions? Perhaps it is instead a good enough cause to rally round and fight for more resources and better utilisation of existing resources?

As to the call for the preservation of minority culture, the same rule which applies to any minority needs to be applied here too: while people should be given the right to preserve their culture, they must also be sufficiently conversant with the majority culture to be able to adequately communicate and interact with it. Furthermore, those who do not wish to remain within the minority culture should be able to leave it.

In any case, the wishes of disabled people should define policy and service priorities over those of their relatives and society, as long as the risk to themselves and others is taken into account.

Yet, as in any group of people, the wishes of disabled people are unlikely to be uniform, and the degree of informed choice exercised by them would also differ widely. The lack of uniformity is due to the simple truth that by virtue of being people disabled people are as heterogeneous as any other large group of people. The variations in degree of informed choice, however, are more likely to be a function, not only of the educational level of each individual, but also of the fact that traditional services in the community - let alone in institutions - tended not to provide service users and relatives with adequate information, as they were based on the assumption that the professional knows best and the client is anyhow unable to make valid decisions.

As outlined above, deinstitutionalisation is based on a repudiation of these assumptions. If this approach is to be taken seriously, disabled people would need to be provided with sufficient, non-jargonised, information early on in any decision-making process for deinstitutionalisation not to remain only a lip-service concept.

The majority of health professions in western Europe have been trained to believe in the almost unqualified usefulness of a "good" institution, and are yet to disabuse themselves of the belief in the inability of people with disabilities to be genuine partners in any professional intervention process.

Every act of violence by a disabled person is frightening. So is a similar act by a non-disabled person.

Yet in Britain the relatively small number of killings by people suffering from mental illness has led to:

- a campaign of defamation by the populistic media of all people with mental illness

- ignoring the fact that they are much more likely to harm themselves than anybody else (DoH, 1992), and that self-harm is often related to predicted deprivations of an emotional and social nature

- calls for reinstitutionalisation and active sabotage of serious attempts to create asylum facilities in the community.

The individual circumstances of any killing by a person suffering from mental illness have to be investigated and lessons learnt from such an investigation beyond the individual case. Yet the media-hyped hysteria around this issue in Britain has no parallel in any other European country, including Italy, which has closed more psychiatric hospitals than Britain, and which hospitalises fewer people annually than Britain (Ramon, 1996, ch.8). So far, the British media, the politicians, the professionals, relatives and pressure groups have refused to learn anything about and from the Italian scene. This refusal leads me to conclude that they are afraid to learn that it can be different, that the British outcomes to date are not inevitable.

Current state of play in western Europe
Varied, complex, multi-sectorised, with and without professionals, with greater say given to users and relatives at times, more flexible yet often non-comprehensive alternative systems have developed where institutions have either closed down in full or demoted sufficiently from being the core of the system. Professionals wavering in their commitments and governments which do not honour their own promises prevail.

The fundamental work on changing professional and public attitudes in the direction of social role valorisation is yet to be completed throughout western Europe. At the same time a momentum to open more-secure units has developed in Britain, while alternative crisis facilities are not encouraged in most countries.

The sense of a system in flux is pervasive. It is not clear where we are going from here, as future directions depend on the simultaneous effect of the political, economic, cultural and professional factors at work.

In the post-modern era in which we live such a variety fits the cultural bill, even if it falls short of what most stakeholders in this field know is needed.

Eastern Europe
A western observer of the way people with disabilities are treated in eastern Europe, especially in the ex-Soviet Union part can easily come to the conclusion that these societies are where western Europe was in the pre-Second World War phase. Large institutions exist for every long-term disability, with very few inter-mediate services between family doctors and hospitals or between hospitals and residential institutions. It is believed that good institutions offer the best intervention available, and therefore groups perceived as "socially deserving", such as soldiers and physically ill children, should be placed in an institution or be there long enough to benefit from it. Of course, the lack of non-institutional services reinforces the validity of such a view.

I have observed:
- Psychiatric hospitals which combine emergency admission, short-term admissions and long term hospitalisation on the same ward. People with alcohol and drug abuse are hospitalised together with people exhibiting psychotic symptoms. People with epilpsey remaining for months on end in the psychiatric hospital to "stabilise their medication". Children who do not suffer from any psychiatric symptoms staying for years in the psychiatric hospital because they have been abandoned by their parents and there are no legal fostering arrangements.

- War veterans needing three hours per day physiotherapy are requested to stay for six weeks in a residential establishment.

- Children with heart problems remain in a boarding school in the same city in which their parents and siblings live.

- A military prison for minor offenders containing 130 prisoners in one - big - room. Their guards live in similar conditions.

- A hospital with carpets and plants for 400 people, run by the Medical Academy in Moscow; and a hospital for 5,000 patients not that far from the first, without carpets but with torn lino and cracks in the walls.

- A netted bed for "agitated patients", now outlawed after a fire in which a patient was burnt to death, can be seen in Polje, near Ljubljana.

- A professionalised alcoholics anonymous service for which people pay in dollars (Odessa) and private psychotherapy services (Budapest, Ljubljana and Moscow).

- A striking lack of interest in older people is noticeable across almost all of eastern Europe (with the exception of the Jewish service to holocaust survivors in Budapest).

I have also observed:

- The work of the Peto Institute in Budapest where dedicated and imaginative long-term work with children with a variety of serious physical disabilities continues.

- Young people after a psychotic episode acting as my interpreters in a study day with relatives (Ljubljana).

- A shelter for children and adolescents who ran away from institutions in Odessa, run on a shoestring by volunteers who are otherwise teachers in special education, who have created together with the children a homelike environment in a basement. These children are not allowed to study in the ordinary schools of the city because they ran away from abuse either at home or in an institution.

- A Sunday school for children with a variety of learning difficulties and neurological problems, initiated by their mothers in Kiev. When the children work in small groups with a teacher the mothers use the time for their own self-help group. During the week the children go to a special school, taking three hours to get there and back on public transport. This precludes the possibility of work for most mothers.

- Two young people, a woman and a man, each with an artificial leg replacing the one lost in the Armenian earthquake, now studying medicine in Yerevan.

Thus eastern Europe too is by now less uniform than we imagine it to be, and perhaps less uniform than it was five years ago.

Yet the belief in the inevitability of institutional living for people with long-term disabilities is as strong as it was before 1990, and very few people envisage a future without them.

In contrast with pre-Second World War western Europe, expressed criticisms in Eastern Europe focus on:

- low standard of living conditions
- lack of medication
- lack of good diagnostic skills by professionals.

Very few people mention non-medical interventions; work for people with disabilities; or even the need to develop non-institutional options.

Many of the professionals who were part of the middle classes before the change in the regime are now struggling to survive, leave the helping professions for business, or try to find additional jobs. There has been little change in training and hardly any access to foreign literature. Only a few nurses are qualified and there are no qualified social workers in all of the CIS countries. Doctors and psychologists spend most of their time diagnosing patients.

Real spending on welfare and health services is steadily going down; staff who leave are not replaced; anything broken is unlikely to be even properly repaired. In some places the professional staff have bought paint and decorated the ward themselves.

New initiatives encouraged by the West are all too often mainly focused on aping the West: upgrading medical knowledge and developing the knowledge and skills of nurses, rather than a differentiated way of learning which could prevent the repetition of the failures of Western medicine, while adopting its positive achievements.

Thus the demoralisation at any level of the system, the very poor record of keeping human rights standards within the existing institutions, the sense of inferiority and suspicion *vis-à-vis* western Europe, the preoccupation with one's own and one's family survival, militate against the likelihood of a real change in policy or practice in any but a few pockets, despite the compelling economic, professional and moral reasons for the move to deinstitutionalisation.

Western Europe can therefore encourage these pockets to survive and expand as models for the future; it can offer training to a few key people abroad and through them to many more in their country of origin. It can support the establishment of new professional groups which are essential to deinstitutionalisation (such as social work, social policy researchers, qualified nurses) as well as encourage the establishment of users and relatives associations.

Approaches to Deinstitutionalisation: Western and Eastern Europe, Social Policy, Social Work and Related Disciplines

I, for one, view the attempt to bring the level of knowledge of doctors and nurses to that of their western counterparts as a waste of time, energy and scarce resources. My objection is based on the fact that the lack of drive towards deinstitutionalisation is not based on ignorance *per se*. More professional western knowledge coming out of medicine will only enhance the belief in an improved version of the existing professional solutions, given that the main professional opposition to deinstitutionalisation comes from medically trained people in western Europe.

Western Europe cannot change the east European system: only the people of each of these countries themselves can do that.

The task of changing the minds and hearts of the majority of west European professionals remains as urgent and demanding as that of changing views, systems and practices in east Europe.

Disciplinary Approaches to Deinstitutionalisation
Although deinstitutionalisation is the single most radical visible and symbolic policy change concerning people with disabilities since the 1960s, the responding analysis and research have been rather unimpressive.

Four disciplines have been engaged in the debate on deinstitutionalisation:

*SOCIAL POLICY: Policy makers and politicians made the decisions to opt for or against institutions as a way of "sorting out" specific types of deviancy and people with disabilities.

For most of the time, the issue of deinstitutionalisation did not interest most social policy theorists and researchers.

A minority demonstrated interests:

- In the concept of community care (Bulmer, 1987).

- In the role/burden of women as carers (often ignoring the fact that women are also the majority of clients and of members of the helping professions). Only recently has there been the beginning of a focus on the process of caring and its implications for women and men alike in terms of their self-and social identity Chamberlyne, 1994, 1996).

- In the process of decision making by formal planners concerning de-institutionalisation (Korman and Glennerster, 1990 and Tomlinson, 1992).This interest did not extend to other stakeholders, such as grass roots workers, clients and relatives.

159

- more social policy became influenced by economics, the more it focused on the *cost* of either institutional or non-institutional solutions and less on the non-cost advantages or disadvantages of different options (Knapp, 1992).

- Southern European and Swedish social policy researchers use the language of *marginalisation and de-marginalisation, exclusion and inclusion/integration* in the discussion of people coming out of institutions, making a clear connection between poverty and exclusion, a connection made less often in Britain.

Social Work as an applied discipline, the knowledge base of social work is taken from more than one discipline.

The critique of institutions, and that of psychiatry, found favour in social work in the 1960s and 1970s to the point of being taken for granted because it fitted well its pro-community stance and its "self-determination" ethical principle. Social workers always worked mainly in the community and placing a person especially a child in an institution, was perceived as a failure of the social work enterprise (Fischer and Marsh, 1986). The interest in the users' perspective, in advocacy and in the Social Role Valorisation approach is more represented in social work than in any other helping profession.

Research on alternatives to institutions has become part and parcel of social work evaluation research (Petch, 1992). The very few studies on the processes of de-institutionalisation in terms of impact on workers and users have been undertaken by social work researchers (Brandon, 1991; Ramon, 1992). The conceptual framework underlying this work utilises psychodynamic research on institutions (Menzies-Leith, 1988), social psychological and sociological approaches to individuals and institutions undergoing change (Jodelet, 1991; Breakwell, 1984; Tomlinson, 1992).

Although social workers are actively involved in the deinstitutionalisation and re-integration processes, rarely did social work scholars and researchers develop their own analytical framework of these phenomena. Those rare attempts include further elaboration of concepts such as self-directed work (Mullender and Ward, 1991), empowerment (Stevenson and Parsloe, 1993, Braye and Preston-Shoot, 1995) and participatory models of change (Ramon, 1992; Ramon and Sayce, 1993; Wistow and Barnes, 1995). This paucity is perhaps related to the tendency to rely on social policy to supply a conceptual framework, overlooking the fact that only rarely do social policy researchers ask the relevant questions from the social work angle. Relevant social work questions are often much more complicated than social policy questions as they span psychosocial issues, putting together individual, group and community levels, as well as the intellectual and emotional facets of existence.

Psychiatry has provided polemical contributions, evaluation of new methods of interventions piloted often by psychiatrists (e.g. home treatment, care management, sectorised services, day services), epidemiological studies (which allegedly have no underpinning ideology or conceptual framework from which questions are being drawn), and cost implications (Holloway, 1988; Holloway, 1994; McCrone and Thornicroft, 1995).

Burden studies of relatives have been conducted by psychiatrists and psychologists (McCarthy, 1988).

The studies add to our knowledge of the usefulness of specific interventions, but all too often do so from the perspectives of either psychiatrists or policy makers, and rarely include users. When users, relatives and frontline workers are included, the tools of inquiry are too rooted within a positivist framework to enable users to speak frankly and elaborate their views and feelings.

While focusing on outcome studies, little attention has been paid within psychiatry to the processes of deinstitutionalisation and to the construction of a conceptual framework.

Sociology has provided us with a critique of medicine and of professionalism (Friedson, 1994) simultaneously with the initial critique of institutionalisation.

Yet the approach to professionalism as mainly being focused on extending social control or making the latter more sophisticated, sounds hollow when in contact with the vast number of people who have a disability, who are vulnerable and poor, and who inevitably turn to professionals for protection and support. Invariably, professionals carry most of the burden that this type of work entails, in addition to that carried by sufferers and their relatives. This is not written in an attempt to argue that most professional activities should continue as they are: far from it. However, it seems to me to be more useful to treat professionals as a reflection of their society as well as a shaping power (in the same way that the media are) than as mere conductors of social control.

While professionals resisted for a long time the notion of abuse, the dedication of some of them and the readiness of many more to take account of abuse – especially sexual abuse – illustrate this mixture of care and control, of reflection and shaping (Kingston and Penhale, 1995).

Although sociology provided a critique on institutions, it did not afford an understanding of the processes of deinstitutionalisation, and in fact seems uninterested in the subject once the main argument has been won.

While early sociological contributions focused on "the moral career of the patient" more recent contributions do not seem to find the client who lives in the community that attractive as a subject of study in terms of the processes of identity formation, but focus more on the superficial aspects of life in the community (Prior, 1993). Rogers's work (Rogers, Pilgrim and Lacey, 1993), which focuses on the experience of psychiatric services by 500 users of mental health services, is an exception. However, this very important study has been largely left at the descriptive level, and therefore remains insufficient in terms of the issues we need to understand.

It is revealing that the many sociologists of deviance are not at all interested in decarceration, the term used by Scull (a British sociologist working in the US) to describe the initial forms of deinstitutionalisation. Instead, they prefer to focus on the penal system, where much less change has taken place.

Why has deinstitutionalisation not attracted the analytical and research attention it deserves?

Only speculation can be offered at this stage:

- the move to focus on outcomes in social policy, social work and psychiatric research meant a shift of focus from analysis to providing what the funders want to get

- the move to focus on outcomes also means a shift from a process-focused framework

- because of the emotive value of deinstitutionalisation it attracted polemical expressions rather than a systematic analysis

- the piecemeal nature of the change, and the co-existence of two systems, obscures the radical nature of the change, as do a number of formal new settings which nevertheless continue to maintain an institutional character.

*Approaches to Deinstitutionalisation: Western and Eastern Europe, Social
Policy, Social Work and Related Disciplines*

References

Basaglia, F. (1968) *L'istutizione negata*, Einuadi, Milano.

Bolwby, J. (1951) *Maternal Care and Mental Health*, World Health Federation, Geneva.

Brandon, D. (1991) *Innovation without Change?* Macmillan, Basingstoke.

Brandon, D. (1991) "Skills for Professionals". In: Ramon, S. (ed.) *Beyond Community Care: Normalisation and Integration Work*, Mind Macmillan, Basingstoke.

Brandon, D. Brandon, A. Brandon, T. (1995) *Advocacy: Power to People with Disabilities*, Venture Press, Birmingham.

Braye, S.& Preston-Shoot, M. (1995) *Empowerming Practice in Social Care*, The Open University, Milton Keynes.

Breakwell, G. (1984) *Threatened Identities*, Methuen, London.

Brown, P. (1985) *The Transfer of Care*, Routledge, London.

Bulmer, M. (1987) *The Social Base of Community Care*, Heinemann, London.

Chamberlyne, P. (1994) "Women and Social Policy in Germany". In: Clasen, J. & Freeman, R. (eds) *Social Policy in Germany*, Harvester Wheatsheaf, London.

Chamberlyne, P. "Changing Cultures of Care: underlying ideologies, policies and practicies in post-communist and post-fordist societies". In: Ramon, S. (ed.) (1996) *The Interface between Social Work and Social Policy*, Venture Press.

Cochrane, D. A. (1991) The AEGIS Campaign to improve standards of care in mental hospitals: A case study of the process of social policy change, Ph.D. Thesis, the London School of Economics, London.

Department of Health. (1992) *Health of the Nation*, HMSO, London.

Fischer, M.& Marsh, P. (1986) *In and Out of Care*, Routledge, London.

Foucault, M.(1973) *The Birth of the Clinic*, Tavistock, London.

Friedson, E. (1994) *Professionalism Reborn*, Academic Press, New York.

Goffman, I. (1961) *Asylums*, Penguin, Harmondsworth.

Goffman, I. (1963) *Stigma*, Penguin, Harmondsworth.

Graham, H. (1993) "Feminist Perspectives on Community Care". In: Bornat, J. (ed.) *Community Care: A Reader*, Macmillan, Basingstoke, 124-133.

Holloway, F. "Day Care and Community Support". In: Lavender, A.& Holloway, F. (ed) (1988) *Community Care in practice: Services for the Continuing Care Client,* Wiley, Chichester.

Holloway, F., Rutherford, D., Carson, J., Dunn, L. (1994) Elderly Graduates and a Hospital Closure programme: A Five year Follow-up Study, *Psychiatric Bulletin*, 18, 534-7.

Jodelet, D. (1991) *Social Representations of Madness*, Harvester, Hemel Hampstead.

Jones, M. (1952) *Social Psychiatry*, Tavistock, London.

Kingston, P. & Penhale, B. (1995) *Family Violence and the Caring Professions*, Macmillan, Basingstoke.

Knapp, M. (1992) *Care in the Community: Challenge and Demonstration*, Personal Social Services Research Unit, University of Kent, Canterbury.

Korman, N., Glennerster, H. (1990) *Closing a Hospital: The Darenth Park Project*, Bedord Square Press, London.

Mauri, D., De Leonardi, O., Gianichedda, M.G. (1984) *La Liberta e Terapeutica?* Fletrinelli, Roma.

McCarthy, B. (1988) "The Role of Relatives". In: Lavender, A & Holloway, F. (eds) *Community Care in Practice: Services for the Continuing Care Client*, Wiley, Chichster, 207-230.

McCrone, M. & Thornicroft, G. (1995) "The Economic Evaluation of Case Management". In: Moscarelli, M. Sartorius, N. (ed) T*he Economics of Schizophrenia* Wiley, Chichester.

Menzies-Leith, I. (1988) *Containing Anxiety in Institutions*, Free Associations, London.

Mosher, L. (1982) Italy's Revolutionary Mental Health Law: An Assessment, *American Journal of Psychiatry*, 139, 199-203.

Mosher, L. & Burti, L. (1989) *Community Mental Health: Principles and Practice*, Norton, New York.

Mullender, A. & Ward, D. (1991) *Self-Directed Groupwork*, Whiting and Birchwood, London.

Nirje, B. (1969) "The Normalisation Principle and its Human Management Implications". In: Kugel, R. & Wolfensberger, W. (eds) *Changing Patterns in Residential Services for the mentally Retarded*, President's Committee on Mental Retardation, Washington D.C., 255-287.

Oliver, M. (1990) *The Politics of Disability*, Macmillan, Basingstoke.

Perske, R. (1972) "The Risk of Dignity". In: Wolfensberger, W. (ed.) *The Principle of Normalisation in Human Services*, National Institute of Mental Retardation, Toronto, 194-206.

Petch, A. (1992) *A Home in the Community*, Avebury, Aldershot.

Prior, L. (1993) *The Social Organisation of Mental Illness*, Sage, Beverly Hills.

Ramon, S. (1985) *Psychiatry in Britain: Meaning and Policy*, Croom Helm, London.

Ramon, S. (ed.) (1990) *Psychiatry in Transition: British and Italian Experiences*, Pluto Press, London.

Ramon, S. (ed.) (1991) *Beyond Community Care: Integration and Normalisation Work*, Mind Macmillan, London.

Ramon, S. (1992) "The Workers' Perspective: Living with Ambivalence and Ambiguity". In: Ramon, S. (ed.) *Psychiatric Hospital Closure: Myths and Realities*, Chapman Hall, London.

Ramon, S. & Sayce, L. (1993) Collective User Participation: Implications for Social Work Education and Training, *Issues in Social Work Education*, 13, 2, 53-70.

Ramon, S. (1996) *Mental Health in Europe: Ends, Beginnings and Re-discoveries*, Mind Macmillan, Basingstoke.

Robb, B. Sans (1967) *Everything: A case to Answer*, Nelson, London.

Rogers, A., Pilgrim, D., Lacey, R. (1993) *Experiencing Psychiatry*, Mind Macmillan, Basingstoke.

Roosens, E. K. (1979) *Mental Patients in Town Life: Geel, Europe's First Therapeutic Community*, Sage. Beverly Hills.

Rose, N. (1985) *The Psychological Complex*, Heinemann.

Sacks, O. (1992) *Seeing Voices*, Penguin, Harmondsworth.

Scull, A. (1978) *Decarceration*, Prentice Hall, Englewood Cliffs, New Jersey.

Stainton, T. (1994) *Autonomy and Social Policy: Rights, Mental Handicap and Community Care*, Avebury, Aldershot.

Stevenson, O. & Parsloe, P. (1993) *Community Care and Empowerment*, Joseph Rowntree Foundation, York.

Swain, J. (ed.) (1992) *Disabling Barriers - Enabling Environments*, The Open University, Milton Keynes.

Tomlinson, D. (1992) "Planning After a Closure Decision: The Case for North East Thames Regional Health Authority". In: Ramon, S. (ed.) *Psychiatric Hospital Closure: Myths and Realities*, Chapman Hall, London, 49-82.

Vernon, A. (1996) "Consumer Choice and Independence", In: Ramon, S. (ed.) *International Perspectives on Health Social Work*, ATSWE Publications, Sheffield.

Wistow, G. & Barnes, M. (1995) "Central Nottinghamshire, England: A Case Study of Managed Innovation in Mental Health". In: Schulz, R. & Greenley, J. (eds) *Innovation in Community Mental Health: International Perspectives*, Prager, Westport and London,.

Wolfensberger, W. (1983) Social Role Valorisation: A Proposed New Term for the Principle of Normalisation, *Mental Retardation*, 21, 234-9.

**Part IV: The Role of Social Policy
and Social Work in Defining, Understanding and
Responding to Social Problems**

The Rediscovery of Child Neglect and Abuse

Marina Oghasian

The studying of child abuse in Armenia is a very difficult process, as it is not officially recognised. The reason for such public indifference is the cultural peculiarities of the Armenian family. The Armenian child is highly valued; s/he is a base of a strong and a happy family, the possibility of continuation of kin, the support in old age and a sense of life. All of these factors make a child "inviolable". But child abuse does exist in Armenia. Interviews with experts - teachers and traumatologists - illustrate its existence. Teachers can show children who are subjects of systematic physical punishment at home. The source of such kind of information is children who tell a teacher not to give them a poor mark, as they will be beaten up by their parents. In such a case when traumatologists were asked if they had ever had suspicious cases in their medical practice, in which the trauma was inflicted intentionally by parents or care-takers, nine out of ten answered "yes, we suspected sometimes, but we did not get into deeper understanding because nobody authorised us to take any initiative in such cases".

In studying child abuse in Armenia we take into account the relative nature of this phenomenon, as the different understanding of acceptable parental behaviour depends upon the culture of a given society. The culturally sensitive approach is the main key in studying child abuse and the first step in this process was the attempt to understand people's views about it.

The present sociological study was designed to explore the following issues:

- The cultural perceptions of children's personalities by adults.
- Parental awareness about children's rights.
- The degree of children's freedom of choice and speech.
- What is acceptable parental behaviour
- Unacceptable, or "bad parenting".

Because of the lack of information about intentionally inflicted trauma on children and taking into consideration the intentional nature of punishment, we also studied parental opinion about punishment methods as the basis for revealing child abuse cases.

The ultimate purpose of these studies was to gain sufficient understanding of this phenomenon so that social policy recommendations and a new legislative act on children could be developed with special social services for children enabling them to begin to function in the Armenian Republic.

According to these goals, we needed to study both parents' and children's views. One hundred parents and one hundred children were involved in the sample stratified according to their social status, their income, educational level and gender. Children's ages ranged from ten to sixteen, half presented by sex. The parent's sex was random, because the children decided which of their parents would fill out the questionnaire. It turned out that a lot of children gave it to their mothers. A questionnaire was used because of the failure of interviewing. This fact could be explained by the sensitivity of the issue: it was easier to share thoughts about child abuse on a paper, than *vis-à-vis* with a person.

Findings
Generally speaking, parental answers showed that most of them are kind and careful in their treatment of children. Yet this finding does not disprove the original hypothesis about the existence of child abuse in Armenia, since such treatment of children is not considered to be a normal behaviour but regarded as a deviation from the acceptable norm.

Typical attitudes of adults
These can be divided into two groups. The first group involved highly educated people who perceive their children as independent personalities with their own basic needs, interests, values and rights (James & Aven, 1985). The level of income does not influence parental opinion and treatment of children in this group.

The second group of parents differ considerably in their attitude. They think of their children as if they are their most favourite, but silent, property. For instance, this type of parents want their children to always live with them, even when the children will have their own families, because this gives the children the opportunity to be grateful to the parents for all their efforts in bringing them up. Also, such parents will forbid their child to have a friend whom they dislike. Such parents will not allow the child to go away in order to get a better education, because it is much more psychologically comfortable to have the child near to them. Children in such families tend to be much more vulnerable under emotional pressure and could be strictly punished when disobedient.

Typical attitudes of children
Children's opinions of parental power, and of their own freedom and rights, differ. We had expected children to be more pessimistic than their parents, assuming parents would be frank in their answers and children more disingenuous.

However, the findings illustrate that the children think about their parents as much less strict than indeed they are. This can be explained in different ways:

- Children are not frank in their answers, they only express their independence and freedom.

- Children choose positive answers about parental attitudes, hiding the real situation. In this way their wishes for their parents to be better are expressed.

These responses may also reflect the impact of gender on parental attitudes. Usually boys are brought up more freely, but the methods of punishing them are much stricter. Girls are treated more conservatively, but the methods of punishment are not heavy.

What type of parental behaviour is considered to be good enough and what kind of parental behaviour is absolutely unacceptable in the Armenian culture? Each respondent was asked to underline three points in the list of answers which corresponds to the concept of a "bad parent". What we have got is as follows:-

- The mother who deserts her new-born child at birth in hospital (72%)
- The parent suffering from alcoholism (40%)
- The mother who could become a prostitute because she has no other way of taking care of her child (30%)
- The parent satisfying all of the child's needs (4%)
- Very strict and cold parent (6%)
- The parent who betrayed his child because of another man/woman (44%)
- The parent whose child is neglected (6%)
- The parent who systematically punishes his children physically (46%)
- The parent who allows his child to earn money instead of going to school (46%)

Parents' and children's opinions about what constitutes bad parenting were very similar.

The use of methods of punishment as the first step on the way to becoming abusive parents

Respondents were given a table in which types of children's bad behaviour were shown vertically and types of punishment were shown horizontally. The respondents (both parents and children, who were asked to imagine that they have their

171

own children) should choose a type of punishment which according to them corresponds to the punishable act. The deprivation of pleasure is the most popular punishment among Armenian parents for children being naughty and disobedient at school and at home. The other methods of punishment used by them are standing the children in the corner of a room or isolating the child in the other room and ignoring them.

Do parents use physical force? *Yes they do*, 18% of adult respondents would beat the child if he hurts other people, 24% of parents would physically punish children when they lie, 22% would beat them up for stealing and shop-lifting, 14% would beat up a child if he commits an act dangerous to himself. Usually parents who are not well educated often use this type of punishment.

The majority of people respond to children's bad behaviour differently. Their first reaction could be aggressive, but then they will try to explain and to talk with a child.

What do children think about physical punishment? We can divide children-respondents into four groups according to their attitude to punishment.

- The first group of children do not choose methods of physical force, because their parents do not use such methods.

- The children who are subject to physical abuse will never use this method of influencing on their own children. They prefer more peaceful methods - a strict glance, a strict voice, explanation, negotiation, or reaching a compromise.

- Children who experience physical punishment tended to be more physically punitive.

- Children who are often beaten by their parents will use a physical force in future. For these children a physical punishment is normal parental behaviour.

It was suggested to the respondents that in many countries the law allows children to inform the police about abusive parents. The answer of both Armenian parents and children was: Parents are not machines and it may happen when parents can get angry with their children and even physically punish them, but it does not mean that they are responsible for it legally (62% of parents and 65% of children). However, parents as well as children felt the need to have established social services which will not only protect children's rights but also participate in the process of bringing up children. Such services should fit in with the cultural reality of Armenia.

In summing up, I should like to emphasise again that the main purpose of this work was making people admit that such problems do exist in Armenia. I have realised that we'll have a lot of obstacles *en route* to making people in Armenia aware of this issue. This study constitutes a first step in this direction.

In Jill Tonkin's words: "Reports of the rarity of child abuse and neglect . . . may be met with a measure of scepticism. It is well documented that the reported incidence of child maltreatment increases dramatically as public and professional awareness of the problem is enhanced and mandatory report laws are put into effect". (1987, p 207).

References
James, A. & Aven, G (1985) *Understanding abusive families*. Lexington Books, Mass.

Tonkin, J. (1987) *Cross-cultural approach to child abuse*. London.

Comprehending and Responding to Elder Abuse

Bridget Penhale and Paul Kingston

It is important when considering social problems to examine those phenomena which could be viewed as somewhat apart from the mainstream social concerns, and which in addition are relatively new "social problems". The purpose of this chapter is to consider the evidence surrounding the recent discovery of elder abuse as a social problem in need of attention to provide a necessary framework for an understanding of the phenomenon. Additionally, the potential strategies of intervention available in situations of the abuse and neglect of elders will be considered.

Introduction

In recent years there has been a gradual increase in concern about the abuse and neglect of elderly people by their carers in the domestic setting. However, recognition of elder abuse and neglect as a social problem in need of attention has been comparatively slow to happen both in the United Kingdom and elsewhere in Europe. In some respects, we are still now only at the early stages of a process of problem identification, and of positive action being taken to try to combat elder abuse and neglect. Elder abuse is not a new phenomenon (Stearns 1986), but it is effectively only since 1988 that the problem has really begun to be explored in the UK. There has been a steady increase in the amount of research and material published about the subject (Phillipson and Biggs, 1992; Pritchard, 1992; Decalmer and Glendenning, 1993; Bennett and Kingston, 1993; Eastman, 1994). Nevertheless, it was not until 1993 that there was any indication on the part of the British government to acknowledge elder abuse as a problem in need of attention (DOH, 1993). In September 1993, the junior Health Minister John Bowis, formerly launched the voluntary organisation "Action on Elder Abuse". This was the first indication that this social problem had been accepted at a political level.

What is known about elder abuse?

There are a number of difficulties in attempts to properly establish the exact scope of the field of enquiry and scale of the problem. Elder abuse and neglect are a complex and sensitive area to investigate satisfactorily (as was child abuse and domestic violence). Comparative norms are hard to come by, and do not seem to exist in the same way as have been established, for example, in work with children who have been abused.

From the work which has been conducted in the field, since Drs. Baker and Burston first remarked on the phenomenon of "Granny Bashing" in *Modern Geriatrics* and the *British Medical Journal* in 1975, a number of distinctive problem areas have been identified and documented. As long ago as 1983 these were characterised by Cloke as being problems with

- definition: there is no agreed definition in the UK or USA
- research: there are many methodological problems, due to small scale unrepresentative samples using different definitions
- incidence: it is difficult to substantiate claims due to the problems in research
- causation: full consideration of the theories of causation have not been developed in the UK
- family violence: insufficient attention to differences between the various forms of family violence may have clouded the issues
- procedures: the need for guidelines has not in general been fully accepted by professionals in this country.

All these points indicate that there have been problems in attempting to establish a comprehensive, sound, theoretical base to the phenomena. This is partly due to the lack of agreement concerning a standard definition, but also because of difficulties in researching the topic (see for example Bennett and Kingston 1993; Ogg and Munn-Giddings 1993). Many of the research samples have been very small and have concentrated on known cases which have already been identified by professionals. Results of surveys in the USA, although it is not entirely appropriate to draw generalisations from that country (due to the problems with definitions and with the research data, as outlined above), originally suggested that somewhere between 4% and 10% of the elderly population are either at risk of, or are experiencing, elder abuse from their caregivers (Crystal *et al.*, 1982; Gioglio and Blakemore, 1985; Pillemer and Finkelhor, 1988; US House of Representatives, 1981).

The only published survey of prevalence in the UK to date has indicated that potentially, 5% of the elderly population experience verbal abuse, and 2% experience physical or financial abuse (Ogg and Bennett, 1992).

From a European perspective, advances in understanding elder abuse and neglect vary widely and may be influenced by the relative developments in health and welfare systems designed for older people, allied to the present state of "gerontological expertise" in each country.

Northern European countries appear to be the most advanced, both in understanding and responding to the phenomena.

Sweden and Denmark

Data from Sweden and Denmark (Tornstam, 1989) suggest that from a survey of 943 men and women aged 18-74 (Sweden) and 1,535 (Denmark), 8% of the interviewees were familiar with a case of abuse that had occurred within the preceding twelve months. Service developments can be seen to follow a traditional social welfare tradition, avoiding the criminalistic route which seems to have been favoured by the US.

Finland

In a study of 1,225 people (480 men and 745 women) born during or before 1923 the rate of abuse for the total population was considered to be 6.7% (Kivela *et al.* 1992).

Greece

A Greek study in 1988-9 of 757 elderly respondents suggests that 117 had suffered some type of abuse; in addition 109 respondents knew of at least one case of elder abuse. The authors, Spinellis and Pitsough-Darrough (1991a, 1991b) suggest that these figures translate into a rate of 154 mistreated older people per 1,000 population.

These three studies are the only prevalence studies found by the authors outside the UK up to 1995. However, knowledge about the phenomena is apparent in other countries.

Ireland

Developments in Ireland have effectively only occurred in recent months; however "claimsmakers" like O'Loughlin (1990) have been arguing for several years that elder abuse exists in Ireland and deserves political attention. The present situation appears hopeful with the Minister of Health requesting a report on elder abuse from the National Council for the Elderly. O'Loughlin suggests that this timely event has ". . . notes of great hope for the hidden victims of elder abuse in Ireland" (1996).

At this point in time it is not possible to present a wholly accurate picture of developments in Europe. However, it can be seen that the emergence of knowledge in certain European countries, most notably the UK, and in Scandinavia has prompted other countries to consider if elder abuse is a social problem that they should be addressing.

Definitions

As previously stated, attempts to define elder abuse and neglect adequately have proved difficult: until now there has not been any firm agreement either in Europe or in the USA. This point cannot be overstated, especially when it is noted that in the USA the debate emerged in 1979. The fundamental difficulty seems to revolve around discussions about what should be included in, or excluded from, any definition of elder abuse and neglect. The sorts of questions which occur are about whether crimes such as muggings against elderly people should be considered as abuse (Pritchard,1992): are there distinctive qualities about elder abuse that distinguish it from other forms of familial violence (Bennett *et al.*, 1993) and should abuse be confined to a consideration purely of physical assault?

Then there are a set of broader issues around definitions generally: what does violation of rights mean; what of intentionality on the part of the "perpetrator" and the duality of direction of abuse in many situations? Recent reflections have started to consider abuse and neglect at three distinct levels: Macro, Mezzo and Micro (Bennett, Kingston and Penhale, 1995). Macro abuse refers to issues at a societal level: pensions, access to health and social care, fuel costs and institutional abuse. All of these issues are broadly encompassed under the sociological frameworks of the political economy of ageing (Phillipson, 1982) and structured dependency theories Townsend (1981) (for a wider analysis of the disempowering nature of these policies see Estes, 1979; Walker, 1986). Mezzo abuse refers to behaviours, attitudes and policies inflicted on older people at the community level (see for example Pritchard, 1992). These would include anti-social behaviours like gang abuse, ageism and forcing people to live what Phillipson (1992) calls "marginal lives".

Until now, the major focus has generally been on elder abuse and neglect at the micro level: conflict between two people in later life, usually in the domestic setting. Future debate may well expand the definition of abuse to encompass a wider range of ideologies and policies that clearly force older people to live on the periphery of society. It is clear also that attention needs to be paid to institutional abuse (Phillipson,1993).

It would seem that if a definition is too tightly drawn, then people get caught up in potentially lengthy and time-consuming considerations as to whether particular instances fall within the scope of that definition. This is to the detriment of a focus on more-pertinent issues, like which intervention strategies to use. This dilemma allows for some abusive situations to be excluded on the grounds that they do not quite fit the definition in use. Conversely, if the definition is too broad then potentially many situations could be considered to be abusive, particularly surrounding situations concerning the violation of the rights of elders (Callahan, 1988).

It is possible that different groups may need different definitions to suit their particular requirements: for example, researchers, politicians and practitioners may all need their own working definitions of what constitutes abuse (Bennett and Kingston, 1993). Perhaps it would be better at this point to acknowledge, accept and work with the different definitions, rather than lose time on searching for the ideal definition, covering all situations, which does not, and probably will not ever, exist.

Hallett (1995) whilst referring to definitions of child abuse suggests that: "what constitutes abuse changes over time and varies from place to place, reflecting differing national problems and professional and societal preoccupations".

This view is also found within the debate concerning elder abuse. It has already been suggested that abuse in the domestic setting is perhaps being overstated as a problem, particularly when compared with institutional abuse, a phenomenon with a lengthy history in the UK (Bennet *et al.*, 1993; UKCC 1994; Biggs, Kingston and Phillipson 1995).

Despite the difficulties already mentioned, in the late 1970s a number of definitions of elder abuse emerged. The usual types included physical, psychological, financial and neglect. A typical breakdown of behaviours falling into each category would include:

- Physical abuse: the infliction of physical harm, injury, physical coercion, sexual molestation and physical restraint

- Psychological abuse: the infliction of mental anguish, verbal and emotional abuse

- Material abuse: the illegal or improper exploitation and /or use of funds or materials, including property

- Active neglect: the refusal or failure to undertake a care giving obligation (including a conscious and intentional attempt to inflict physical or emotional stress on the elder)

- Passive neglect: the refusal or failure to fulfil a caretaking obligation (excluding a conscious and intentional attempt to inflict physical or emotional harm on the elder) (Wolf and Pillemer 1989).

It is also possible to list indicators of abuse, although it is very difficult to diagnose mistreatment with these indicators in isolation; linking a bruise to mistreatment, for example, would require more evidence than just the injury. The following are examples of some of the indicators that should raise a "high index of suspicion" especially if the explanation for the acquisition of the injury does not fit the presentation (Kingston and Penhale, 1994).

Physical indicators of abuse
- Unexplained bruises and welts on the face, lips, mouth, torso, back, buttocks, thighs, in various stages of healing
- Clustered, forming regular patterns
- Reflecting shape of article used (cord, buckle)
- On several different surface areas of the body
- Regularly appear after absence, week-end or holidays
- Unexplained burns; cigar, cigarette, especially on soles, palms, back or buttocks
- Immersion burns (sock-like on feet, glove-like on hands, doughnut-shaped on buttocks or genitalia)
- Patterned like an iron or rope burns on arms, legs, neck, torso
- Unexplained fractures: to skull, nose, facial structure, in various stages of healing
- Multiple or spinal abrasions
- Unexplained lacerations or abrasions to mouth, lips, gums or eyes, to external genitalia

Sexual abuse
- Difficulty in walking or sitting
- Torn, stained or bloody underclothing
- Pain or itching in genital area
- Bruises or bleeding in external genitalia, vaginal or anal areas
- Venereal disease
(Bennett *et al.*, 1993).

In recent years, terminology has developed in the US to include the concept of "inadequate care", suggesting that elder abuse could be defined as:

"actions of a caretaker that create unmet needs for the elderly person" and neglect as the "failure of an individual responsible for care-taking to respond adequately to established needs for care" (Fulmer and O'Malley, 1987).

Fulmer and O'Malley's rationalisation for usage of the terminology "inadequate care" was pragmatic. They argued that it is easier to reach consensus on what is considered adequate, or inadequate, care than what are endorsed as acceptable behaviours within families. In addition, health and welfare professionals would be less averse to use the description "inadequate care" than to define the interaction as abuse or neglect, with all the emotive and negative connotations which may be attached to such labels. Fulmer and O'Malley (1987) present a list of injuries and behaviours that could be found in situations of inadequate care, but do not categorise them under separate headings:

Manifestations of Inadequate Care

Abrasions	Dehydration
Lacerations	Malnutrition
Contusions	Inappropriate clothing
Burns	Poor hygiene
Freezing	Over sedation
Depression	Under medication
Fractures	Untreated problems
Sprain	Dislocations

The fundamental problem with all these definitions relates to their subjective nature.

Reports of which type of abuse is most common vary greatly depending on the survey considered. Some early research from the US suggested that most instances of elder abuse are recurrent and part of a pattern, rather than a single incident (O'Malley *et al.*, 1981). Other researchers in the US have found that neglect is the most prevalent (Valentine and Cash, 1986), whilst yet further research from the US has suggested that psychological abuse (Block and Sinott, 1979) or physical abuse (Lau and Kosberg, 1979) are the most common. These early studies were, however, small-scale samples using different definitions.

How large is the problem?

The scale of the problem of elder abuse and neglect has also been very difficult to ascertain. It has been suggested that:

"Research in the preceding nine years before Pillemer's (1988) prevalence study ... had addressed every conceivable perspective of elder abuse without knowing what percentage of the population is abused, or are potentially at risk of abuse". Kingston (1990).

There are now several prevalence studies all indicating similar prevalence rates of abuse and neglect.

Table 1: Comparison of prevalence rates of US/UK/Canada			
Types of abuse	Rate%		
	US	UK	Canada
All types	3.2	—	—
Physical	2.0	2.0	0.5
Verbal	1.1	5.0	1.4
Neglect	0.4	—	0.4
Financial	—	2.0	2.5

Source: US study: Pillemer and Finkelhor (1988); UK study: Ogg and Bennett (1992); Canadian Study: Podnieks (1989).

Table taken from Bennett and Kingston, (1993). Reprinted with kind permission of Chapman and Hall.

The Boston study by Pillemer and Finkelhor (1988) was the first prevalence study that prompted other researchers to consider replication. It was conducted in the Boston metropolitan area, the sample comprised 2,020 people aged 65 years and over. The interview schedule was divided into abuse and neglect, the physical abuse category was operationalised using the Conflicts Tactics Scale (Straus, 1979). Psychological abuse was rated by repeated insults and threats, forming a category of "chronic verbal aggression". Neglect was defined as having any one of ten activities of daily living withheld by a close family member more than ten times in the preceding year. The overall prevalence rate of 32 per 1,000 led the researchers to suggest that "if a survey of the entire United States were to find a rate similar to the one in Boston it would indicate between 701,000 and 1,093,560 abused elders in the nation" (Pillemer and Finkelhor, 1988).

The methodology utilised in the UK used questions which formed part of a larger household survey asked at random sites throughout the UK (Ogg and Bennett, 1992). The total sample of the survey was 2,130, of which 593 respondents were aged over 65 years. The questions were loosely based on the Conflict Tactics Scale (Straus, 1979). If the UK figures are translated into 95% confidence intervals, victims of verbal abuse could range from 561,000 to 1,123,000 people; victims of physical abuse 94,000-505,000 and victims of financial abuse 94,000 to 505,000. These figures are clearly substantial, but there are strong reasons to suggest that they may well underestimate the true number of victims of abuse and neglect.

Firstly, it is likely that many frail, impaired older people would not be in a position to answer the questions in numbers representing their volume in the population; they may thus be under-represented in the research sample. Secondly, the responses of the 1,366 adults aged sixteen and over asked whether they abused an older person must be considered with caution. Of the respondents, 129 (9%) acknowledged verbally abusing someone of pensionable age and twelve (0.9%) stated that they had physically abused an elder. It is apparent from research data that when "sensitive topics" (Lee and Renzetti, 1990) are approached considerable ethical difficulties are experienced (Bennett and Kingston, 1993). Respondents to research on sensitive issues often reply in a "socially respectable" way, often denying the size of the problem; this needs to be taken into account when considering the findings.

The third difficulty relates again to the 593 older people who responded to the survey, with 32 (5%) reporting being victims of verbal abuse; nine (2%) reporting being physically abused; and nine (2%) victims of financial abuse. It is highly likely that these reports represent an underestimate from the total population: US research suggests that victims of abuse often do not report the situation (Tomita, 1982; Fulmer and O'Malley, 1987).

The dynamics of abuse
In attempting to determine the dynamics of elder abuse, most of the early research concentrated on trying to establish a profile of victims of abuse. Initial studies did, unfortunately, settle on the "typical victim" as being a frail, dependent female of

75+ years who is impaired (either physically or mentally or both) and living with an adult child (O'Malley *et al.* 1981; Lau and Kosberg 1979). The levels of dependency due to the degree of impairments experienced were considered to be a source of extreme stress for the caregiver. Additionally, the degree of frailty of the victim was felt to put the victim in a position of high vulnerability and high risk of abuse occurring. There seemed to be an assumption within such studies that the abuser was not really concerned with the well-being of the victim and that they were motivated by greed. Such a view of elderly people as being dependent and vulnerable may add to widely held negative views and attitudes about elderly people which appear throughout western society. One commentator from the US has suggested that one of the reasons that elder abuse gained the status of a legitimate social problem there may be strongly connected with the fact that it accorded with the predominant focus of research on ageing in the US: a focus on the problems associated with ageing (Baumann 1989).

Research which followed some of the early studies in the US has tended to focus on the characteristics of abusers. These studies should be considered to be empirically more informative because of their improved methodology. The assumptions outlined above about the stress of caring have generally not been upheld. Instead, abusers appear to be more likely (when compared with non-abusive carers) to have alcohol- or drug-related problems and mental health psychological problems (Pillemer, 1986; Bristowe and Collins, 1989; Wolf, 1986; Homer and Gilleard, 1990; Grafstrom, 1992; Anetzberger, 1994). These patterns seem to be particularly relevant in situations involving physical or psychological abuse. There may also, in such situations, be a history of long-term difficulties in the relationship between the parties (Homer and Gilleard, 1990; Grafstrom, 1992). In the debate concerning dependency, some investigators have indicated that abusers may be highly dependent on their victims: financially (Hwalek *et al.*, 1986) and possibly also with regard to housing and transportation (Pillemer, 1986).

From research in the US, it would seem that there are different characteristics in victims, depending on the type of abuse which is apparent. To expand slightly, Wolf (1989), after considering the US research of the past 20 years, suggests that elders who are neglected appear to fit the characteristics of the stereotypical victim (as presented above), and are a source of extreme stress to their caregiver. Those elders who are physically or psychologically abused are less likely to be physically dependent but may have emotional difficulties. This group of elders usually live with their abuser who is dependent on them, especially financially. Elders who are victims of financial abuse are also likely to be less dependent on physical care from relatives and more likely to be unmarried and to live alone (but in comparatively isolated situations) (Wolf, 1989 cited in Bennett and Kingston, 1993).

Although there is still uncertainty regarding the rates of elder abuse either as an overall figure or with regard to the various sub-types, it can be stated with some certainty that abuse within the domestic setting occurs across all ethnic and socio-economic groups and in both urban and rural areas (Steuer and Austin, 1980). Abusers may be partners or adult children. Finkelhor (1983) suggested that when the probability for abuse is adjusted to relate to the amount of time that the abuser spends with the victim, men are much more likely to be involved in abusive acts, particularly physically violent acts.

With regard to the gender of abusers, many of the early studies reported that those who abuse were more likely to be female, usually relatives (Eastman, 1984). Further analysis of such data, which distinguished between physical abuse and neglect, discovered a significant gender difference: that men were more likely to be involved in physical violence and women in neglectful acts (Miller and Dodder, 1987). These researchers suggested that because categories of neglect (including self-neglect) were very high in the studies they reviewed, this to a large extent explained why it had appeared that the majority of perpetrators were women. In a later study, Pillemer and Finkelhor (1988) discovered that abusers were more likely to be spouses than adult children or non-relatives. In most cases, however, perpetrators were close family members, usually living with the victim.

This same study found nearly equal numbers of men and women in their sample of victims. When the figures were adjusted to account for the actual numbers of men and women in the total population of elderly people, the risk of abuse for men was twice that existing for women. However, in terms of the severity of abuse, this tended to be greater for women (Pillemer and Finkelhor, 1988). There are a number of possible reasons why a higher proportion of women may come to the attention of professionals. It may be that women are more likely to seek assistance or to report abuse than men. Additionally, the populations surveyed may be made up largely of women or of very elderly people most of whom are female (O'Malley *et al.* 1981). It is also possible that more assistance is necessary for women due to the severity of their injuries, resulting in them coming to the attention of professionals which then leads to the conclusion that the risk to older women of being abused is higher than the risk to men (Pillemer and Finkelhor, 1988). Abusive behaviour by women, which is more likely to be psychological or passively neglectful, may be much less likely to result in any treatment (of injury) for the male victim and may thus be comparatively unnoticed by professionals. These aspects require further research effort in future.

Barriers to identification
Recognition and identification of elder abuse and neglect is difficult because there is uncertainty about definitions, and a lack of agreement as to what actually constitutes abuse. There are a number of issues surrounding the detection of abuse and abusive situations. One of the most relevant points is that some ageing processes cause changes which are difficult to distinguish from aspects of assault, so it can be difficult for doctors to be sure how an injury might have occurred (Homer and Gilleard, 1990; Bennett *et al.*, 1993). Additionally, there are other complex reasons why abuse is not recognised. These include

- societal views about the family which promote a view of family life as harmonious and protective
- societal views about violence which promote a view of "normal" violence which is acceptable provided it doesn't go "too far"
- societal views about ageing which promote a view which may mean that abuse is undetected as it is seen as due to the ageing process.

The following factors may also be relevant here:

- the social isolation of many elderly people may mean that abuse is undetected (elderly people do not attend school or work or may be house bound)
- problems in obtaining access to victims due to their isolation or the reluctance of carers (or victims) to allow access
- reluctance to report (or discuss) abuse by victims (see below)
- professional difficulty in detecting abuse (see below)

A reluctance to report abuse by victims can make detection even more difficult. One US survey of professionals and agencies involved in elder abuse consisted of 336 completed questionnaires of which 183 contained reports of abuse occurring over an eighteen-month time frame (O'Malley *et al.*, 1981). From this survey it appeared that only 24% of known cases of abuse were reported by the victims involved and in 36% of these situations although the case had already been identified, the victims did not acknowledge that abuse had occurred.

There are a number of reasons why this might happen. These include:

- Fear of making the situation worse, or of retaliation
- Fear of being removed from home
- Assumption of blame for the abuser's behaviour (seen also within child and spouse abuse)
- Guilt at having an abusive child (Steinmetz, 1978)
- Bonds of affection which are stronger than any desire to alter a situation
- Societal views about "happy families" and rights to privacy.

Within society generally there is a reticence to accept that abuse exists. Associated with this taboo is a stigma which is attached to perpertrators of all forms of abuse. This may result in a reluctance by abusers to seek assistance for their difficulties (for fear of attracting stigma). Alternatively, there may be absolute denial of the existence of any problems.

As seen above, barriers to identification may arise at the level of societal views and attitudes and also at a more individual level for both victims and abusers. A further series of problems may arise at the professional level within the decision-making process involving abusive situations. These may be due to: a lack of knowledge and/or training about abuse; a lack of clear procedures concerning action to be taken; inadequate resources (financial and other); priority given to rights of privacy of individuals and families; personal and professional attitudes and biases (Penhale, 1993; Kingston and Penhale, 1994; Kingston and Phillipson, 1994). Such attitudinal difficulties can be overcome but there must be an awareness of their existence and a willingness to deal with them if such problems are to be appropriately resolved.

Interventions in elder abuse

There are also possible difficulties concerning intervention strategies for victims of elder abuse and for the treatment of abusers. One of the most crucial professional dilemmas to deal with is that of attaining and maintaining a balance between the right to self-determination and protection of the individual. Elderly people have the right in most cases to be autonomous. It is not uncommon for elders to refuse offers of assistance; generally unless individuals are mentally incompetent, in a legal sense, their decisions about such offers should be accepted. Fulmer and O'Malley (1987) found that elderly people preferred independence over safety and protection. Professionals need to be able to accept and work with such situations when they occur.

Another area of difficulty within intervention surrounds the fact that due to the lack of strategies which have so far proved to be effective, workers may not feel they can deal with abusive situations. They may then either avoid such situations or set low-level objectives. Another possibility is that, in their desire to do something (anything) to help, an inappropriate intervention may be offered.

In addition, the severity of some situations may not be fully appreciated by professionals. Many of them would appear to consider their options for intervention as consisting in a continuum from least to most disruptive in terms of the effects on those involved (Phillips, 1989). Those strategies which are viewed as the most disruptive seem to be reserved for use very much as a last resort (SSI, 1992). A reluctance to employ such strategies "unless absolutely necessary" may mean that a situation which requires intensive intervention may be inaccurately perceived by the professional. The result may be a mismatch between the possible severity of the situation and the methods employed to deal with it (Phillips, 1989). Those involved in such situations need to find ways of preventing such tendencies from occurring if possible.

It can be difficult, too, for professionals to work effectively with both victims and abusers; people may show particular skill with one or other group and should to be able to develop expertise in these areas. It is also important that workers do not become over-protective towards victims of abuse. Respecting the elder's right to autonomy can be difficult, but is essential. The principle of empowering the individual is crucial in this type of work (Bennett and Kingston, 1993): individuals may require support and assistance but they must also be empowered to find their own solutions to their problems. Phillipson (1992) proposes that policies to address elder abuse should develop within the context of empowerment and advocacy. For him, the emphasis should be on the enabling of elders to live lives free from abuse (including neglect) and on the promotion of abilities for self-care in later life.

Generally, health and social care workers are trained in therapeutic rather than corrective methods. There may thus be a reluctance to use what legal remedies exist due to connotations about punishment, blame and control. Such issues need to be addressed by professionals if they are to be successful in working in these complex situations. Despite recent indications in the UK that some reform of the law may be necessary (Law Commission, 1993), any legislative change is likely to take several years to effect. At present, practitioners need to help individuals to use the existing law properly, in order to gain some measure of protection and redress.

Intervention strategies are still in the early stages of development in the UK. It appears that, currently, intervention tends to focus on the provision of practical services to alleviate situations (although as Homer and Gilleard,1990 found, this may not resolve the problems). The main emphasis seems to be on maintaining people in the community wherever possible (SSI, 1992). Additionally, some therapeutic interventions are employed by practitioners for situations involving relationship difficulties, and there have been suggestions that some "family therapy" techniques might be adapted and used with elders and their families and carers (Browne, 1989; Rathbone-McCuan *et al.*, 1983).

What is apparent is that there is a pressing need for a number of different techniques and interventions within this field: from well-developed and co-ordinated practical services to more-intensive therapeutic methods; from education and counselling about the intrinsic costs of caring to the provision of "safe houses" (akin to refuges, but for elders) or alternative accommodation for those who abuse. Access to services on an emergency basis may be required and assistance for abusers needs to be developed (McCreadie, 1991; Riley, cited in SSI, 1993).

Also necessary is careful and continuous monitoring of the number and type of cases reported, alongside the service responses that occur, in order to ensure that the needs of individuals are being met in the most appropriate ways (SSI, 1993). As well as training to provide knowledge about elder abuse in its many forms, there is a need for information about which strategies work and in what circumstances (Penhale, 1992). This then needs to be shared with all professionals involved in cases of elder abuse and neglect. It is hoped that these further developments will evolve alongside attention being paid to the goal of prevention of abuse. The challenge of this latter part of the century is to formulate and provide acceptable and appropriate solutions to this most pernicious of social problems.

References
Anetzberger, G. J., Korbin, J..E. and Austin, C. (1994) "Alcoholism and Elder Abuse", *Journal of Interpersonal Violence*, 9 (2):184-193.

Baker, A. A. (1975) "Granny Bashing," *Modern Geriatrics* 5, (8):20-4.

Baumann, E. (1989) "Research Rhetoric and the Social Construction of Elder Abuse" in Best, J. (Ed.) *Images of Issues: Typifying Contemporary Problems,* Aldine, New York.

Bennett, G.C. and Kingston, P.A. (1993) *Elder Abuse: Theories, Concepts and Interventions*, Chapman and Hall, London.

Bennett, G.C., Kingston, P.A. and Penhale, B. (1995) *Elder Abuse: Health and Welfare Perspectives.* Chapman and Hall, London,.

Biggs, S., Kingston, P. A. and Phillipson, C. (1995) *Elder Abuse in Perspective.* Open University Press, Milton Keynes

Block, M. R. and Sinott, J. D. (1975) *The Battered Elder Syndrome: An exploratory study*, College Park, University of Maryland Centre on Ageing.

Bristowe, E. and Collins, J. (1989) "Family mediated abuse of non-institutionalised frail elderly men and women in British Columbia." *Journal of Elder Abuse and Neglect*, 1 (1): 45-64.

Browne, K. (1989) "Family Violence: Elder and Spouse Abuse" in Howells, K. and Hollin, C. R. (Eds) *Clinical Approaches to Violence*, John Wiley and Sons, London.

Burston, G. R. (1975) "Granny Bashing," *British Medical Journal*, 3 (6): 592,.

Callahan, J. J. (1988) "Elder Abuse: Some Questions for Policy Makers", *Gerontologist*, 28, 4: 438-458.

Cloke, C. (1983) *Old Age Abuse in the Domestic Setting - A Review*, Age Concern, Mitcham,.

Crystal, S., Dejowski, E., Daiches, S. and Fleming, C. (1982) *Adult protective services: The state of the art.* Project Focus. New York Human Resources Administration: New York.

Decalmer P. and Glendenning, F. (Eds) (1993) *The Mistreatment of Older People*, Sage, London.

Dept. of Health (1993) *No Longer Afraid: The Safeguard of Older People in Domestic Settings*, HMSO, London.

Eastman, M. (1984) *Old Age Abuse*, Age Concern, Portsmouth.

Eastman, M. (1994) *Old Age Abuse: A New Perspective*, Chapman Hall, London.

Finkelhor, D. "Common Features of Family Abuse". in Finkelhor, D., Gelles, R. J., Hotaling, G. and Straus. M. (Eds) (1983) *The Dark Side of Families: Current Family Violence Research* Sage, Newbury Park.

Fulmer, T. and O'Malley, T. (1987) *Inadequate care of the elderly: A health care perspective on abuse and neglect*, Springer, New York.

Gioglio, G. R. and Blakemore, P. (1985) *Elder abuse in New Jersey: The knowledge and experience of abuse among older New Jerseyians.* Trenton: New Jersey Division of Youth and Family Services, Bureau of Reserach and New Jersey Department of Community Affairs, New Jersy Division of Ageing.

Grafstrom, M., Nordberg, A. and Wimblad, B. (1992)Abuse is in the eye of the beholder: reports by family members about abuse of demented persons in home care, A total population based study. *Scandinavian Journal of Social Medicine*, 21 (4) 247-255.

Hallett, C. (1995) "Child Abuse: an Academic Overview", in Kingston, P. and Penhale, B. (Eds) *Family Violence and the Caring Professions*, London, Macmillan.

Homer, A. and Gilleard, C. (1990) "Abuse of Elderly People by their Carers". *British Medical Journal*, 301: 1359-1362.

Hwalek, M.; Sengstock, M. and Lawrence, R. (1986) "Assessing the probability of abuse of the elderly," *Journal of Applied Gerontology*, 5, 153-173.

Lau, E. E. and Kosberg, J. I. (1979) "Abuse of the elderly by informal care providers" *Ageing* 299, 10-15.

Kingston, P.A. (1990) *Elder Abuse*. Unpublished MA thesis, University of Keele, Staffordshire.

Kingston, P.A. and Penhale, B. (1994) "Recognition of a major problem: Assessment and management of elder abuse and neglect." *Professional Nurse*. 9 (5): 343-347.

Kingston, P.A. and Phillipson, C. (1994) "Elder Abuse and Neglect". *British Journal of Nursing*, 3 (22): 1171-90.

Kivela, S.L.; Paivi, K.S.' Kesti, E.; Pahkala, K. and Ijas, M.L. (1982) Abuse in Old Age - epidemiological data from Finland. *Journal of Elder Abuse and Neglect*, 4(3):1-18.

Lau, E. and Kosberg, J. (1979) "Abuse of the elderly by informal care providers." *Ageing* 299:10-15.

Law Commission (1993) *Mentally Incapacitated and other Vulnerable Adults*: *Public Law Protection* Consultation paper 130, HMSO, London.

Lee, R. and Renzetti, C.M. (1990)"The problems of researching sensitive topics." *American Behavioural Science*, 33 (5):510-28.

McCreadie, C. (1991) *Elder Abuse: An Exploratory Study*, Age Concern Institute of Gerontology, London.

Miller, R. B. and Dodder, R. A. (1989) "The Abused: Abuser Dyad; Elder Abuse in the State of Florida" in Filinson, R. and Ingman, S. R. (Eds) (1989) *Elder Abuse: Practice and Policy*, Human Sciences Press, New York.

Ogg, J. and Bennett, G.C. (1992) "Elder Abuse in Britain", *British Medical Journal*, 305: 998-9.

Ogg, J. and Munn-Giddings (1993) "Researching elder abuse", *Ageing and Society* 13 (3): 389-414.

O'Loughlin, A. (1990) Old age abuse in the domestic setting: definition and identification, *Irish Social Worker* 9(2):4-7.

O'Loughlin, A. (1996) Elder Abuse: A perspective from Ireland. *Special Edition: Social Work in Europe.*

O'Malley, H.; Segars, H. and Perez, R. (1981) *Elder Abuse in Massachusetts: A Survey of Professionals and Paraprofessionals* Legal Research and Services for the Elderly, Boston, Massachusetts.

Penhale, B. (1992) "Elder Abuse: an overview", *Elders*, 1, 3, 36-48.

Penhale, B. (1993) "The Abuse of Elderly People: Considerations for Practice", *British Journal of Social Work*, 23, 2, 95-112.

Phillips, L.R. (1983) "Abuse and neglect of the frail elderly at home: an exploration of theoretical relationships." *Journal of Advanced Nursing*, 8:379-392.

Phillips, L. R. (1989) "Issues Involved in Identifying and Intervening in Elder Abuse," in Filinson, R. and Ingman, S.R. (Eds) *Elder Abuse: Practice and Policy* Human Sciences Press, New York.

Phillipson, C. (1982) *Capitalism and the Construction of Old Age.* Macmillan, London.

Phillipson, C. (1992) "Confronting Elder Abuse". *Generations Review* 2 (3): 2-3.

Phillipson, C. and Biggs, S. (1992) U*nderstanding Elder Abuse: A Training Manual for Helping Professions* . Longman, London.

Phillipson, C. (1993) "Abuse of Older People: Sociological Perspectives" in Decalmer, P. and Glendenning, F. (Eds) *The Mistreatment of Elderly People*, Sage, London.

Pillemer, K. A. (1986) "Risk factors in elder abuse: Results from a case-control study" in Pillemer, K. A. and Wolf, R. S. (Eds) *Elder Abuse: conflict in the Family* Auburn House, Dover, Massachusetts.

Pillemer, K. A. and Finkelhor, D. (1988) "The prevalence of elder abuse: A random sample survey," *Gerontologis*t, 28 (1): 51-57.

Podnieks, E. and Pillemer, K.A. (1989) *Survey on Abuse of the Elderly in Canada.* Ryerson Polytechnical Institute, Toronto.

Pritchard, J. (1992) *The Abuse of Elderly People: A Handbook for Professionals* Jessica Kingsley, London.

Pritchard, J. (1993) "Dispelling some myths", *Journal of Elder Abuse and Neglect.* 5 (2): 27-37.

Rathbone-McCuan, E.; Travis A. and Voyles, B. (1983) "Family Intervention: the task-centred approach", in Kosberg, J. I. (Ed.) *Abuse and Maltreatment of the Elderly: Causes and Interventions* J. Wright, Boston, Massachusetts.

Riley P. (1993) in Social Services Inspectorate *No Longer Afraid: The safeguard of older people in domestic settings* HMSO, London.

Social Services (1993) *No Longer Afraid: the safeguard of older people in domestic settings* HMSO, London.

Social Services Inspectorate (1992) *Confronting Elder Abuse* HMSO, London

Spinellis, C. D. and Pitsough-Darrough, (1991a) *Elder victims of abuse and neglect* EKLOGH, Athens, Greece.

Spinellis, C. D. and Pitsough-Darrough, E. (1991b) "Elder abuse in Greece: A descriptive study". in G. Kaizer, H. Kurry and H. J. Albrecht (eds) *Victims and criminal justice* (pp311-38) Freiburg: Eigenverlag Max-Planck-Institute.

Stearns, P. (1986) "Old Age Family Conflict: The Perspective of the Past". In Pillemer, K. A. and Wolf, R.S. (eds) *Elder Abuse: Conflict in the Family.* Auburn House, Dover Massachusetts.

Steinmetz, S. K. (1978) "Battered Parents", *Society* 15, 5, 54-5.

Steuer, J. and Austin, E. (1980) "Family Abuse of the Elderly", *Journal of the American Geriatrics Society,* 28 (8): 372-6.

Straus, M. A. (1979) Measuring intra-family conflict and violence: the conflict tactics (CT) scales. *Journal of Marriage and the Family.* 41:75-88.

Tomita, S. K. (1982) (1982) "Detection and treatment of elderly abuse and neglect: A protocol for health care professionals." *Physical Therapy and Occupational Therapy in Geriatrics,* 2 (2) 37-51.

Townsend, P. (1981) (1981) "The Structured Dependency of the Elderly: The Creation of Social Policy in the Twentieth Century." *Ageing and Society,* 1 (1):5-28.

Tornstam, L. (1989) Abuse of the elderly in Denmark and Sweden:Results from a population study. *Journal of Elder Abuse and Neglect.* 1(1):1-18.

United Kingdom Central Council for Nursing, (1994) Midwifery and Health Visiting *Professional Conduct: Occasional Report on Standards of Nursing in Nursing Homes.* UKCC, London.

United States House of Representatives, Select Committee on Aging (1981) *Elder Abuse: The Hidden Problem.* Washington, DC: US Government Printing Office

Valentine, D. and Cash, T. (1986) "A definitional discussion of elder mistreatment" *Journal of Gerontological Social Work*, 9, 17-28.

Walker, A. (1986) Pensions and the Production of Poverty in Old Age. In Phillipson, C. and Walker, A. (eds) *Ageing and Social Policy: A Critical Assessment.* Gower, Aldershot.

Wolf, R. S. (1986) "Major findings from three model projects on elder abuse" in Pillemer, K. A. and Wolf, R.S. (Eds) *Elder abuse: conflict in the family* Auburn House, Dover, Massachusetts.

Wolf, R. S.; Godkin, M. and Pillemer, K. A. (1984) *Elder Abuse and Neglect: Final report from three model projects* University Centre on Aging: University of Massachusetts Medical Centre, Worcester, Massachusetts.

Wolf, R. S. (1993) "Testimony before the Subcommittee of Human Services: Select Committee on Aging; US House of Representatives Hearings on Elder Abuse" in Bennett, G. and Kingston, P. *Elder Abuse: Concepts, theories and interventions* Chapman & Hall, London.

Wolf, R.S. and Pillemer, K.A.(1989) *Helping Elderly Victims: The reality of elder abuse.* Columbia University Press, New York

Social Integration of Children with Disabilities in India

Mithu Alur

Introduction

Social integration, which means "to be an integral part of a society, to participate within a community with a degree of equality", is a far cry for Indian disabled people. Programmes of poverty alleviation, caste and gender issues, and rural upliftment take a higher priority, putting the disabled last on the list of developmental activity. The disabled are very much a part of these areas, but, mainly due to political weakness they remain a neglected segment, kept out of the political and social framework of social policy. India is one of the few developing countries where the State still relies heavily on the voluntary sector for providing basic services for the disabled. More services are provided by non-governmental agencies than government. Due to the fact that voluntary agencies can only serve on a micro level the services remain patchy and not uniform around the country, they cover only the tip of the iceberg. Rural areas still remain out of reach and, considering the fact that the majority of disabled people live in these areas, this very significant group of the Indian population remain unserved. Far from being socially integrated into society, the vast numbers of India's disabled are marginalised out of mainstream society.

This chapter records the development of services within India's historical perspective, the size and definition of the problem, the services that exist in the governmental and non-governmental (NGO) sectors and concludes with an analysis of why social integration has not happened as far as the disabled are concerned. I do not want to sound too negative since over the years there have been many success stories of talented individuals who have been employed as lawyers, chartered accountants, publishers, librarians, musicians. In fact, in every field of life in India, hundreds of disabled people have shown their competency, their skills and abilities. But these are exceptional people who have achieved *despite* the lack of social integration policies provided by the State. This chapter proposes to analyse the State's policy and legislation, the work of the NGOs and how this has impeded or facilitated integration on a macro level. The ground realities show that a vast majority of India's disabled population remain out of mainstream society, due to faulty attitudes, lack of services, lack of political lobby, lack of statute and legislation and above all due to the country's lack of a national policy. This chapter highlights what is happening to the majority, in a country which has the world's largest number of disabled people.

A Short Historical Perspective
Educational Policy and Marginalisation

The history of modern Indian education commences from the time India became a part of the British Empire. The British were not anxious to introduce education to the masses in India. Colonial education was not complementary or supplementary to indigenous educational practices, but was in fact planned as an alternative: indigenous models which existed, such as, the gurukul system of education, were removed and replaced by the western model.

A dichotomy was created, between the élite upper class, whose sons and daughters were educated to be Anglicised "more British than the British" and those who could not speak the Queen's English were considered to be socially of a lower level.

The idea behind education was to create a cadre of Indians who would think and express themselves like the British . . . well reflected by Macaulay's famous statement : "We want a class of persons, Indian in blood and colour, but English in tastes, in opinions, in morals and in conduct" (Sharp, 1952).

The nationalists' point of view was that efforts should be directed to create "not a lesser England but a greater India" and that a national system of education should be evolved, based on Indian traditions and suited to the life, needs and aspirations of the Indian people. However, the pleas of national stalwarts like Dadabhai Naoroji, Gokhale, and Gandhi fell on deaf ears and education remained restricted to the upper and upper-middle classes. It became compartmentalised, including the "haves" and excluding the "have nots", resulting in a split and alienation of the masses. Due to the imported model of education, this divide dominates the country and even today raises many questions about social integration of a marginalsed group such as the disabled coming from low socio-economic levels of our society.

When India obtained her independence on 15 August 1947, a massive movement was started towards educating the masses. In 1964, the Government of India appointed an educational commission to look into all aspects of education and to formulate a policy for developing a national system of education for the first time. The national system of education was to emphasise education of the people, removal of illiteracy and universalisation of elementary education. Unfortunately, the education of a certain segment of society, namely the disabled, was neglected.

Today, some of the most conspicuous failures of the Indian educational system have been not achieving universalisation of primary education and high enrolments, and acquiescing in high drop-out rates and exclusion of disabled children firmly out of the main framework of the educational system. Although India has been a signatory to the accomplishment of UPE by the year 2000, there is very little chance of achieving "Education for All", as pious as the plans are, if the disabled remain segregated out of the educational system of the country.

Social Policy and Marginalisation
Researchers in the past 50 years, both Indian and foreign, are poorly informed about India's disability issues in the nineteenth century, due to insufficient documentation. Many inaccurate data have been copied from secondary sources which seem to lack reliability (Miles, 1994).

According to published material regarding the pre-independence period, there was "no government action concerning services for the disabled until India became independent: before this time, voluntary bodies had provided the only services available" (Taylor and Taylor, 1970). This was refuted by Miles who states that "whereas there was no nation-wide plan to provide disability services, there were voluntary organisations taking care of the needs of disabled people and the Presidency Government gave financial aid and other assistance to institutions serving people with disability from the nineteenth century onwards as shown in many official records" (Miles, 1994). As we shall see later, such a state of affairs still continues.

In England, the Education (or the Butler) - Act was passed, in 1944. This was the first mandate recognising children with disability and directing the State to provide appropriate services for the different categories. In India, in the same year, the Central Advisory Board of Education published a comprehensive report on the Post-War Educational Development of the Country also popularly known as the Sargent Report. This was the first official attempt to analyse the problem of educating physically handicapped children.

It is interesting to note that, in this Report, provisions for the handicapped were to form an essential part of the national system of education and were to be administered by the Education Department. Whenever possible, the Report stated, handicapped children should not be segregated from normal children. Only when the nature and extent of their defect make it necessary should they be sent to special schools (Sargent Report, Chapter IX of the Cabe Report, Post-War pp76-82, 1944).

However, in 1956, India put the clock back, and responsibility for the handicapped became the jurisdiction of the Ministry of Social Welfare with no plan for educating them or integrating them into existing services. A retrogressive step, no doubt, as it is a universally accepted fact that the disabled need education, training and employment just as any other human being, and not welfare or custodial care.

The Ministry of Welfare was entrusted with the responsibility of providing services for the scheduled classes, the other backward classes, drug addicts, cancer patients, those affected with leprosy, women and child welfare, and the welfare of the disabled.

The social welfare activities in post-independent India were based on Article 38 of the Indian Constitution which directed the State "to strive and promote the welfare of the people by securing and protecting as effectively as it may, a social order in which justice – social, economic and political – shall prevail in all the institutions of the national life".

Article 46 placed the responsibility upon each state government for the upliftment of the weaker sections of society. Directorates of social welfare in each state were established in 1956 with responsibility for the handicapped. The welfare measures were broadly categorised under education, training, employment, self-employment, supply of aids and appliances, recreation and cultural activities. Grant awards are as incentives, reservation, concessions and exemptions. Presently the thrust of the schemes for the disabled are implemented through governmental and non-governmental organisations.

The disabled are segregated into special schools and labelled and categorised according to the medical definition of their disability, somewhat similar to what existed in the western countries 30 years ago. The Ministry of Welfare's agenda does not include setting up schools for the disabled as they give grants to voluntary organisations to do this.

UN and WHO and our own statistics show that there are 10% disabled in India. Developmental work, encompassing nearly 400 million people, directly or indirectly, was given the lowest of priority. One ministry to take care of child and women's welfare, tribal welfare, scheduled caste, other backward classes, drug addiction, leprosy and the disabled. This heterogeneous group of people, who constitute over 60% of the country's weakest and most vulnerable, have been dumped in one ministry ever since independence. No government has thought it fit to change this and the result is chaos. Chaos for the poorest sections of society, those needing most attention and care (Alur, 1992).

Healthcare and Marginalisation

In 1974, government launched the Integrated Child Development Scheme (ICDS). This programme is the world's largest package of services for the most vulnerable sections of the population (Swaminathan, Issue 12, 1992). Disabled under 5s are not admitted in the Anganwadi and Balwadis, nor is the family given any support system, and when asked why they do not attend the ICDS clinics, the mothers seem embarrassed and say "no that is not for us". The anganwadi workers too confirm that there's no place for disabled children and that they are not their responsibility.

Since the ICDS works in the slums, the tribal and the rural areas, it is the most appropriate service to include disabled children who are mainly amongst the most vulnerable sections of society. Yet professionals associated with early childhood care while designing manuals and curricula for training of paraprofessionals in early learning have not made provision for pre-school disabled children. The policy-makers too are aware of the critical 0- to 5-years-olds and a large resource allocation has been made to the ICDS, yet children with special needs are not a part of the social policy concerning even basic needs, such as health, nutrition and pre-school facilities. *Clearly such a major social policy in the country has excluded the disabled from its agenda.* The argument usually proffered by policy-makers is that the paraprofessional workers are overloaded and have no knowledge of how to handle a handicapped child.

Socio-Economic Marginalisation
Prevalence and incidence of disability
Numbers and statistics about the disabled vary in India. The 1991 National Sample Survey estimates 16.5 million (1.9%) persons with physical disabilities in the country including the orthopaedically, visually and hearing handicapped.

Table 1
Number of Disabled Persons in India (in millions)

Type	Total	%	Rural	Urban	Male	Female
Locomotor	5.4	21	4.3	1.1	3.5	1.9
Visual	3.4	13	2.9	0.6	1.4	2.0
Hearing	3.0	12	24	0.5	1.6	1.3
Speech	1.7	7	1.4	0.4	1.1	0.6
Physical	11.9	47	9.6	2.2	7.0	5.1
%			81	19	57	43

UN and WHO and our own studies show a 10% figure, making the number of disabled people in India 80 million and if one were to include parents and even one child per family, 240 million people are directly or indirectly affected.

The Periurban Areas

Disability and poverty being closely related, the disabled are mostly living in rural and tribal belts and in the urban slums of cities. Increasing urbanisation, recording a growth rate of 38%, shows that more than half the population of every city live in expanding shanty towns, squatter settlements and slums. The meaning of a slum in India is the absence of proper housing a lack of basic amenities such as water, drainage and sewage; an unhealthy and unhygienic environment, with high levels of pollution, all a result of excessive urbanisation and population explosion (Desai and Pillai, 1970). In India, the slum settlements are known as "chawls, bustees, or jhopadpattis"

Diagram1: The Vicious Circle

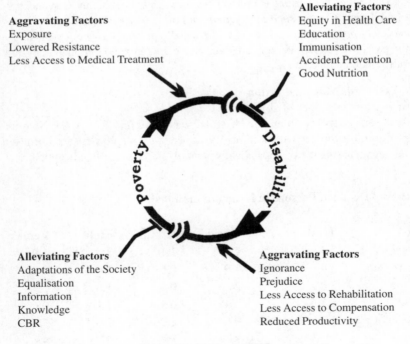

Aggravating Factors
Exposure
Lowered Resistance
Less Access to Medical Treatment

Alleviating Factors
Equity in Health Care
Education
Immunisation
Accident Prevention
Good Nutrition

Alleviating Factors
Adaptations of the Society
Equalisation
Information
Knowledge
CBR

Aggravating Factors
Ignorance
Prejudice
Less Access to Rehabilitation
Less Access to Compensation
Reduced Productivity

Source: Tiroler/Kumlin 1995

In 1986 the Spastics Society of India (one of India's larger NGOs dealing with disability) mounted a survey of 11,829 households, examining the prevalence and incidence of disabilities among children in the city of Bombay and found that 4% of households had disabled children. Four indicators of housing, income, education and occupation were selected to get an insight into their socio-economic background from which certain demographic patterns emerged. The data revealed that 78% of families with handicapped children lived in chawls or temporary structures 62.9% had a monthly income of less than 1,000 rupees (around £25) a month. On examining parents' education, it was found that 13.2% of fathers and 35% of mothers were illiterate.

Among 8-10% were to be found in the slum areas. In Dharavi, reputedly Asia's largest slum, where the author has been working for the last ten years, the majority of the work-force belong to the unorganised sector comprising of what are known as "C" and "D" category workers. They are engaged in trades such as broom-making, rag-picking, tanning and leather work and fishing and were usually domestic servants, as maids, cooks, drivers and sweepers. Other, skilled ,labour included plumbers, electricians and carpenters. Most families in the area fell well below the poverty line due to large family sizes (*per capita* income Rs.300 or £7). Housing mainly consists of a hut measuring 10 ft x 10 ft, with an average family of seven living there crammed together in sub-human conditions. Sanitary arrangements were practically non-existent and water was scarce, available only once during the day - at 4 am. The disabled in these conditions are considered a curse and a liability. Little or no services exist, their very presence being ignored. Even the ICDS services are not available for them (Alur, 1988).

The Rural and Urban Divide
Seventy per cent of India is agricultural, spread over the rural areas and remains basically unreached. Families have little or no access to information and services. Able-bodied members of the family are hard-pressed to hold their jobs down and in the absence of any rehabilitative services families are exposed to acute stress.

According to the National Sample Survey Report (1983) data, excluding mental retardation, mental illness and other psychiatric disorders, there are 11.11 million disabled in the rural areas and just 2.60 million in the urban.

Table 2
Number of disabled, by type of disability, in Rural and Urban Areas:

Disability	Rural		Total	Urban		Total
	(M)	(F)		(M)	(F)	
Locomoter	2.81	1.53	4.34	0.69	0.41	1.1
Visual	1.2	1.71	2.92	0.25	0.32	0.57
Hearing	1.37	1.11	2.48	0.29	0.25	0.54
Speech	0.87	0.5	1.37	0.26	0.13	0.39
Total	6.25	4.86	11.11	1.49	1.11	2.60

Source: GOI, NSSO Report 1983, Vol.VII

The above data suggest that under each category of disability, the rural population is four times the urban population. This is not surprising, as medical facilities, awareness, access to information, and physical medicine, etc. are all lacking in the rural areas.

Social Beliefs, Customs and *Mores*
Faulty social attitudes prevail resulting in ostracism and stigmatisation. India, essentially a country where religion plays a strong and powerful part in the community, has its own religious beliefs about disability. There is a deep belief in past life or "Karma" amongst the Hindus, who believe that a bad past life may have led to having a disabled person. A counter-philosophy to this very detrimental belief has been promoted by some of us, that the child could have had a blessed past and has the strength to carry the burden it has in this life and, being a very special person, the child has been born to a special family.

In a set-up where a child is regarded as either a support system to look after children and household needs or a wage-earner, the child with disability is normally looked upon as a burden. The mother seems to be the main caretaker along with female siblings. Often the female sibling is made to dropout from school to take care of the disabled sibling, especially if it is a boy. The mother is almost always blamed for the disability. It is conveyed very directly and harshly by family members, neighbours and relatives. In some Muslim families, the husbands have left the wife saying "she was only capable of producing disabled children", in some Hindu homes the mother-in-law used it as yet another tool for persecution against the daughter-in-law.

In the slums, often the mothers tied up the child inside the house so that nobody could see, accuse or tease him or her. Since the child was mostly inside the house, he or she was often exposed to much more of crime, hostility, sex, etc., which an able-bodied could avoid by just running out to play with siblings which this child was forced to witness. In these areas, rather than social integration, the disabled are caught in an acutely distressing situation of social rejection and stigmatisation (Alur and Kalra, 1995).

The Spastics Society of India's research studies in the rural belt of Maharashtra showed that, suffering from negative attitudes, discrimination and prejudice, the disabled often fall prey to open ridicule. An orthopaedically disabled person is never called by his name, but is referred to as "Langada", a very derogatory reference as someone crippled or lame; a blind man as "Andha" and a mentally retarded as "Pagal" - mentally ill, deranged.

Although national statistics on the education of disabled children are not available, micro-level studies in 32 villages in rural Maharashtra indicated that only 13% of disabled girls as apposed to 56% of boys received primary education (Kalra, Pai, and Bidwe, 1992).

Strong undercurrents of caste systems, beliefs in superstition, fear of contracting disability by association, gender bias, are dominant features hindering social integration.

Provisions
Government Services :
The Ministry of Welfare operates schemes of assistance to voluntary organisations to provide services to people with disabilities. Assistance up to 90% in urban and 95% in rural areas is given to NGOs for education, training and rehabilitation of the disabled. In 1988 four premier national institutes working in specific disability areas were set up to develop models of care and services, conduct research and promote human resource development. Artificial Limbs Manufacturing Corporation at Kanpur was established with the object of promoting, developing, manufacturing, marketing and distributing artificial aids and appliances.

Each year, on the occasion of the International Day of Disabled Persons, national awards are presented by the President of India to the best employer of the handi-capped, the best handicapped employee and self-employed, Best individual working for handicapped welfare and the best institution working for handi-capped welfare.

The District Rehabilitation Centres have been set up to provide comprehensive rehabilitation services in areas of training, employment aids and appliances on the district levels. In an endeavour to contribute to multisectoral follow-up with respect to rural development in India the Council for Advancement of People's Action and Rural Technology under the aegis of the Ministry of Rural Development was set up as part of the ESCAP Agenda (Capart, 1995)

Currently, a slight shift in policy is noticeable. The Ministry of Human Resources, looking after education in the Indian eighth Five Year Plan 1991-6 increased the budget for children with impairments by more than five times. The District Primary Education Programme (DPEP) covering over 40 districts intends to make primary schools available to all children including children with special needs

The Government of India surveys show that 98% in the urban and 98% in the rural areas are not being covered by any service. Government's services are miniscule compared with the magnitude of the problem, and segregation of the disabled from their normal peer group has occured, not least due to the ineffective inter-ministerial networking.

Non-Government Organisations
The Government relies heavily on the efforts of the non-governmental sector for the provision of services for children, women, the handicapped and other vulnerable groups.

A recent survey of organisations working for the disabled in the entire country was carried out by the government. There are more than 2,456 voluntary organisations in the disability area and 1,200 special schools, 450 of which receive grants from the Government towards their operational costs. The majority of voluntary organisations are autonomous. (Source: Government of India, Directory of Voluntary Organisations, 1995).

The voluntary agencies in India, since independence, have provided the backbone of services in the different categories of disabilities with a phenomenal spread, putting disability on the map of the country The work has been in the areas of identification of disabilities, education, manpower training, vocational training, placement and employment. However, concentration has been not so much on adulthood and employment as on the early and school years. Some of the larger ones, such as the Spastics Society, the National Association for the Blind, the National Federations for the Mentally Handicapped, Hearing Impaired, have produced sterling services in socially integrating their clients through school and higher education, and employment some have even introduced a scheme of arranged marriages for their clients. Since it is not within the purview of this chapter to go into too much detail of the workings of these worthy organisations where each one plays an excellent part on a micro level, an attempt will be made to give an overview of some of the larger ones, the exemplars selected according to their annual budgets, usually an indicator of an organisation's size.

The Spastics Society of India, created in 1972 in Bombay because of a lack of awareness and services for cerebral palsied children, is today one of the largest autonomous organisations in the non-government sector, dealing with physical disability and other associated handicaps in the country. Several identification camps, clinics, centres and schools have been set up combining education and treatment under one roof of a special school setting. Training teachers, therapists, parents and doctors to help decentralise services in this large country have been started ensuring the very essential spread of services. Twenty-five years have culminated in the building up of two national centres:

1. The National Centre for Cerebral Palsy, Research and Training and Other Physical Handicaps in Bandra

2. The National Job Development Centre, in Chembur.

Basically, the organisation used has a community-based approach and has helped several NGOs around the country to build up their technical base in the way of schools, post-graduate studies and training courses within a socio-educational format encouraging flexibility and autonomy, thus decentralising the service on a macro level. This model has been shown to be highly replicable and, today, the spread extends to over fifteen of the 28 states, reinforcing its generaliseability and the fact that it was a much needed one.

The organisation has been able to work on a micro as well as a macro level. On the macro level, the Society has been able to introduce educational reform through the school boards and universities ensuring extension of examination timings, scribes who have been used to write up answers, and a slight modification of the syllabus. Facilities such as these have also been pushed by those groups dealing with visual and hearing impairment. This has enabled a large group of children with different types of disabilities to pass the school and university examinations. These educational reforms have been made statutory with most school boards and universities across the country. Some amount of social integration has been introduced with changes and modifications of the existing examination systems, allowing disabled people to pursue higher studies.

Continuing the emphasis on integrated education of visually handicapped children, particularly in rural areas, the National Association for the Blind, another large NGO, was instrumental in serving 1,694 students with the help of 188 teachers. These children were from 1,114 regular schools covering 999 villages/towns in fifteen states (NAB Report, 1992).

However, one of the main problems of the voluntary sector is the very limited and fast-dwindling capacity to raise funds and its increasing dependence on grants-in-aid from the central and state governments. As they obtain a major portion of their funding from the government, their main allegiance remains with the Government, weakening their position to question governmental policy.

"NGO's and State are often locked in an institutional embrace, not simply the product of minimalist regulation by registration but more directly through finance and through capture and substitution. A society relying on NGO's as the mechanism for the delivery of social welfare, accepts their insecurity of funding and their social costliness. Such a society accepts the minimal regulations of NGO's service provisions and their sometimes quirky allocative priorities" (Harris-White, Oxford, 1995).

The NGO sector has pioneered valuable services, ensuring social integration into the community, however, with limited infrastructural services, and limited funds, the voluntary sector can only serve on a micro level.

Community Based Rehabilitation Intervention

Community Based Rehabilitation (CBR) is another alternative, cost-effective intervention promoting social integration being carried out by well-known NGOs (such as The Spastics Society, Seva in Action, Amar Jyothi Trust, Action Aid, NAB), with the main aim of building up the community members with an objective of relying less and less on highly specialised professionals and more on local people around in the community. There is no one sacrosanct model that can be used for the diverse problems faced in India, and for the sake of brevity, two excellent models of CBR intervention – a rural CBR project established in 1981 by The Spastics Society of Northern India, in a village called Dayalpur, where they have created an interesting model of an integrated service delivery programme at three levels – basic, intermediate, and specialised with100 disabled people and families from more than 30 villages. Poverty, unemployment, health-care, integration, illiteracy and women's problems are some of the areas addressed (Burrett, 1992). Again doing excellent work in social integration is the

CBR model, working in 30 villages of South 24 Parganas district of West Bengal called Sanchar (Chaudhury and Sanchar, 1992). These are just a few of the exemplars which have helped promote social integration on a micro level

Employment

Three per cent vacancies are reserved in "C" and "D" posts in central government and public sector undertakings. However, the prospects of obtaining work in the open market for the disabled are minimal, unless they have been well trained and the community has been educated to accept them. The National Job Development Centre, started by The Spastics Society of Northern India, researched the difficulties of employment and found that the disabled often do not get jobs for the following reasons: lack of proper technical training, access problems - most buildings do not have ramps or lifts and are therefore inaccessible; transportation – no buses are available allowing wheelchair access; negative employer and community attitudes.

Access

A total lack of access – environmental barriers, lack of special transportation facilities, access to public buildings and offices – prevents hundreds of disabled people from joining mainstream society in India. "I could never move around on the streets on my own, with the roads and pavements full of potholes, and the shops, libraries, theatres, museums, cinema halls, restaurants, inaccessible to wheelchairs. To top it all, if one moves out on a wheelchair, you will soon have a whole crowd around you making pitiful noises. In a country where there are no ramps in shops, in colleges, in offices, no disabled toilets, the pavements are inaccessible, where everything is geared for the normal, where there are social, psychological, emotional, and mental blocks against the disabled, it makes me wonder, after 49 years of Independence, are we really citizens of India? Are we Free?" (Alur, 1995).

Legislation

In India, poverty, caste and gender push disability to the lowest of priorities. Within the ambit of the overall perspective, the Constitution of India has attempted to focus on the needs of persons with disabilities in Article 41. This Article is part of the Constituent Assembly's attempt to direct the State's effort in areas which are considered desirable but which cannot be enforced.

Article 41 reads "The State shall within the limits of its economic development make effective provision for securing the rights to work, to education and to public assistance in cases of unemployment, old age, sickness, disablement and in other cases of undesired want." Article 41 is the only one explicitly to mention disabled people.

"Political manifestos of the last 45 years in India have not included disability as an issue. The scattered disabled population does not have political clout, as it is not organised to campaign for its rights" says a disabled activist Venkatesh (ADD, 1995).

Initiatives to promote legislative provisions for persons with disabilities suffer from what Alston rightfully said: " . . . but Rights without mechanisms to claim and without obligation to provide are empty" (quoted in Harris-White, 1995).

Historically, in the western countries, it was around the mid-twentieth century that education for the disabled became statutory and Acts of Parliament entrusted the responsibility of providing services for handicapped people to the State. Legislation backed with fiscal support, empowered disabled people and their families to avail themselves of litigation and go to courts of law if they found statutory services not complying with the law and discriminating against them. Today a vast network of rehabilitative services exists for disabled people which seeks to integrate them into society as a matter of right and not charity. India relies on philanthropy, charity and good Samaritans to set up facilities for the large segment of their citizens.

The Ethics of Disability
Diagram II - The Tentacles of Human Oppression

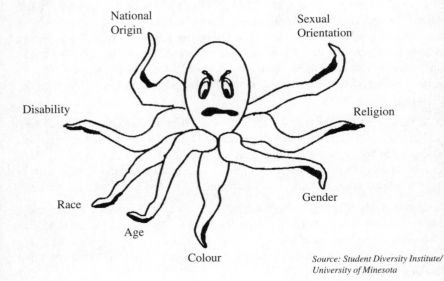

Source: *Student Diversity Institute/ University of Minesota*

Disability is considered one of the major tentacles of human oppression, as shown in the illustration. Questions of morality and ethics, raised by philosophers over centuries, are: who oppresses whom? In the ultimate analysis, what is the norm? Who is normal?

In the Indian context, the prevailing deep-rooted prejudice creates the split between normal and disabled; negative attitudes towards people perceived as deviants affect the common man on the streets as well as the policy makers in the Government, thus imprisoning and locking up the disabled people in their homes, barring disabled people from being a part of the norm.

Conclusions
The economic and political marginalisation of the disabled from the mainstream of life has four main reasons.

The Indian nation has not recognised the fundamental rights of the disabled nor made any critical attempt to remedy the lacuna that exists in their policies since independence. Policy and practice during the post-independence period seem to be similar to what was happening in pre-independent India a hundred years ago where a policy of paternalism (of doling out grants in aid) was applied to charitable institutions. This state of affairs has continued due to political weakness and a lack of a political lobby for change from disabled people and their families.

The Government's continued reliance on the NGO sector absolves it of its responsibilities towards the disabled as citizens of India, and this policy is responsible for only a micro-level spread resulting in only a 2% coverage. The Government's lack of networking with existing resources to ensure that each ministry includes rather than excludes disability has resulted in the economic and political marginalisation of that ministry. Today, not only the disabled remain segregated in their own sub-culture cut off from the mainstream: so is the Ministry of Welfare which is cut off from other ministries, its clients excluded from services.

The non-government sector needs to become independent of a type of Stalinistic control that exists: it needs to press for change to raise the quality of life on a macro level, for the disabled, trapped in their impoverished lives. To merely work for one's own organisation when clients have no rights in the country is being self-indulgent and not seeing the woods for the trees.

International agencies have greatly helped, but on a micro level. They should give direction in changing social policy and legislation towards mainstreaming.

UNDP's HDI (Human Development Index) for each country for 1995 does not include disability. A GDI is specified quantifying various areas of social development, and reflecting government and state participation in the area of women. To go into a further derivative, as is the GDI of the HDI, a DDI, (Disabled Development Index) which compares the plight of the disabled against the HDI is critical, considering that the disabled amount to half a billion world-wide, the maximum number in India. This will determine the areas of development needing maximum infrastructure and development.

Finally, a broader view must also recognise that armed conflict is not the only force which is affecting the normal development of millions of children in the 1990s. More quietly, the continued political and social marginalisation of the poorest nations, and of the poorest communities within the nations, is depriving far larger numbers of children of their basic human rights.

"An underclass is therefore being created, undereducated and unskilled, standing beneath the broken bottom rungs of social and economic progress, victims of past poverty, of falling real wages, and of the fraying of social safety nets in the 1980s" (World Books, 1995).

For many millions of families in the poorest villages, in the remote tribal belts and in the urban slums, the daily oppression of poverty takes its toll, victims unable sometimes to have one square meal for their family, unable to keep a job down, unable to clothe themselves, unable to send their children to school and in the midst of this despair and destitution is their disabled child, caught in the net of oppression, treated like pariahs of society.

References

Action Aid (1995) *Disability News*, Vol. 6.

ADD (1995) *India, Action on Disability and Development* India.

Alur, M.(1992) *Proceedings of National Network Seminar on Vocational Rehabilitation and Employment* Paper available at The Spastics Society of India, Bombay.

Alur, M. (1988) *"Sixteenth World Conference for the Disabled, New York, Comprehensive Services for Multiply Handicapped Children in India, Rehabiltation International*, Paper available at The Spastics Society of India, Bombay.

Alur M., & Kalra D. (1995) *Multidimensional Implications of Children and Youth with Special Needs in Socially Disadvantaged Settings and Relevant Strategies of Intervention,* International Society Chandigarh, Paper available at The Spastics Society of India.

Billimoria, R., & Krishnaswamy S. (1986) *Prevalence of Disabilities Among Children in Bombay,* available at the National Centre for Research, and Training Library, The Spastics Society of India, Bombay, India.

Burrett, G., & Nundy, M. (1994) *The Convention of the Rights of the Child, The Disabled Child,* available at The Spastics Society of Northern India, New Delhi.

Burrett G. (1992-3) *Volunteers and Experts Give the Best of Both Worlds,* South Asia Children's Save the Children Fund Magazine, The Spastics Society of Northern India.

Capart, (1995) *Strategy to Integrate - Disability Concerns of Rural People with Development & Participation in the Poverty Alleviation Programmes & Projects.*

Chaudhury, G. Sanchar, A. (1992) *An Experience of Community Based Rehabilitation of Disability,* 24 Parganas, West Bengal, India.

Chib Alur, M. "Are We Truly Free". *The Bombay Times Edition of The Times of India,* August 1995 (available at The Spastics Society of India, Bombay).

Children, Disabiity and Development, (1994) UNICEF.

Director of Institutions Working for the Disabled in India, (1995) CACU-DRC Scheme, Ministry of Welfare, New Delhi.

Directory of NGOs receiving Grants-in-Aid Under Various Schemes of Ministry of Welfare, (1995) Government of India.

Harris-White. B.(1995) *Onto A Loser: Disability in India,* Oxford University, paper available with the author at Elizabeth House, Oxford.

Harris-White. B (1995) *The Political Economy of Disability & Development with Special Reference to India.* Paper available at Elizabeth House. Oxford.

Human Development Report, (1995) United Nations Development Programme (UNDP), Oxford University Press.

Integrated Child Development Services (ICDS) (1990) Department of Women and Child Development, Ministry of Human Resources Development, Government of India, New Delhi.

Kalra, D.; Pai, M.; and Bidwe A. (1992) *Prevalence of Disabilities in Rural Maharashtra,* Available with The National Centre for Research and Training and other Disabilities, The Spastics Society of India, Bombay, India.

Macaulay, T. B. (1952) *A Minute on Indian Education* reprinted in *Prose and Poetry,* Cambridge: Harvard University Press.

Majumdar K. (1995) *Perspectives of Social Work.*

Miles, M. (1994) *Research on Disability, Care and Education in 19th Century; some dates, places and documentation*, Action Aid Disability News, Vol.5, No.2, Supplement.

Ministry of Welfare, (1995) *Provision of Aids and Appliances.*

Naik, J.P. (1975) *Elementary Education in India*

National Association for the Blind India (1992-4) *Biennial Report* .

National Sample Survey Report. (1991) Government of India .

National Sample Survey Report. (1983) Vol. VII.Government of India.

Rama Mani, D. (1988) *Physically Handicapped in India..*

Rane, A. *Status of Children in Villages of Rural Maharashtra.*

Rao, S.G. A (1995) *Different Vision - ADD India (Action on Disability and Development India).*

Report of a National Consultation,(1995) UNICEF.

Sargent Report, Chapter IX of the CABE Report, Post-War pp76-82.

Sen, A. *Poverty and Famine*, Oxford Publishers.

Sharp, E.D. "Macaulay's Minute", op. cit.

Singh and Pothan, *Slum Children of India*, Deep & Deep Publications.

Social Welfare Department, (1992) Maharashtra, *Information on Welfare Schemes.*

Swaminathan, (1992) Issue 12, UNICEF, *The Coordinators.*

Taylor, W.W., and Taylor I.W., (1970) *Services for The Handicapped In India*, International Society for Rehabilitation of the Disabled.

Tilak, Jandhyala B.G (1990) *The Political Economy of Education in India,* Special Studies in Comparative Education, No. 24, Comparative Education Center, Graduate School of Education, State University of New York of Buffalo.

The State of the World's Children, (1995) UNICEF.

World Development Report, (1995) World Bank Publication.